Critical Political Theory and Radical Practice

Series Editor
Stephen Eric Bronner
Department of Political Science
Rutgers University
New Brunswick, NJ, USA

The series introduces new authors, unorthodox themes, critical interpretations of the classics and salient works by older and more established thinkers. A new generation of academics is becoming engaged with immanent critique, interdisciplinary work, actual political problems, and more broadly the link between theory and practice. Each in this series will, after his or her fashion, explore the ways in which political theory can enrich our understanding of the arts and social sciences. Criminal justice, psychology, sociology, theater and a host of other disciplines come into play for a critical political theory. The series also opens new avenues by engaging alternative traditions, animal rights, Islamic politics, mass movements, sovereignty, and the institutional problems of power. Critical Political Theory and Radical Practice thus fills an important niche. Innovatively blending tradition and experimentation, this intellectual enterprise with a political intent hopes to help reinvigorate what is fast becoming a petrified field of study and to perhaps provide a bit of inspiration for future scholars and activists.

More information about this series at
http://www.palgrave.com/gp/series/14938

Nils C. Kumkar

The Tea Party, Occupy Wall Street, and the Great Recession

palgrave
macmillan

Nils C. Kumkar
University of Bremen
Bremen, Germany

Critical Political Theory and Radical Practice
ISBN 978-3-030-08836-1 ISBN 978-3-319-73688-4 (eBook)
https://doi.org/10.1007/978-3-319-73688-4

Cover illustration: Anke Wittkowski / EyeEm

Printed on acid-free paper

This Palgrave Macmillan imprint is published by Springer Nature
The registered company is Springer International Publishing AG
The registered company address is: Gewerbestrasse 11, 6330 Cham, Switzerland

Acknowledgements

I want to thank Stephen Bronner, whose presentation on the Tea Party at the Rosa-Luxemburg-Foundation in Berlin is one of the sources from which the original plan for this project sprang, who discussed the vicissitudes and niceties of the topic with me time and again and whose commentary, criticism, and advice, together with that of the three anonymous reviewers, have helped me transform my doctoral thesis into this book.

With regard to my thesis, I first of all want to thank my two supervisors, Monika Wohlrab-Sahr and Ralf Bohnsack, who, on incredibly short notice, kindly offered their support and encouraged me to complete this thesis the way I always wanted to but had begun to doubt. I want to express my gratitude to the DFG-Research Group 1261 "Critical Junctures of Globalization" and especially its director, Ulf Engel, and the director of the Centre for Area Studies, Matthias Middell, for the inspiring working environment, the generous funding, and the helpful advice, without which my research would not have been possible.

The most continuous fellow travelers of this project's trajectory were the members of our small qualitative data analysis and PhD self-help group. The long evenings and the heated debates with Falk Eckert, Lisa Vollmer, and Antje Winkler have shaped my perspective on my research in ways that I can often not even retrace. They encouraged me over and again to follow my often very vague intuitions and to "just go back to the material" when I was about to lose my nerve.

Of the great scholars I was allowed to meet at conferences from Yokohama to New York and whose advice, criticisms, and encouragements carried me through the inevitable doldrums of my thesis, I especially want to thank Ruth Milkman of the City University in New York and Michael Shalev of the Hebrew University in Jerusalem, whose panel at the ISA in Yokohama was the first international forum I presented my research in and who continued to advise me throughout its development. I furthermore thank Oliver Decker of Leipzig University, whose book on the *Secondary Authoritarianism* became the home of my research strand on the German AfD that had become homeless in my own concept of the thesis; Helena Flam of Leipzig University, who discussed large parts of this thesis with me and helped me sharpen my argument; Arlie Hochschild of the University of California, Berkeley, who, when I was overwhelmed by the familiarity of some of her findings in her research on the TP she presented at the ESA in Prague, at this very same evening and in the middle of the opening party, began to discuss the results of her (and my) research with me.

I am profoundly grateful to my family, and especially my parents, Brigitte and Matthias Kumkar, my friends, and my office colleagues at Metrogap for the conversations, the coffee, the moral support, and the distractions I needed. I especially want to thank those of you that additionally even read and commented on parts of this book at different stages of its development: Anna Danilina, Blair Taylor, Christian Banse, Claudia Baumann, David Bebnowski, Holger Kuhn, Jan-Felix Kumkar, Kai-Moritz Kumkar, Karoline Dietel, Kim Holtmann, Matthias Claussen, Micha Fiedlschuster, Nicholas Dietrich, Robert Ogman, and Sina Arnold.

When I wrote that the analysis group were the most continuous fellow travelers, I was deliberately leaving aside somebody I wanted to save a special thank-you for: my best friend and partner in crime, Verena Letsch, who has endured and accompanied me in this project from the first night on which I pondered comparing crisis-protests, over stressful field-research in pre-Christmas New York, up until this very moment. I probably could not have finished this without you and I am pretty sure I would not have finished it, and I am deeply grateful for this and everything else you've done and been for me.

Last, and most importantly, I want to express my gratitude to all the participants in my group discussions and to all my interviewees that made space in their often incredibly crammed agendas to sit down for sometimes quite personal discussions with a stranger that could not offer more than a cup of coffee and some cookies in exchange. Even though our politics surely differ quite substantially at times, I hope that those of you that may end up reading these lines find, not only yourselves regarded with the highest respect, but also some valuable insights in my reflections throughout this work that you have so importantly shaped. I, for sure, have learned more from listening to you than from most books cited in the bibliography.

Contents

List of Figures

List of Tables

CHAPTER 1

Introduction: Protests in the Wake of the Great Recession

The election of Donald Trump as the 45th president of the USA came as a shock to most observers and commentators. As such, it was the (preliminary) culmination point of a decade of surprising events: In 2008, the bankruptcy of the investment bank Lehman Brothers precipitated the worst economic recession since the Great Depression. One year later, the Tea Party, an explosively growing, right-wing conservative protest mobilization, helped to dampen or to stop the reformist programs of the newly elected Obama administration and injected radical ambition into the Republican Party which many had already seen as being in inevitable decline after Obamas election. In 2011, just as the economic indicators seemed to suggest that the crisis was over, a group of young, left-wing activists, inspired by the uprisings around the Mediterranean, began a symbolic encampment in the heart of the financial district of New York City. After a short incubation period, Occupy Wall Street spread to cities all over the USA and many other countries, voicing sharp criticism of rising inequalities. In 2015, observers of the primaries of the two large US-American parties began to register signs of anomaly: In the Democratic Party, the social democrat and self-proclaimed socialist Bernie Sanders managed to win important primary elections against Hillary Clinton, who had already been considered the de facto crowned presidential candidate. The leadership of the Republican Party began to abandon their favorite candidate Jeb Bush and to support the so-called

N. C. Kumkar, *The Tea Party, Occupy Wall Street, and the Great Recession*, Critical Political Theory and Radical Practice,
https://doi.org/10.1007/978-3-319-73688-4_1

Tea Party candidates Ted Cruz and Marco Rubio as contenders against the rise of Donald Trump—as we know, ultimately in vain.

It is striking how similar the political public reacted to these events: Almost nobody saw them coming. Early signs were ignored and those that did warn about them were ridiculed or excluded from 'serious' debates. When the dynamic of the event became undeniable, its scope was first talked down before the mood quickly turned: The events were now seen as unprecedented, tide turning, and teaching 'us all' important lessons. And after their momentum faded, they were either forgotten or relegated to the dustbin of the anecdotic.

Freud theorized that the symptom is to be understood as the return of something repressed, and such a recurring surprise by seemingly random events nurtures the suspicion that there is something we avoid to confront and which therefore continues to haunt us. It is the wager of this book that this is indeed the case. There is something the public debate was avoiding to confront and which threatened to resurface in these moments of shock. And however fleeting their appearance and disappearance might have seemed, the protests of the Tea Party (TP) and Occupy Wall Street (OWS) offer a window into the social processing of the hard subjective and objective reality that subterraneously connects the Great Recession and the election of Donald Trump—and even points beyond it. The economic crisis was no "black swan" that interrupted the normal course of events out of the blue.[1] Instead, it represented the escalation of deep economic imbalances rooted in the contradictions of the current state of global capitalism. In the same vein, these protests should not simply be reduced to a (more or less) consequential but ultimately random event. Rather, they should be seen as symptoms of the very crisis they reacted to, thereby revealing social tensions at the heart of contemporary capitalism. Given that the political economic contradictions that became visible as the Great Recession are far from resolved, it is all but surprising that the wishes, tensions, and grievances that drove these protests surfaced again—and with force.

This book understands and analyzes the protests therefore as symptoms of an underlying socioeconomic crisis. Its *guiding question*, which will be further theoretically and methodologically nuanced and unfolded in the rest of this introduction, is: *How can the lived experience of the Great Recession by the social classes that drove these mass protests be understood as shaping and informing their very protest-practice?* Or, the other way around, *how can the protests as a social practice be interpreted as a symptom of the socially specific lived experience of the political economic crisis?*

To answer this question, I focus on the first, explosive phase of OWS and the TP. The aim is to *analyze the respective protest-practices' rootedness in the socially specific lived experiences* of those that expressed their longings and discontents in them. I did not choose these examples because they effected or initiated important political changes, nor because I deem them politically more relevant than other protests in the same period of time. Instead, I chose them for two main reasons. First, pragmatically speaking, they were accessible to me. Thanks to generous funding provided by the Deutsche Forschungsgesellschaft (DFG), I was able to travel to the USA for three extended periods of field research. My experiences with both Leftist activism (especially of the college campus variety) and with interviewing conservative activists and personal ties provided an opportune combination that allowed me to quickly establish friendly and open relationships to people active in the TP and OWS. Drawing on Georg Simmel's metaphor, it does not matter much from which point of the surface of a given moment we lower the lead (Simmel 1994, 71)—if we proceed carefully, it will start to swing with the same deep currents.

Second, beyond pragmatic considerations, it was the hopes and fears projected onto and articulated through them, and the diffuse and often contradictory claims and issues raised by them, that made me think of them as a promising starting point for sketching out the fault lines and discontents that built up with the escalation of social contradictions during this socioeconomic crisis. True, their constituencies were not among those objectively hit the hardest by the Great Recession. Yet, through mobilizing hundreds of thousands and being vocal about their discontents, they prove to be very sensitive indicators of the developments. Furthermore, the class-generational units from which the core constituencies of the respective protest mobilizations were drawn—the older cohorts of the classical petty bourgeoisie in the case of the TP and the younger, aspiring cohorts of the new petty bourgeoisie in the case of OWS—tend to be very involved in the processes of political opinion building in the USA. As important factions of the so-called middle classes, these groups' importance for the legitimacy of the political system can hardly be overestimated. Their perceptions of the crisis and their criticisms must therefore be carefully interpreted—independent of the degree of legitimacy that one intuitively is willing to grant them.

At first I was, for example, irritated by the son of two philosophy professors, himself a student and scholarship-recipient in a prestigious graduate program at New York University, somewhat martially declaring that *his* "generation" was hit by the Great Recession "with the force of a bomb" and that he experienced "wrenching periods of underemployment" before he joined OWS (Gould-Wartofsky 2015, 4). However, there is no denying that he and his fellow occupiers were the ones who articulated the most vocal criticism of rising social inequality and a general discontent about the way the crisis was politically and economically processed. Connecting the criticism to its social roots should therefore not be misunderstood as a veiled attempt at disqualification qua social reduction. Instead, connecting it to the social conditions of the possibility of its occurrence hopefully contributes to the overall potential of a critique of the very social conditions that underlie the suffering and the discontent driving the critique.

In the following, I will sketch out my practice-oriented, materialist approach through which I address this challenge and the corresponding reconstructive, critical-hermeneutic methodology employed in collecting and making sense of the empirical data. I hope that what otherwise might strike some readers as crude reductionism camouflaged in overly arcane jargon will instead be understood as a very careful, iterative attempt at identifying a limited number of essential determinants in the chaotic multiplicity of empirical 'facts' through which the inner logic of the protest-practices and their relation to the Great Recession presented itself. Following this explanation of the general theoretical and methodological perspective, the research question is reformulated through the lens of this approach, concluding with a short summary of the structure of the book.

1.1 Theoretical-Methodological Considerations: Protests as a Social Practice

Although OWS was a rather short-lived episode in the wave of protest that emerged three years after the beginning of the Great Recession, it captured the imagination and attention of the academic and journalistic public more than most other protests in the last decade: "(...M)easured by words published per square foot of setting, Zuccotti Park may well be the most intensely scrutinized landscape in recent journalistic history. (...) Measured in terms of words published per political results (sic), on the other hand, OWS may be the most over-described historical event of all time" (Frank 2012). This polemical statement by Thomas Frank might be a slight exaggeration, especially given the difficulty of properly measuring the political results of OWS.[2] Published in late 2012, Frank's article nevertheless evocatively describes the flood of journalistic, activist, and/or academic publications that sprung up after OWS marked the arrival of the wave of protests in the epicenter of the economic turbulences that had triggered the Great Recession. Despite this strong interest in OWS and the TP, throughout these accounts, three aspects of the protest mobilization remain under-researched and under-theorized. These aspects are crucial for answering this book's guiding question and therefore together constitute the research gap which this book seeks to close (or at least narrow):

(1) On the macro-level, despite a broad consensus among those researching especially the Occupy protests, according to which the Great Recession is an important factor for explaining the protests (e.g. Della Porta 2015; Benski et al. 2013; Langman 2013), the exact nature of this link between the political economic dynamics and the protest-practice itself is still underexplored. (2) This corresponds, on the meso-level, with largely unsystematic accounts on the demographic composition of the protests, especially regarding social class, as I will discuss in more detail in Chap. 3. (3) On the micro-level, finally, there is a lack of reconstructive, qualitative studies on the experiences and motives of the participants, especially regarding the Occupy protests. It is the wager of this dissertation that these three desiderates cannot be treated separately from each other but are in fact attributes of one and the same research gap, and that filling this gap allows for a more systematic comparison of the different protests in this wave of contention, especially for a more symmetrical comparison with right-wing protests thus far excluded from comparative studies on the protests in the wake of the Great Recession.

To formulate these three research desiderates as attributes of one integrated complex already points to the theoretical and methodological perspective that informed the construction of this book's research object. My practice-theory-oriented, materialist assumption problematizes the separation of micro-, meso-, and macro-level phenomena. I assume that the practice of the protests can be explained (to a relevant degree) via the socially specific experiences of their constituencies before and during their participation in the protests, and these experiences are (again to a relevant degree) determined by the dynamics of their socio-material living conditions. The key term, 'socially specific experience', points to the meta-theoretical assumption that the explosive yet clearly demographically structured growth of the protests is, on the one hand, grounded in the fact that members of specific social classes (or rather class-generational units) are very likely subject to specific, shared, or at least similar, objective developments of their socioeconomic living conditions. On the other hand, because of their experienced as well as their (consciously and non-consciously) anticipated biographical trajectory, they also share similar predispositions to interpret and act upon these dynamics.

This understanding of socially specific experiences as the key mediating link between the objective dynamics of the Great Recession and the social practice of protest shapes the whole perspective of this book. This perspective is theoretically informed by the theory of practice in the tradition of Bourdieu. In the research practice of this study, this theoretical approach implies the use of a reconstructive, critical-hermeneutical methodology.

1.1.1 The Perspective: The Theory of Practice as Socio-Analysis

In a sociological critique of opinion polls, Bourdieu points out that there are at least three different ways in which an answer to a question "deemed political" by the pollsters can in fact be generated by those being polled: through (a) a practical "class ethos," a habitus, which as an implicit generative formula also allows practically coherent answers to everyday problems to be produced, (b) a systematic political concept, and (c) a "decision of the second degree" which aligns the answer with the "line" of a political party. Since the probability that any one of these options dominates the production of the answer is distributed unequally among social classes, he concludes that the "public opinion" portrayed is very likely an artifact (Bourdieu 1994, 655 f., see also 1979b).

This criticism not only applies to how one understands the social logics of opinion polls, but can also be extended to other observations of behavior deemed political. In their ground-breaking study on the TP, Skocpol and Williamson argue that the TP should primarily be understood from the vantage point that their supporters are very conservative (Skocpol and Williamson 2012, 26ff.). This hypothesis theoretically implies that one subsumes the decision to support the TP under one of two latter categories: Either one supported the TP because these protests suited one's general, very conservative, conception of what the world should (or should not) look like, or because very conservative political authorities had endorsed the protests. In philosophical terms, we could call the perspective implied in these two possibilities the *idealist* perspective, in that they imply a conscious decision or some system of beliefs as having the primacy over the socio-material living conditions in predetermining the practical behavior.

Without denying that these kinds of mechanisms played a role in the mobilizations of protest, my basic theoretical, *materialist*, approach rests on the assumption that, in order to unearth the experiential core of the articulated criticism, one should focus on the mechanism behind the first possible explanation mentioned by Bourdieu to understand the logic of the protests' explosive growth. In the case of the relation between being "very conservative" and the support of the TP, this perspective leads us to suspect the set of statements and behaviors which denotes them to be "very conservative" in the eyes of Skocpol and Williamson is de facto produced by the very same pre-reflexive generative formula that also produced the support for the TP. As will be shown in Sect. 4.1, being a 'true believer' in a world that is not 'what it appears to be' is an important feature of the TPers socio-materially rooted experiential structure—which not only explains their affinity to conspiracy theories but also answers why they detest the ambiguities inherent in any 'lukewarm' answer. Positioning oneself as "very conservative" in this sense is neither primarily an indicator of a coherent system of beliefs nor of a form of political loyalty, but rather an expression of one's 'authenticity' and 'firmness', and as such located at the same level as the engagement in the TP—both observable behaviors flow from the same shared source rather than explaining each other.

This also sheds some light on another peculiarity of the polls on the TP that was noticed by Skocpol and Williamson, namely, that TP supporters disproportionately identified as Independents rather than as Democrats or Republicans, yet in fact almost exclusively reported voting Republican. Here too, self-identification has to be primarily read as a display of a pre-reflexive attitude to the surrounding life-world, as a 'real' and 'simple' person, with 'firm', 'principled opinions', who cannot be subsumed under a 'political' label, rather than as an indication of an actual political stance governing (or even just coherent with) a voting behavior.[3] As such, it is the product of a practical ethos that also underlies their preference to drive the large, sometimes flag- and always sticker-decorated SUVs that filled the parking lots in front of the TP meetings I attended and their preference to eat in 'real' American roadside diners to which they invited me for first meetings.

What makes my perspective on practice *materialist* is the assumption that this class-specific ethos or habitus is ultimately grounded in the objective relations of the socio-material environment through which the subject is socialized and which it in turn embodies. The structured perception of the world that guides one to act in the world is constituted through moving and acting in an objective surrounding that is itself already socially and materially structured (cf. Bourdieu 1987, 142) (in this sense, *social being determines consciousness*, to borrow Marx' classical formulation of the materialist stance [Marx 1971, 9]). From this perspective, the regularities observable in people's everyday routines and actions cannot primarily be understood as guided by a systematic set of rules, be they anthropological givens (in the sense of natural laws) or explicated in some sort of discourse (in the sense, social conventions) but rather as the outcome of the requirements of practical coherence in a world experienced as patterned both by explicit rules and implicit regularities to be reckoned with—the logic of practice is logical only insofar as (and because) it is practical (Bourdieu 1987, esp. 157–170, 1979a, esp. 203–227, 248f.).

Thus, the theory of practice rejects the dichotomies of 'objective' and 'subjective', of 'structure' and 'agency', of 'micro' and 'macro', and conceptualizes them not only as mutually constitutive but as two sides of the same coin, which is the constant dialectic of embodied and objectified history, or of the social and mental structures at different points of social space (cf. Wacquant 1996, esp. 17–34; also Müller 2002). This does not mean to ignore so-called non-economic motives and focus on some sort of 'objective interest' but rather to mistrust the very dichotomy of economic and non-economic motives and to instead reconstruct the dialectic through which both are emerging from the same social dynamics and contradictions. It is for this reason that this perspective offers an original and promising angle for an analysis of the relation of different classes' socio-specific experience of the Great Recession with their respective protest-practice, since it urges us to ask not only how experiences are translated into grievance and then expressed as protest, but how all three of them—the experience, the translation, and the expression—are in fact not only interrelated but structured and connected through a shared predisposition which itself is ultimately grounded in the living conditions of the members of the respective group.

To approach the protests from the angle of a theory of practice rather than from the angle of other theories usually referred to in social movement studies is plausible not only because it is a promising and original way of addressing the research gap identified but also because the very nature of the protests sunder scrutiny seems to call for a shift of attention toward their pre-reflexive and practical aspects: As Kerbo already argued in 1982, in his critical engagement with Resource Mobilization Theory (RMT), mainstream social movement theories' criticism of the older theories of collective behavior was implicitly connected to a shift in attention from one type of 'movement' to another type. The anomie and deprivation-oriented collective behavior approaches tended to focus on what Kerbo calls "movements of crisis", which are defined (among other factors) by their spontaneity and often unclear strategy. RMT theory implicitly privileged "movements of affluence" (that might in fact better be called movements in times of relative socio-political stability), which are defined by rather moderate and defined aims and long-term strategic planning and mobilization of participants (Kerbo 1982). The explosive growth of the early phase of OWS and the TP, which mobilized so many first-time activists with such a vague, undefined message, clearly indicates that at least their early development, which is the focus of this book, belongs to the category of the crisis movement.

Skocpol and Williamson's observation that the TP meetings they visited did not differ much in style from a "run-of-the-mill meeting of a homeowners' association, or a Bible study group (...) or the Elks' Club" (Skocpol and Williamson 2012, 16) also seems to support this line of reasoning: It is plausible that for the TP and OWS, differentiation between the constitutive logics of the protest practice and that of other genres of social practice of the protesters might not be as pronounced as in the case of social movements under more stable circumstances. Another example illuminating this subterranean connection between different forms of practice, this time taken from OWS, might be a participant, himself a *schoolteacher*, who, interviewed about the occupation of Zuccotti Park, sums the whole scenery up as that of "*a classroom*" which "people didn't want to leave" (Wedes, Justin. Cited in: Gould-Wartofsky 2015, 70, emphasis added).

My perspective on the protests can be summarized as an understanding of the protest-practices as reacting to the lived experience of socioeconomic crisis, which in its form and content is shaped by the habitus as a socio-specific logic of practice as it is formed in (and forms) the whole everyday practical engagement of the members of the respective social classes with their socio-material environment. On the one hand, this requires breaking with pre-constructed notions of protests and movements as specific genres of practice. On the other hand, it calls for the use of a conceptual and methodological toolkit that allows one to understand the protests as products of an underlying practical class ethos or habitus. This double requirement explains (and hopefully justifies in the eyes of the reader) why this book at times might seem to travel with unusually heavy baggage of philosophical and political economic terminology, yet at the same time unusually light in regard to references to what could be considered object-related theories by a reader versed in social movement studies.[4]

As Wacquant clarified to critics, *Body and Soul*, which is based on his ethnographic study in a Chicago Boxing Club, is not a book "about sport," or about "an occupational or ethnic 'subculture'", but about "a *bodily craft* and its practical logics" (Wacquant 2005, 442, emphasis in original, cf. 2003). I would therefore also like to issue a warning: This book is not so much about social movements or the (sub) culture of certain political or social milieus. Rather, it aims to deal with the way in which the habitus of certain class-generational units both structures and is structured by the experience of the Great Recession. It is for this reason that I avoid the terminology of social movement studies and rather refer to the more open concept of *protest-practices*—understood as the social practice of articulating and enacting discontent as a form of public critique—and *protest mobilization* to refer to the complex of protest-practices that, from the inside and outside, are identified as one integrated protest.

For two reasons, *social class* is the main identifying dimension of the core constituencies in this book. First, although the protests themselves clearly evolved around (maybe displaced, yet clearly discernible) questions of class conflict, as documented in Santelli's call for "all capitalists" to join him for another Boston Tea Party which is often mentioned as the founding moment of the TP and in the whole "producerist" ideological narrative structuring the TP's political rhetoric (Berlet 2012), as well as in OWS' slogan that "we are the 99%", this dimension was only insufficiently taken up in studies on the protests. The focus on this dimension is not only the attempt to fill a gap but also to counter a problematic trend—as della Porta noted, where social movement studies did mention the "class cleavage" in the last decades, it was usually only to declare its diminishing significance for contemporary societies (Della Porta 2015, 12)—a fact which has to almost be considered active denial, given that social inequality has risen unambiguously in most of these societies during the very same period.[5] Second, and more importantly, however, class is the central social structuring principle of capitalist societies when seen through the lens of the analysis of the political economy. This is explicitly *not* to say that other social categorizations do not structure the exposure and experience of social developments such as the Great Recession, or even that class is the most central category for this experience and the institutions shaping the exposure to the crisis, but that, seen from the perspective of the political economic crisis, this exposure enforces these differences primarily *as* class differences.

This is one reason why, as Bourdieu noticed, the mobilization of social groups on the basis of other structuring principles than class is most promising in those cases (such as 'race' in the USA) in which the social groups delineated by these categories at least roughly coincide with the fault lines of social class (Bourdieu 1985, 13f.) or that scholars in political science identified the class cleavage as the cleavage most persistently shaping the political landscape in many European countries (Rokkan 1999, 334ff.). In capitalist economies, in which the iron laws of commodity exchange and the ever-extending reevaluation of capital through the exploitation of labor determine the material reproduction of society, class is not simply one among several 'axes of inequality' but is in its specific logics directly implicated in the defining basic structure of this society itself. While one can at least try to imagine a non-racist capitalist society, classless capitalism is a *contradictio in adjecto*.

Analytically, the identification of the class-generational units therefore also functions as the hinge to another level of analysis—that of the structural crisis of the finance-dominated accumulation regime as the crisis-protests' defining horizon. In order to understand and not only replicate these classes' experience of crisis and its relation to their protest-practice, and especially to be able to grasp the critical potential of the protest-practice, the identification of the classes and their socio-biographic trajectories needs to be analytically reembedded into the changing social morphology of the direct environment of the practice (which in the case of more established forms of social practice would be a *field*) and social space more generally. This is all the more pertinent, since, other than in the case of less spontaneous, more differentiated social practices, the protests in times of crisis cannot be unambiguously identified with a specific social field. Rather, as discussed in Chap. 6, they unfold at the conjuncture of synchronized yet relatively autonomous developments in different social fields. This conjuncture, however, is itself not accidental, but it is the structural dominance of the economic over all other spheres of social life that allows for this process of synchronization.

My practice-oriented approach can thus be summed up as the reconstruction of the overdeterminancy of the protest-practice as arising from the interaction of the socially specific subjectivations of the development of the social structure and the objective development itself at different points in social space. To fill this rather abstract formula with the concrete experiences, conflicts, and contradictions that arise at these meeting points is the task of the book. Before the next subsection turns to the methodological implications of this approach, it now seems appropriate to also write something about the *libido sciendi* underlying the choice of this perspective. In other words, what did *I* wish to learn and do through this approach, beyond filling or at least reducing the manifest research gap identified above?

First, to understand the protest-practice through this lens helps in better understanding the genesis and social meaning of some of the often observed peculiarities, especially of OWS' protests, such as the occupation of public space, or its refusal to formulate explicit demands. As discussed in Chaps. 5 and 7, these elements of the practice can be modelled as resulting from different, sometimes even contradicting latent and manifest interests of the core constituency of the protest, and of those of other class-generational units that were aligned with—or participating in—the protests, as well as of opportunities and limitations of the broader social context in which the protests unfolded. This critical reconstruction allows for a sober understanding of the social meaning of these practices in the historical conjuncture they unfolded in and thus to reach beyond the opposition of making them the signature of the emphatically new—the "new new social movement" (Langman 2013) that "changes everything" (Gelder 2011)—and reducing them to yet another instance of "simulative democracy" (Blühdorn 2013).

Second, and more generally, this practice-oriented reconstructive approach implicates a stance toward the protests which allows for productively surmounting the tension between *identification with* and *objectivation of* the protests, between acting as a loudspeaker for (or against) and a schoolmaster of the protests. Using a term coined by Bourdieu for his own scientific strategy, I decided to call this project of the "sympathetic interpreter"—as Roland Roth praised Herbert Marcuse's stance toward the new social movements (Roth 1985, 8)—*socio-analysis* (Bourdieu and Wacquant 1996, 95ff.; see also King 2014; Steinmetz 2006). In focusing on the tension between the different layers of the subjective meaning of the protest-practice as well as between different social predispositions in the respective protests and between these predispositions and the objective social context that these conflicting predispositions unfold in, this approach contributes to a process of reflexivity and self-understanding that untangles the social conflicts, discontent, and desires that surfaced in this short but turbulent phase of critique as protests as a consequence of the Great Recession.

1.1.2 *Methods I: Reconstructive and Critical-Hermeneutic Methodology*

The practice-oriented perspective implicates a certain methodological stance that aims at reconstructing both the meaningful lived experiences of the actors and the objective determinacy of the condition of the possibility of these experiences, as well as reconstructing the social practice that bears witness of these experiences by productively and creatively intervening in the subjects' environments. The concrete methods chosen to address this triple task will be discussed in the context of the respective chapters. This subsection intends to clarify the general methodological stance's relation to the practice-oriented perspective as well as some decisions made in setting up the research design and to thereby already help the reader estimate the scope and validity of what s/he will find in this book. Thus, this subsection discusses two main issues: (i) the specificity of the reconstructive approach this book employs in reconstructing the habitus, which is substantially different from quantitative approaches, but also differs strongly from subsumptivist approaches as employed, for example, in Mayring's qualitative content analysis (Bohnsack et al. 2003, 89ff.; Przyborski and Wohlrab-Sahr 2014, 27, fn. 26; cf. Mayring 1993), and (ii) the type and scope of the material used for the different parts of the analysis.

As discussed, my practice-oriented approach presupposes that the key link between experience and practice is the socially specific, pre-reflexive rationality of the habitus—the reconstruction of this habitus therefore is the key methodological challenge.[6] If this approach is to differ epistemologically from ascribing analytically derived (or otherwise pre-constructed) interests onto actors—as the deployment the trope of the 'objective class interest' in the Marxian tradition often meant—or from simply tautologically labeling the habitus the totality of what the subjects have observably done anyway, then this rationality must be studied via a reconstruction of the immanent logics of practices and experiences. In the terminology of Bourdieu, one must attempt to reconstruct the logic of the *modus operandi* from the homologies detectable in the multiplicity of *opus operati*, which alone are observable (cf. Bourdieu 1979a, 209).

An open reconstruction of the inner logics of the practice requires factoring out knowledge on the object that would theoretically pre-structure the case and thereby potentially impose an external structure of meaning on the research object (cf. Hoffmann-Riem 1980). This extends both to theories on social movements but also to existing studies or other contextual knowledge on the 'culture' of the social classes and political milieus involved in the two mobilizations. Two main reasons for doing so should be named. First, as discussed in Chap. 3, the definition of the class-generational unit is different from many other notions of class that circulate in the social sciences. That something has been argued to be part of the typical 'American middle class culture', for example, does not mean that it is also a relevant element in the practical unfolding of the discontent of the older cohorts of the classical petty bourgeoisie and of the younger cohorts of the new petty bourgeoisie alike—in fact, this is highly unlikely.[7]

Furthermore, the focus of my interest is the immanent logic of the practical unfolding of critique as protests as a social practice of the respective class-generational units. This unfolding is understood not as a determined program, but as a process of practical appropriation of the socio-symbolic and material surroundings. Thus, the observable accordance with pre-existing discourses and interpretative schemes is something that in itself needs to be explained rather than being an explanation for anything. It is, for example, true that the TPers display a strong anti-communist resentment in their protest-practice, and of course US history provides a rich tradition of red-baiting linked to this resentment. What interests me the most, however, is not the coincidence of these two empirical facts, but the question of how TPers integrate and (re-) produce this resentment in their own, habitually structured appropriation of the world around them.

Systematically setting aside contextual knowledge does of course not mean pretending that the interpreter 'forgets' them during the analysis, which would be both impossible and counterproductive. As, for example, Oevermann, as the main proponent of one of the most rigorous reconstructive approaches, convincingly argues, this kind of contextual knowledge is very important to informing the reading of the cases and help to build hypothesis on their logics. However, the only solid touchstone for falsifying and validating these hypotheses are the protocols of the cases itself (Oevermann 1996, esp. 99f.). Strictly focusing on the immanent logics of the cases does however not imply that the generalizability of the results is not of interest—but it is aimed not via the size of the 'sample' but through the careful reconstruction of the decisive patterns of the inner structure of the cases (Oevermann 2005, 12–16). In this approach, the generalizability of the results rests mainly on the fine-grained understanding of the *type*, not the number of *tokens* in which the type might be realized (Oevermann 2005, 13).

This focusing on the *typical* instead of the *representative* means that the material on which this reconstruction is based has to be selected according to carefully meta-theoretically derived empirically informed criteria. It was explicitly not the aim to interview and observe activists who were as diverse or different as possible, but rather to focus on those identified as belonging to the core constituency of the respective protest mobilization. Practically, however, the identification of this core constituency and the recruitment of my interviewees was rather an iterative, dialectical process. When I began my research project in the fall of 2012, I traveled to the USA as soon as possible to establish access to social groups, which, as I feared, would become more difficult over time as the heydays of the mobilizations had, in both cases, already passed. Nonetheless, the mass mobilization of Occupy Sandy, intertwined with the last attempts to revive the overall networks of OWS, and the TP's mobilization around the presidential election proved to be an opportune window of access to the groups. Since my theoretical framework and my empirical knowledge on the demographics of the mobilization was still, however, in a very fragmentary state, I basically collected all data I could get my hands on—I observed every meeting I was invited to, spoke to pretty much every activist who was willing to talk to me, and collected every leaflet or piece of literature that I could get my hands on.

Following this first "long preliminary soak" in the material (Hall 1975, 15) and informed by the available surveys and a process of ongoing theoretical reflection, the focus of the project was consequently narrowed down. While I theoretically derived *class-generational unit* to be the conceptual category to define the core constituency of the protests, my impressions of the protests and the available surveys led me to identify the respective core constituencies as the older cohort of the classical petty bourgeoisie and the aspiring youth of the new petty bourgeoisie. The process resulted in numerous protocols of participant observations at group meetings of all protests, and a total of 30 interviews and seven group discussions with 63 activists, transcribed in approximately 1400 pages, constituting base of material for the analysis. The habitus reconstruction proper drew on ten interviews and six group discussions.

1.2 Structure of the Book

As already indicated, understanding the protests as a social practice is of course not reducible to reconstructing its habitual structuring. It also requires identifying the social subject of the practice and the crisis dynamics they are exposed to, as well as the social environment in which they articulate their protest. This multi-level approach is reflected in the structure of this book.

When I started my research, the events around which the analyzed practices unfolded were still clearly present to most people I spoke to. Recently, however, I had to explain what the Tea Party was to an otherwise well-informed listener at a presentation on my research, bringing to my mind the sobering yet also somewhat comforting banality that even though I spent the last four years contemplating the very same series of events, most others have found different questions to ponder. Indeed, a decade has now passed since the collapse of the US housing market triggered the Great Recession, and more than half a decade has passed since Time Magazine declared the protester to be the person of the year 2011 (Andersen 2011). After this introduction and before the first chapter, a kind of prelude to the study itself therefore recalls the early development of the two protest mobilizations—thereby hopefully bringing back the memory of countless newspaper articles, television news segments, blog entries, and personal experiences through which the reader learned about these protests—and with it a more nuanced image of the protests than can be possibly offered in this short subsection.

The second chapter, *The Structural Crisis and the Emerging Patterns of Class Conflict*, provides a brief discussion of the political economic causes of the Great Recession and its political processing in the years leading up to the protests mobilizations. This both prepares the ground for an understanding of the developments in the US class structure over the last decades and allows for critically evaluating the relation of the protest-practice to the politics of crisis and the latter's objective limits.

The main argument of this chapter is that these concrete phenomena are driven by a series of escalating contradictions, which amount to a *structural crisis of the finance-dominated regime of accumulation*, the roots of which are to be sought in the falling profit rates around the globe. The mutual blockade of different factions of the dominating classes in the USA hinders an effective solution of the crisis via a large-scale devaluation of surplus capital and a shift in the productive base of the accumulation regime. Using a concept developed by Gramsci, I call this period of a blocked transition during a structural crisis—in which "the old is dying", yet "the new cannot be born"—an *interregnum*.[8] This means that the protests have to be understood in the context of a *disintegrating hegemonic block*, which is expressed in conflicts between the factions of the ruling classes on question of economic redistribution, economic restructuring, and austerity as ways to deal with the crisis, heightening the potential social resonance of protests addressing political economic questions.

The third chapter, *The Demographics of the Mobilized: the Core Constituency of the Protests*, aims at identifying what I call the *core constituency* of the respective protest mobilizations and their *experiential background* or *corridor of experience* in the years before the protests began. The term core constituency is used to refer to the class-generational units whose shared experiential background and corresponding class ethos decisively shaped the 'style' of the respective protest-practice.

Using the available statistical data on the protests, this chapter identifies the older cohorts of the *classical petty bourgeoisie* as the core constituency of the TP. Mainly small property owners, usually from the middle and upper-middle income quintile, they were directly impacted by the crisis via a devaluation of their safety assets. Furthermore, the crisis ended the brief period of a temporary reversal of the secular decline of the relative size of this class between 2001 and 2007, resulting in the eclipse of their economic horizon. The core constituency of OWS is shown to be the aspiring, yet *biographically blocked youth of the new petty bourgeoisie*. Highly educated, usually in the arts, social sciences, or humanities, yet with no or relatively little economic capital at their disposal, they are confronted with a devaluation of their cultural capital which increasingly erodes their distinct class position.

The fourth, methodological chapter, *Theoretical and Methodological Considerations: Habitus and Habitus Reconstruction*, first explains the concept of the habitus as the way in which social structure folds back on itself through subjectivized mediating structures, thereby outlining this category's potential for understanding the lived experience and the predisposition toward resonating with specific protest-practices. Second, it outlines the methodological premises and the basic steps of interpretation of the so-called documentary method, which I use in the reconstruction of the protest mobilizations' habitus.

In the fifth chapter, the empirical heart of this study, *Experiencing the Crisis: Results of the Habitus Reconstruction*, passages of interviews and group discussions with core constituency participants from all three protests as well as two images used in the propaganda of the TP and OWS are analyzed to reconstruct the respective habitus structuring both these class-generational units' experiences of the crisis and their *investment* in the respective protest-practice. The accounts of the participants in the two American protest mobilizations reveal a torn *modus operandi* of processing the way in which the crisis escalated the contradictions already inherent in their respective class position.

The TPers *conformist rebellion* can be understood in this light as the expression of a painful socio-symbolic crisis, resulting from their feeling duped by the very same social order and authority that they base their claims to wealth and social recognition on—a contradiction I sum up as *disappointment while refusing to be disillusioned.* In other words, the refusal/repression of the knowledge that one's socioeconomic position is systematically undermined by the dynamics of capitalist accumulation, which returns as the apocalyptic imaginary of the end of the world. The investment of OWS' core constituency in protest-practice, in contrast, is shown to be structured not around the repression of an inevitable loss but around the insistence on the ethos of a social role which is more and more at odds with its objective chances for realization. For example, the style in which the much cited *prefigurative politics* were realized have to be understood at least partially as produced by the desire for the *continuation of the university by other means*, sometimes in *contradiction to the explicit political content* of the protest-practice. These contradictions contribute to what I call the tragedy of the crisis protest, namely, that important motivational forces of the protest mobilizations in fact block or at least hinder the strategic engagement with the very social causes of the underlying discontent.

The sixth chapter, *Fields and Conjunctures: The Thick Opportunity Structure of the Mobilizations*, again zooms out to the broader social context of the protest-practice. The different dynamics in a number of social fields, especially the economic, the political, and the journalistic field, but also the sub-space of the political field which we can identify as the social movement field, together explain why the protest-practice was able to resonate with the broader social space and to reach beyond the immediate surroundings of the early constituency. This in some sense closes the circle that began with the chapter on the economic crisis, which is now understood more concretely as articulated as (semi-)autonomous developments in different social fields, the conjuncture of which culminated in the protest-practices.

In the case of the TP, the synchronicity and homology between conflicts in three social fields not only in part explains the mobilization's explosive growth but also its direct impact on the public beyond it. From the economic field, the mobilization against the specter of a 'Green New Deal' spilled over into the political field, where it merged with the mobilization of the far right of the Republican Party in crisis after the election of Obama, all further fueled by a polarized journalistic field. In the case of OWS, the social movement field had become increasingly professionalized and many actors were directly aligned with actors in the political field in the past decades. When these political actors became increasingly discredited in the first years of the Obama administration, the field itself did not seem to offer a possible outlet for the resulting frustration. Inspired by the protest-practice of other protests in Europe and Northern Africa and motivated by the initial success of OWS, the core constituency of OWS de facto attempted to secede from the social movement field. But while this demonstrative cutting of all ties allowed for large initial mobilization successes, the core constituency was not able to institutionalize and stabilize their early successes in the face of state repression and disintegration tendencies.

The seventh chapter, *The Acid Test: Reconstructing the Meaning of the Park as a Socially Determined Practice of Protests*, turns toward two often noticed peculiarities of the protest-practice of OWS, namely, the centrality of the occupation of Zuccotti Park and the apparent refusal to formulate explicit demands and set up institutionalized decision-making structures. Bringing together the determinants of the practice developed in the analytical part, they demonstrate that the findings of these chapters can indeed explain peculiarities of the protest-practice: The centrality of the occupation for the practice of OWS is shown, on the one hand, to be rooted in the affective investment into the dialogical and caring practices reflecting the habitus of the biographically blocked new petty bourgeoisie, while, on the other hand, the crisis state of the social movement field especially in NYC hindered the development of other practice-settings that could have channeled these investments in a similar way.

1.3 Prelude: Explosions and Implosions. A Very Short History of the Protest Mobilizations

On February 19, 2009, Rick Santelli, a CNBC editor, reporting from the floor of the Chicago Board of Trade, had an angry outburst accusing the government of promoting bad behavior by not supporting those that "carry the water instead of drink(ing) the water"; he called for "all capitalists" to join him for a new *Tea Party* in Chicago on July 4.[9] The occasion for this outburst was the *Homeowners Affordability and Stability Plan*, which President Obama had announced the day before to counter the swelling wave of foreclosures that had precipitated the financial meltdown of the US economy a few months earlier.

In the next few hours, the "rant heard 'round the world"[10] was played in all cable news networks, dozens of Facebook Pages supporting Santelli popped up, and the website reTeaParty.com that was set up to coordinate Tea Party (TP) rallies nationwide reported to have 11,000 visitors per day on March 4, 2009 (Last 2009). However, on February 27, 2009, when the first 'official' TP protests, organized by lobbying organizations such as *Freedom Works* and the *Sam Adams Alliance*, took place in dozens of cities, they drew only comparatively small crowds (Williamson 2011, 26). The numbers grew substantially when, on April 15, 2009, the so-called Tax Day, rallies were held in 750 cities with a total of more than half a million participants (Robbins 2009). In the weeks before, six nationwide operating organizations had worked on publicizing this event—three of them already existing, like the mentioned Freedom Works, three newly founded, but all of them heavily backed by existing right-wing think tanks and lobbying organizations.[11] Another important mobilizing force was *Fox News*: It had run more than 100 promotion clips for its coverage of the TP events in the days leading up to April 15, 2009 (Carr 2009).

In the following year, the TP remained a highly visible and vocal presence in the political public of the USA. It mobilized tens of thousands of demonstrators, united by their mistrust and anger toward the new administration and especially Barack Obama, to large rallies in Washington DC. TPers interrupted (or very persistently participated in) town hall meetings, for example, on the proposed healthcare reform (*Obamacare*) and held roadside rallies all across the country. In the lead-up to the midterm election of 2010, TP groups (in many cases successfully) backed very conservative Republican candidates and thereby shifted the party notably to the right. Their enthusiasm and involvement without doubt further contributed to the Republican victories in this midterm election itself, which, similar to the so-called Gingrich-Revolution in 1994, broke the majority of the Democrats in congress and thereby allowed for a politics of blockade—something that observers had not deemed possible when the Republicans had hit their historic low in popularity in 2008 (e.g., Solty 2013, 35f.).

After the midterm election in 2010 however, and latest after the near-bankruptcy of the USA in the summer of 2011 that followed after a conflict over raising the so-called debt ceiling (in which many TP groups backed the uncompromising positions within the Republican Party), the popularity of the TP declined notably (Cooper and Thee-Brenan 2011; CBS News 2014). With this loss in popularity the mobilization also lost its momentum and the impact on decisions in the party itself diminished significantly, culminating in the nomination of the moderate Mitt Romney as the presidential candidate of the Republican Party in 2012. Since then the TP as a brand continued to draw attention in inner-party conflicts but, as a protest mobilization 'on the ground', never really regained momentum.

In fall 2011, another protest mobilization began to capture the headlines instead: inspired by the uprisings around the Mediterranean Sea—from Tunisia and Egypt to Greece and Spain—the Canada-based magazine *Adbusters* called to "#OCCUPYWALLSTREET" (Adbusters 2011). At a small public assembly on August 2, 2011, which was supposed to discuss this suggestion, after conflict over the use of loudspeakers and the conduct of the meeting itself, a group of (mostly) Anarchists broke off and formed the *New York City General Assembly* (NYCGA), which began to organize the symbolic occupation of a public square in Downtown Manhattan (Gould-Wartofsky 2015, 42–52; see also Kroll 2011). On September 17, 2011, a group of between 2000 and 5000 people attended several small actions in Downtown Manhattan (Kraushaar 2012, 73) and finally met for the first large General Assembly in *Zuccotti Park*, a space chosen because it, as a privately owned public space, had no curfew, as opposed to NYC's other public parks. They decided to rename the Park *Liberty Plaza* and to declare it to be a permanent occupation (NYCGA 2011). *Occupy Wall Street* was born. Frequent smaller confrontations with the police seemed to display insecurity in how to deal with the new form of protest and led to a few arrests, but not to the eviction of the park, which seemed imminent several times (Schneider 2013, 33f.).

The protesters famously refused to raise any demands but rather focused on the building of direct-democratic practices for negotiating the multiplicity of different interests and goals among themselves, insisting that "this is a process, not a protest". However, the very form of the protest—the occupation (symbolically) aiming at Wall Street—and slogans such as "we are the 99%" made it clear that social inequality stood at the center of the criticism that was articulated in this protest-practice. A much referred-to webpage of the protest mobilization, the "wearethe99perscent.tumblr.com" blog that featured personal stories and statements of people supporting OWS, supports this reading. The overwhelming majority of the entries are personal stories in which people describe having difficulties to even just get by, and that they feel like the whole 'game is rigged' against them.

Newspapers such as the *Guardian* published some smaller articles on the occupation and demonstrations around it, but overall press coverage remained low. This started to change with an incident on September 24, when a video of a police officer pepper-spraying young women already trapped in an orange plastic net was published on the internet and led to some prominent support for the movement by left-wing intellectuals and celebrities.[12] On the next Saturday, the police arrested around 700 protesters crossing Brooklyn Bridge. However, the final breakthrough onto the stage of international public attention was in mid-October: The city had announced to clear out the park for "sanitary reasons" on the night of October 13/14, but at the very last minute refrained from doing so, confronted with solidarity demonstrations that mobilized thousands to defend the park while the occupiers demonstratively cleaned the park themselves. The Spanish *15M/Democracya Real Ya* movement, which had occupied central public squares in Spain already in May 2011 and which had been an important inspiration to the OWS planning group, had called for an international day of action on October 15, which, also because of the large media attention drawn by the recent events in New York,[13] saw an explosion of the protests-demonstrations in 911 cities in 82 countries led to numerous new occupations, and the media spoke of an "Occupy Movement" emerging (Kraushaar 2012, 85–92).

In the weeks that followed, in what appears to have been a coordinated effort of several government agencies and corporate actors (e.g., Wolf 2012), the occupations in almost all major American cities were evicted. Afterward, the movement stagnated and then imploded. In NYC, the following spring and summer saw some major demonstrations and attempts to rescale and regroup. However, attempts to build democratic, shared decision-making structures failed and ended in heated conflicts. Lacking central spaces for coordination and decision-making, the protests differentiated and fragmented rather quickly.

In fall 2012, the grassroots attempts to help the victims of Hurricane Sandy in NYC under the label of *Occupy Sandy* once more brought together tens of thousands in the name of OWS, among them many first-time activists, but in doing so probably blew apart the last remnants of identifiable structures organizationally uniting OWS. Latest in 2013 and increasingly so, OWS was something that most participants I talked to regarded as history. Albeit many observers agreeing that OWS played some role in the shift of the political discourse in the USA, in which social inequality played a much more prominent role after the Fall of 2011 (e.g., Milkman et al. 2013, 37ff.), politically and socially, the impact remains difficult to estimate.

Notes

1. The "black swan event" is a metaphor popularized by the philosopher Taleb to describe an event that is originally not expected, then has major consequences, and often gets superficially rationalized with the benefit of hindsight (Taleb 2007). The extreme popularity of his book on the topic in the years of and after the Great Recession is surely no accident. By emphasizing the 'shock' of the improbable against the backdrop of the illusion of a control of risks, it captured the insecurity of many people facing the sudden meltdown of the economy. This emphasis on the unpredictable and unexpected, however, threatens to elide that the crisis did not just result from us being unable to fully understand risk, but instead exposed systemic contradictions. To confront this rootedness in objective contradictions would require to avoid the false dichotomy of *both* hasty rationalizations and of subsuming it under the existential rather than critical-historical category of the unpredictability of the future.
2. OWS did not raise any explicit demands or goals. Measuring the 'success' therefore requires attributing 'objective' political goals to OWS. Another possibility would be, as Milkman et al. have done, to try to measure the discursive shift in the general public, in which the issues raised by OWS became more topical in late 2011. Another factor mentioned by Milkman et al. is the politicization of a new generation of activists, even though evidence for this remains at the anecdotal level (cf. Milkman et al. 2013, 38ff.).
3. This might be a good point to illuminate the logics behind my use of quotation marks with regard to the use of everyday language. Of course, where it is quoted, it is quarantined by double quotation marks to avoid importing pre-constructed objects of social life into the analysis. However, these pre-constructed objects themselves structure the practices of everyday life and as such of course should also become objects of analysis, even where nobody directly refers to them. The concepts of 'firmness' or 'simpleness', for example, even though they denote guiding principles of the everyday practice of many TP activists, are not necessarily directly named by them—neither, however, are they scientific concepts (and their practical relevance

would very likely be obscured by translating them into scientific terms, since that would eliminate their quality of bundling a multiplicity of social connotations, the "semantic halo", as Bourdieu once called it [Bourdieu 1991, 22]). Where these objects and object-properties are referred to in this book, this is indicated by the use of single quotation marks.

4. This also extends to the work of scholars who, for example, Crossley, reconceptualize classical social movement theories through the lens of Bourdieu's theory of praxis. As fruitful as these are in offering a fresh perspective on certain aspects of social movement praxis, they, too, are exclusively focused on single identity and issue-based movements and therefore do not help to critically challenge the pre-constructed object of 'social movement' as it is conceptualized in mainstream social movement studies (cf. Husu 2012; Crossley 2002).
5. Even if one abstracts from the macro-social development of increasing social inequality and instead focuses on the positivist counting of protest events themselves, the withering importance of class conflict is not a simple given. Barker has argued that all periods with increasing 'new social movement' protest activity were in fact simultaneously periods of heightened industrial conflict. Hetland and Goodwin furthermore argued that at the heart of many so-called new social movements were also conflicts with a mediated or direct link to class conflict. Finally, Biggs has shown (for the British case) that the relative numerical importance of protest events aside the industrial conflict might be a statistical artifact resulting from the way in which 'protest' is conceptualized in many surveys. All in all, we might conclude that the diminishing role of class conflict in social movement studies might be more of an interesting question for a critical reconstruction of academic field dynamics than a reflection of any real trend (cf. Biggs 2015; Hetland and Goodwin 2013; Barker 2010).
6. This is not to say that it is the only methodological challenge. As Lorenzer has cautioned, the analyses of objectivized social structures and of subjectivized social structures, even though these two phenomena are mutually constitutive, and even though the analysis of both has to break with the Diltheyian dichotomy of *verstehen* and *erklären*, still have to be understood as following different research logics. Since the logic of the analysis of objectivized social structures, however, seems to provoke less misunderstandings, it might suffice to briefly sketch out its proceeding in the respective chapters (cf. Lorenzer 1977).
7. The same is true for general cultural diagnoses such as 'neoliberal subjectivity' or 'colorblind racism' which at best produce unfalsifiable, essayistic musings and at worst impose a structure of meaning onto the observed practices and interpretations which hinders to understand their inner logics. For example, Skocpol and Williamson rightly caution that the fact that

TP members disproportionately agree with the statement "if blacks would only try harder, they could be just as well off as whites" must be interpreted with care. And indeed, even though the politics resulting from such a political stance very likely will hurt (poor) people of color disproportionately, my reconstruction of their habitus implies that the logic producing this statement is the unshakable belief that your standard of living unmistakably reflects your work ethics (and interestingly, as Skocpol and Williamson point out, TPers also rate the work ethic of 'whites' far more unfavorable than other Americans do). To label this, in consequence no doubt politically dangerous, basic interpretational structure a mere strategy to "prove" one's "idyllically" "color-blindness" and thereby to deny one's racism, as Haltinner has done in her frame analysis, means imposing a structure of thinking derived from one's own understanding of the world onto a practical way of reasoning that developed in a different environment and therefore deprives itself from the very tools for effectively criticizing the resulting arguments (Haltinner 2015; Skocpol and Williamson 2012, 69).

8. "das Alte stirbt und das Neue (kann) nicht zur Welt kommen" (Gramsci 1991, 354), translation NK.
9. *CNBC's Rick Santelli's Chicago Tea Party* 2009. A transcript of the video can be found at http://freedomeden.blogspot.de/2009/02/rick-santelli-tea-party.html (accessed October 8, 2013).
10. The phrase, with which supporters of the Tea Party describe Santelli's outburst, is a reference to the line "a shot heard 'round the world" from the opening stanza of Ralph Waldo Emerson's "Concord Hymn" and thereby connects the event rhetorically to the collective memory of the US-American war of independence (cf. Chapman 2012).
11. *1776 Tea Party* was founded on February 20, the *Tea Party Patriots* on March 10, and *Tea Party Nation* on April 3 (Burghart 2012).
12. In a vein similar to (and maybe inspired by?) the TP founding myth of the "rant heard 'round the world", the OWS media collective that published one of the first books on the movement referred to this incident as "the scream heard 'round the world" (Writers for the 99% 2012; cited in: Gould-Wartofsky 2015, 79).
13. Research on LexisNexis shows 16 newspaper articles worldwide for the period from September 17 to 23, 2011, featuring "Occupy Wall Street", most of them smaller side notes, 76 from September 24 to September 30, 225 from October 01 to 07; and 229 for October 14–20, including front-page coverage and extensive commentary (accessed October 10, 2013).

Bibliography

Adbusters. 2011. #OCCUPYWALLSTREET A Shift in Revolutionary Tactics. https://www.adbusters.org/blogs/adbusters-blog/occupywallstreet.html. Accessed 15 Mar 2013.

Andersen, Kurt. 2011. Person of the Year 2011: The Protester. *Time*, December 14.

Barker, Colin. 2010. *Class Struggle and Social Movement – An Effort at Untangling*. Working Paper, Manchester Metropolitan University. https://docs.google.com/file/d/0Bz3wUg3e6r_4NzYzMzEzNGQtMjEyZC00NzJmLWJmMzItNDY2ZTIzM2VkYWE1/edit?hl=en&pli=1. Accessed 20 Nov 2017.

Benski, Tova, Lauren Langman, Ignacia Perugorría, and Benjamín Tejerina. 2013. From the Streets and Squares to Social Movement Studies: What Have We Learned? *Current Sociology* 61 (4): 541–561.

Berlet, Chip. 2012. Reframing Populist Resentment in the Tea Party Movement. In *Steep. The Precipitous Rise of the Tea Party*, ed. Christine Trost and Lawrence Rosenthal, 47–66. Berkeley: University of California Press.

Biggs, Michael. 2015. Has Protest Increased Since the 1970s? How a Survey Question Can Construct a Spurious Trend. *The British Journal of Sociology* 66 (1): 141–162.

Blühdorn, Ingolfur. 2013. *Simulative Demokratie: Neue Politik nach der postdemokratischen Wende*. Berlin: Suhrkamp.

Bohnsack, Ralf, Winfried Marotzki, and Michael Meuser. 2003. *Hauptbegriffe qualitativer Sozialforschung: ein Wörterbuch*. Opladen: Leske + Budrich.

Bourdieu, Pierre. 1979a. *Entwurf einer Theorie der Praxis auf der ethnologischen Grundlage der kabylischen Gesellschaft*. Frankfurt am Main: Suhrkamp.

———. 1979b. Public Opinion Does Not Exist. *Communication and Class Struggle* 1: 124–130.

———. 1985. *Sozialer Raum und „Klassen" und Leçon sur la leçon: Zwei Vorlesungen*. Frankfurt am Main: Suhrkamp.

———. 1987. *Sozialer Sinn: Kritik der theoretischen Vernunft*. Frankfurt am Main: Suhrkamp.

———. 1991. *The Craft of Sociology: Epistemological Preliminaries*. Berlin: Walter de Gruyter.

———. 1994. *Die feinen Unterschiede: Kritik der gesellschaftlichen Urteilskraft*. Frankfurt am Main: Suhrkamp.

Bourdieu, Pierre, and Loïc J.D. Wacquant. 1996. Die Ziele der reflexiven Soziologie: Chicago-Seminar, Winter 1987. In *Reflexive Anthropologie*, 95–249. Frankfurt am Main: Suhrkamp.

Burghart, Devin. 2012. View from the Top: Report on Six National Tea Party Organizations. In *Steep. The Precipitous Rise of the Tea Party*, ed. Lawrence Rosenthal and Christine Trost, 67–97. Berkeley: University of California Press.

Carr, David. 2009. Cable Wars Are Killing Objectivity. *The New York Times*, April 20. http://www.nytimes.com/2009/04/20/business/media/20carr.html.

CBS News. 2014. *Tea Party Support Hits New Lows: Poll.* http://www.cbsnews.com/news/tea-party-support-hits-new-lows-poll/. Accessed 28 Oct 2017.

Chapman, Roger. 2012. Not Exactly an American Cup of Tea: The Foreign Context of the Nativist Movement Known as the Tea Party. In *Social Scientists Explain the Tea Party Movement. With A Selection of Primary Documents*, ed. Roger Chapman, 51–72. Lewiston: The Edwin Mellen Press.

CNBC's Rick Santelli's Chicago Tea Party. 2009. http://www.youtube.com/watch?v=zp-Jw-5Kx8k&feature=youtube_gdata_player. Accessed 28 Oct 2017.

Cooper, Michael, and Megan Thee-Brenan. 2011. Public Views Congress as Top Culprit in Debt Debate, Poll Finds. *The New York Times*, August 4.

Crossley, Nick. 2002. *Making Sense of Social Movements.* Buckingham: Open University Press.

Della Porta, Donatella. 2015. *Social Movements in Times of Austerity: Bringing Capitalism Back into Protest Analysis.* Cambridge/Malden: Polity Press.

Frank, Thomas. 2012. To the Precinct Station – How Theory Met Practice…and Drove It Absolutely Crazy. *The Baffler* 21.

Gould-Wartofsky, Michael A. 2015. *The Occupiers: The Making of the 99 Percent Movement.* Oxford/New York: Oxford University Press.

Gramsci, Antonio. 1991. 3. Heft. In *2.-3. Heft*, ed. Wolfgang Fritz Haug, vol. 2, 327–448. Hamburg: Argument.

Hall, Stuart. 1975. Introduction. In *Paper Voices: The Popular Press and Social Change 1935–1965*, ed. Anthony Charles H. Smith, 11–24. London: Chatton & Windus.

Haltinner, Kristin. 2015. Individual Responsibility, Culture, or State Organized Enslavement? How Tea Party Activists Frame Racial Inequality. *Sociological Perspectives* 59 (2): 395–418.

Hetland, Gabriel, and Jeff Goodwin. 2013. The Strange Disappearance of Capitalism from Social Movement Studies. In *Marxism and Social Movements*, ed. Colin Barker, Laurence Cox, John Krinsky, and Alf Gunvald, 83–102. Leiden: Brill.

Hoffmann-Riem, Christa. 1980. Die Sozialforschung einer interpretativen Soziologie: der Datengewinn. *Kölner Zeitschrift für Soziologie und Sozialpsychologie* 32 (2): 339–372.

Husu, Hanna-Mari. 2012. Bourdieu and Social Movements: Considering Identity Movements in Terms of Field, Capital and Habitus. *Social Movement Studies* 12 (3): 264–279.

Kerbo, Harold R. 1982. Movements of 'Crisis' and Movements of 'Affluence': A Critique of Deprivation and Resource Mobilization Theories. *Journal of Conflict Resolution* 26 (4): 645–663.

King, Vera. 2014. Pierre Bourdieu als Analytiker des Sozialen: Methodologische und konzeptionelle Bezüge zur Psychoanalyse sowie sozialpsychologische Perspektiven im Werk Bourdieus. *Sozialer Sinn. Zeitschrift für hermeneutische Sozialforschung* 15 (1): 3–28.

Kraushaar, Wolfgang. 2012. *Der Aufruhr der Ausgebildeten: vom Arabischen Frühling zur Occupy-Bewegung*. Hamburg: Hamburger Edition.

Kroll, Andy. 2011. How Occupy Wall Street Really Got Started. *Mother Jones*, October 17. http://www.motherjones.com/politics/2011/10/occupy-wall-street-international-origins?page=1. Accessed 28 Oct 2017.

Langman, Lauren. 2013. Occupy: A New Social Movement. *Current Sociology* 61 (4): 510–524.

Last, Jonathan V. 2009. A Growing ‚Tea Party' Movement? *Weekly Standard, Reprinted By CBSNews.com*, April 3. http://www.cbsnews.com/8301-215_162-4843055.html. Accessed 28 Oct 2017.

Lorenzer, Alfred. 1977. Zum Verhältnis von objektiver und subjektiver Struktur. In *Sprachspiel und Interaktionsformen*, 195–217. Frankfurt am Main: Suhrkamp.

Marx, Karl. 1971. Zur Kritik der Politischen Ökonomie. In *MEW 13*, 3–160. Berlin: Dietz.

Mayring, Philipp. 1993. *Qualitative Inhaltsanalyse*. Weinheim: Deutscher Studien-Verlag.

Milkman, Ruth, Stephanie Luce, and Penny Lewis. 2013. *Changing the Subject: A Bottom-Up Account of Occupy Wall Street in New York City*. New York: Joseph S. Murphy Institute for Worker Education and Labor Studies. https://www.documentcloud.org/documents/562862-changing-the-subject-2.html. Accessed 28 Oct 2017.

Müller, Hans-Peter. 2002. Die Einbettung des Handelns. Pierre Bourdieus Praxeologie. *Berliner Journal für Soziologie* 12 (2): 157–171.

NYCGA. 2011. General Assembly Minutes 9/17/11. *NYCGA* (blog). September 17. http://www.nycga.net/2011/09/general-assembly-minutes-91711/. Accessed 14 Oct 2013.

Oevermann, Ulrich. 1996. Beckett's ‚Endspiel' als Prüfstein hermeneutischer Methodologie. Eine Interpretation mit den Verfahren der objektiven Hermeneutik. Oder: Ein objektiv-hermeneutisches Exerzitium. In *Neue Versuche Becketts Endspiel zu verstehen. Sozialwissenschaftliche Interpretation nach Adorno*, ed. Hans-Dieter König, 93–249. Frankfurt am Main: Suhrkamp.

———. 2005. *Klinische Soziologie auf der Basis der Methodologie der objektiven Hermeneutik: Manifest der objektiv hermeneutischen Sozialforschung*. http://publikationen.ub.uni-frankfurt.de/volltexte/2005/540/. Accessed 28 Oct 2017.

Przyborski, Aglaja, and Monika Wohlrab-Sahr. 2014. *Qualitative Sozialforschung: ein Arbeitsbuch*. München: Oldenbourg Verlag.

Robbins, Liz. 2009. Tax Day Is Met With Tea Parties. *The New York Times*, April 16. http://www.nytimes.com/2009/04/16/us/politics/16taxday.html. Accessed 28 Oct 2017.

Rokkan, Stein. 1999. Cleavage Structures and Party Systems. In *State Formation, Nation-Building, and Mass Politics in Europe: The Theory of Stein Rokkan*, ed. Peter Flora, Stein Kuhnle, and Derek Urwin, 275–340. Oxford: Oxford University Press.

Roth, Roland. 1985. *Rebellische Subjektivität: Herbert Marcuse und die neuen Protestbewegungen*. Frankfurt am Main: Campus.

Schneider, Nathan. 2013. *Thank You, Anarchy: Notes from the Occupy Apocalypse*. Berkeley: University of California Press.

Simmel, Georg. 1994. *Philosophie des Geldes*. Frankfurt am Main: Suhrkamp.

Skocpol, Theda, and Vanessa Williamson. 2012. *The Tea Party and the Remaking of Republican Conservatism*. Oxford: Oxford University Press.

Solty, Ingar. 2013. Einleitung: Die Innen-Außen-Dialektik des American Empire in der globalen Krise. In *Die USA unter Obama: Charismatische Herrschaft, soziale Bewegungen und imperiale Politik in der globalen Krise*, 15–71. Hamburg: Argument.

Steinmetz, George. 2006. Bourdieu's Disavowal of Lacan: Psychoanalytic Theory and the Concepts of 'Habitus' and 'Symbolic Capital'. *Constellations* 13 (4): 445–464.

Taleb, Nassim Nicholas. 2007. *The Black Swan: The Impact of the Highly Improbable*. London: Allen Lane.

van Gelder, Sarah Ruth. 2011. *This Changes Everything: Occupy Wall Street and the 99% Movement*. San Francisco: Berrett-Koehler Publishers.

Wacquant, Loïc J.D. 1996. Auf dem Weg zu einer Sozialpraxeologie. Struktur und Logik der Soziologie Pierre Bourdieus. In *Reflexive Anthropologie*, 17–93. Frankfurt am Main: Suhrkamp.

———. 2003. *Leben für den Ring: Boxen im amerikanischen Ghetto*. Konstanz: UVK.

———. 2005. Shadowboxing with Ethnographic Ghosts: A Rejoinder. *Symbolic Interaction* 28 (3): 441–447.

Williamson, Vanessa, Theda Skocpol, and John Coggin. 2011. The Tea Party and the Remaking of Republican Conservatism. *Perspectives on Politics* 9 (1): 25–43.

Wolf, Naomi. 2012. Revealed: How the FBI Coordinated the Crackdown on Occupy. *The Guardian*, December 29. http://www.theguardian.com/commentisfree/2012/dec/29/fbi-coordinated-crackdown-occupy. Accessed 28 Oct 2017

Writers for the 99%. 2012. *Occupying Wall Street: The inside Story of an Action That Changed America*. Chicago: Haymarket Books.

CHAPTER 2

The Structural Crisis and the Emerging Patterns of Class Conflict

The understanding of the political economic logic behind the dynamics of the Great Recession is important for the understanding of the crisis-protests as a social practice in three ways: (i) First, these dynamics function as objective determinants of the protesting subjects' experience of crisis. The social classes that form the constituency of the respective protest mobilization were subjected to very different social developments in the Great Recession, which also took shape against the backdrop of what 'normal' socio-biographical trajectory they could expect on pre-crisis terms. This aspect of the 'being-subjected-to' the crisis (and with it a more concrete picture of what actually 'happened' as the crisis unfolded) will be treated more concretely in Chaps. 3 and 6. (ii) Second, the political economic logic behind the Great Recession as it will be discussed in this chapter allows us to understand how the different ways in which these groups were exposed to the crisis are rooted in the same crisis tendencies of the capitalist economy. This is an important element of the critical understanding of how they interpreted and reacted to the crisis. (iii) Third, and most importantly for what will be discussed in this chapter, the dynamics of crisis create and reinforce social conflicts crisscrossing social space and thereby decisively structure the morphology of the ground on which the protest-practice itself is enacted. The way in which the contradictions of global capitalism surfaced across different economic sectors predisposed factions of capital in the USA to develop quite different preferences for

N. C. Kumkar, *The Tea Party, Occupy Wall Street, and the Great Recession*, Critical Political Theory and Radical Practice,
https://doi.org/10.1007/978-3-319-73688-4_2

how to react to the crisis in the short and midterm. The political tensions that arose around the resulting conflicts formed an important body of social resonance for protests which focused on questions that were topical in these conflicts.

The chapter will be structured into four subsections. The first section (2.1) will explain my choice to rely on a Regulation Approach informed understanding of the crisis and why this understanding is a theoretically compatible and fruitful background for the theory-of-practice perspective on protest that I will develop in the following chapters. Drawing mainly on the Marxist literature on the crisis, the next section (2.2) then outlines the political economic dynamics that surfaced in the crisis—it explains the Great Recession as an acute stage of the escalating structural crisis of the finance-dominated accumulation regime.

To explain how the crisis contributed to the building up of tensions that then functioned as a resonance body for the protests, the following (2.3) section concretizes this abstract analysis by outlining the diverging class-interests and -relations that confronted each other in the Great Recession. With regard to factions of capital and their strategies in dealing with the crisis, it shows that, in the USA, the crisis polarized capital into two camps. On the one hand, the adherents of a potential Green New Deal that supported the presidential candidacy of Obama. On the other hand, the opponents of such a political economic restructuring rallied behind Obama's opponent McCain. The last concluding section (2.4) will discuss some of this chapter's findings' implications for the understanding of the emergence of the protests—as a 'first cut theory of the crisis-protests', which however, through its gaps and indeterminacies, already prepares the stage for the following chapters.

2.1 Theory of Practice and Regulation Approach

My understanding of the crisis is centered on the Regulation Approach inspired concept of the *structural crisis of the finance-dominated accumulation regime*. I chose this conceptual framework for two main reasons: On the one hand, it allows one to understand social conflicts and developments and economic dynamics and crises as part of one articulated political economic whole without simply deducting the one from the other. On the other hand, the Regulation Approach's open "*ex-post* functionalism" (Lipietz 1998, 81 emphasis in original) enables us to grasp the systemic character of the Great Recession without pre-constructing it as the inevitable end of capitalism or some similarly apocalyptic scenario.

The Regulation Approach developed as a strand of Marxist theorizing on the critique of political economy concerned with the periodization of different stages of capitalism across time and space and the processes of crisis, transformation, and stabilization that connect these stages.[1] It takes as its starting point the observation that the capital relation cannot reproduce itself through itself, but is dependent on historically and politically shaped—and therefore ultimately contingent—arrangements that are to be understood as anchored outside the capital relation itself. Such an arrangement of "processes which permit what exists to go on existing" (Aglietta 2000, 12) does not dissolve the fundamental contradictions that—in tendency—constantly push the capital relation to its limits, but manages and channels them in a way that brings them to contribute to the dynamic of capital's own, extending reproduction. In other words, regulation stabilizes the inherently unstable mode of production that is capitalism into a temporarily (and socio-spatially) stabilized regime of accumulation. Alain Lipietz summed this up using the metaphor of a weaving loom, in which the warp threads regulate the continuous work of the filling thread (Lipietz 1998).

However, this ever-extending reproduction alters the very landscape of hierarchized constitutive relationships of the arrangement that stabilize it temporarily. It, via the process of quantitative changes, drives the whole toward the qualitative point of rupture that marks the escalation of contradictions that are making the reproduction more and more difficult to sustain. Such was the case when in parts of the so-called global north the Fordist regime of accumulation that had guaranteed relatively stable growth for two or three decades drifted toward structural crisis from the 1960s onward.[2]

This regime of accumulation was driven by a strong internal demand and secured by an incorporation of the institutionalized labor movement into the governing structures. However, this temporarily stable regime in the long run resulted in an over-accumulation of capital. Especially the increasing organic composition[3] of capital exerted heavy pressure on the rate of profits—a pressure that was heightened by a strong unionized workforce demanding steady increases in wages. When the capitalist class reacted with austerity measures and offshoring, they partially devalued the capital accumulated in the capitalist centers and, via wage depression, heightened the profits realized by the remaining capital via an increase in the rate of exploitation. However, they also strangled effective demand in the global north exactly when technological improvements would have made an expansion of supply necessary to exploit the productive potential thus gained.

This contradiction was also shaped and overlapped by other lines of conflict: Younger generations articulated and experimented with expectations for a fulfilled life that could not be satisfied by the promise of an ever-extending supply of consumer goods, and the feminist movement attacked the model of the male-breadwinner nuclear-family that was one cornerstone of the socio-cultural regulation of this mode of accumulation. Decolonization and struggles by immigrant workers and other subaltern parts of the workforce called into question the separation between the mostly white and male parts of the working class that were included into the Fordist-corporatist deal and all those that were not (cf. Hirsch und Roth 1986, 46–101).

Already this very superficial sketch allows pointing out three reasons why the Regulation Approach can offer important elements for a theory of protests in times of crisis. (i) It insists on the historical character of modes of accumulation as dynamic, hierarchized ensembles of social relations, which cannot be reduced to the duality of seemingly ahistorical economic laws and socially/culturally shaped institutional surroundings that are then subject to political conflict. Instead, contradictions and conflict are built into every part of the system, potentially politicizing elements which at first sight do not seem to belong either to the realm of the political or to what is usually understood as "economic regulation".[4] Other than 'objectivist' Marxist theories on the periodization of capitalism, such as the 'long waves' of technological innovation which is implied in Wallerstein's world system theory, the Regulation Approach emphasizes the contingency of capital reproduction on the outcome of social conflicts and therefore for social movements and protest.

(ii) Even though contradictions are understood as an omnipresent feature of social life, the Regulation Approach conceptualizes them as being articulated in a specific, hierarchized whole. Which conflicts are pushed into latency and which are assuming politically and socially explosive characteristics has to be understood from the point of view of the developing regime of accumulation and the changing class relations at least as much as from the mobilization work of 'movement entrepreneurs' working on pushing their respective agendas.[5] (iii) Along similar lines, it also allows the differentiation of "minor crises" and "major" or structural crises.

While the former are part of the dynamic regeneration of the regime of accumulation, the latter mark a crisis of exactly this regime: A structural, major crisis is reached when the material reproduction of society threatens to come to a grinding halt because the complex mode of regulation and its corresponding regime of accumulation are not able to dynamically process their own contradictions.

It is in relation to these major crises that the notion of the protest mobilizations as part of the movements of crisis exhausts its full metaphorical weight: In the transition of the *war of position* to a *war of maneuver* (Gramsci), they can play an important part in shaping the further trajectory through and out of the crisis. Even more, their work as *the old mole* (Marx) contributes decisively to the maturing of the complex of contradictions into a major crisis. In this double sense, they are coupled with the movement of the crisis as a socio-historical tendency of the whole of society. But on the other hand, the totalizing tendency of the crisis, which undermines the whole complex of the regime of accumulation, also shakes the very ground on which these protest mobilizations operate—they are themselves also *in* crisis.[6]

Granted, all this is rather a gradual difference from 'regular' social movements and protest mobilizations, who are also caught up in the dynamic development of society as a whole and might also contribute to its driving toward crisis. But it suggests a change in perspective from the mainstream of social movement *theory*: Social movement studies often implicitly privilege movements that successfully build organizations and power to achieve a defined goal *ceteribus paribus*. This focus on *mobilization* instead of *emergence* makes crisis-protests often appear as deficient movements: They fail to scale up, to formulate demands, to bridge frames, and to push for reform.[7]

In their seminal text "Das neue Gesicht des Kapitalismus" ("The New Face of Capitalism", N.K.), published already in 1986, Joachim Hirsch and Roland Roth took up the task to spell out the relationship between the crisis of the Fordist regime of accumulation, the emergence of the so-called New Social Movements (NSM), and the development and possible trajectories of a post-Fordist regime of accumulation (Hirsch and Roth 1986, esp. 78–104; 168–236). Even though their approach was clearly guided by the authors' sympathies for much of the NSM's political goals, it nevertheless led to one of the most sober and nuanced estimations of the movement's potentials and limitations. Since they locate their emergence and potential in the very crisis of the social formation that gave rise to them, they see a political potential of these movements that clearly reaches beyond Habermas' resigned notion of the "*Verteidigung der Lebenswelt*" ("Defense of the Life-World", N.K.) against the colonization by market and state. However, since the movement's chances are seen as limited to 'only' influencing the regulation (Fordism) of an unquestioned mode of production (Capitalism), and their actual chances to achieve substantial change get slimmer the closer they get to the "productivist cores" (Hirsch and Roth 1986, 204), their potential for shaping society is also clearly limited as measured not only against their own ambitious goals but also the sometimes chiliastic hopes that they were invested with in some of the writings on NSM, where they were heralded as showing the transition to an entirely new, "informational", "post-industrial" society (Hirsch and Roth 1986, 194).

As symptoms of the crisis, they rather have an ambivalent relation to the new conflicts in which they are not necessarily clearly positioned "on one side of the barricades" (see also Barker 2013): rather, they find themselves shaping the post-crisis regime in intended and unintended ways, while parts of their discourse and goals become recuperated and others are socially repressed and excluded. The "successful failure" which has been the common fate of many social movements and protest mobilizations (Roth and Rucht 2008, 28) bears witness to this complex relation of a movement toward society as a dynamic changing whole, a complexity that might get lost if one focuses too much on a clearly delineated aim (be it put forward by outspoken actors within the movement or projected onto the movement by the researcher) that the movement sets out to achieve.

It is in this sense that the understanding of the political economic logic of the crisis dynamics that surfaced in the Great Recession and the resulting political economic fault lines that will be discussed in the rest of this chapter will prepare the ground for the theory-of-practice inspired understanding of the protests that will be developed in the following chapters. Especially the topics addressed in Chaps. 3 and 6, the trajectory of the social classes participating in the protests and the social fields or "thick opportunity structures" in which these protests unfold require an understanding of the nature of the political economic dynamics driving the economic crisis beyond its articulation in what one could call the economic field proper: Chap. 3, because the changing chances for economic and social reproduction of class positions are linked to the macroscopic changes in the class structure as it corresponds with the political economic development that escalates in the crisis, and Chap. 6, because the 'state of energy' of the different fields that are connected to the emergence of the protests is linked to these dynamics. As will be outlined in the third section of this chapter and elaborated in Chap. 6, for example, while Skocpol's and Williamson's claim that the election of Obama as the president of the USA was central to the emergence of the Tea Party (TP) is undoubtedly correct, one should not underestimate the degree to which the conflicts in and around the political field that accompanied his presidency are themselves overdetermined by tensions that arose from the economic crisis.

2.2 The Structural Crisis of the Finance-Dominated Regime of Accumulation

Understanding the Great Recession as an acute stage of the structural crisis of the *finance-dominated regime of accumulation* emphasizes a central insight in the nature of the crisis. First, it means to refuse the commonsensical notion that this crisis has been primarily caused by irresponsible and 'detached' financial speculation upsetting an otherwise sound capitalist economy. Instead, the crisis ultimately is rooted in the inherent contradictions of the capitalist mode of production itself. This however does not mean that the processes of Financialization are not relevant for understanding the crisis. Rather, Financialization has to be understood as processing the inherent contradictions of global capitalism in its current historical form, which however does not solve these contradictions but only postpones and shapes their escalation into crisis—which broke into the open in 2008.

The finance-dominated regime of accumulation—as it developed mainly in the USA, but also shaped the accumulation regimes of other, ecologically dependent economies—itself is the outcome of a large number of crisscrossing strategies and practices by different social actors that attempted to overcome the crisis of the Fordist regime of accumulation. The phenomenon labelled "Financialization"—the transformation of more and more spheres of social life and reproduction intertwined with the rise of the relative share of income of the financial sector in the overall economy—in this light has to be understood not only as a crisis-prone and destabilizing development but also itself as the response to a crisis (Panitch and Gindin 2010, 9).[8]

When different capital factions from the 1970s onward increasingly offshored their production in order to avoid the high labor costs at home, they not only devalued capital at home and created new spaces of accumulation abroad. In the process, they also created longer and more arcane commodity chains which for their functioning depended on inverse circuits of financial assets (Panitch and Gindin 2010, 10; Radice 2010, 33).[9] These assets furthermore had to be securitized against the increasingly volatile exchange rates that followed the end of the Bretton Woods agreement (McNally 2009, 471).

At the same time this outsourcing in combination with wage depression (which was facilitated by the historic defeat of the US labor movement) not only increased the rate of exploitation, it also resulted in a lack of demand for consumer goods—a gap that neither investment nor the stagnating proportion of public spending was able to fill. Instead, the credit sector expanded: Private households compensated for their lack of increases or even the decrease in real wages by relying on credit—partially to finance access to higher education, housing, and health, the costs of which also exploded in the same period due to their privatization (Demirović und Sablowski 2013, 200 f.).[10]

Yet, while in the short run cushioning the impact of social inequality, the increase in private credit in fact evolved into a secondary circuit of exploitation of labor through capital: The already smaller wage, which was supplemented by credit, was now chipped away even further by the interest to be paid on the loans. Furthermore, the dependency on credit disciplined the working class and thereby additionally lowered their leverage in wage negotiations (Demirović und Sablowski 2013, 201 f.). While the wage share as a percentage of the GDP plummeted from almost 70% in the USA in 1974 to below 66% in 2007, the portion of value appropriated by the financial sector over the same period of time has increased constantly (Lapavitsas 2013, 188 f., 211).[11]

The effects on different social classes beyond this tectonic shift between wages and profits (and toward profit appropriated through the financial sector specifically) are unfortunately difficult to estimate, even though they would be of high interest for the inquiry presented in the following chapters. This is partially an outcome of the very logic of Financialization itself: One element of this process was the integration of the reproduction of large parts of the population into the financial sphere—not only as debtors by the mentioned expansion of private credit but also as creditors through privatized pension funds and insurances. It nevertheless seems reasonable to conclude from the overall development of the income distribution, which became unambiguously more polarized (Foster und Wolfson 2009), that it primarily facilitated redistribution from the bottom and the middle to the top of the income distribution. As Sablowski and Alnasseri argue, the creditor integration of the middle- and lower-income groups was primarily of ideological importance (Sablowski und Alnasseri 2001), meaning that it made especially the so-called middle classes 'feel invested' in a political economic process which was hurting them economically.

On the supply side, the rising power of shareholders in the decision-making of companies had double-edged effects: It on the one hand helped to renovate the profitability of companies, especially by eliminating their less profitable branches and by putting pressure on wages. On the other hand, the pressure to increase the shareholder value also led to under-investment, since profits were often used to buy back one's company stocks or to distribute bonuses in order to increase the company's stock market value to diminish the chance of hostile takeovers and to increase one's creditworthiness for further rounds of refinancing (Sablowski und Alnasseri 2001).[12] While Financialization in theory made credit more accessible for private enterprises, especially in the USA, they tended to not invest the money in productive capacities, but instead used it to speculate in financial assets themselves (Brenner 2006, 278).

Even this short sketch should suffice to illustrate that Financialization is nothing external 'happening' to an otherwise sound economic environment, but is intimately linked to this very environment's processing of its immanent contradictions. On the one hand, Financialization allows and presses for the constant expansion of the geographical and social scope of accumulation; on the other hand, it also tends to build up 'bubbles' which implode when the expected returns on investment fall short of the expectations that were already priced into the growing amount of fictitious capital. The finance-dominated accumulation regime is inherently unstable, yet it is nevertheless a coherent regime in which different contradictions and institutions temporarily stabilize each other or, in Boyer's words: "Finance is an element in, but not the whole of, this complex (…) regime" (Boyer 2000, 111).[13]

This accumulation regime, albeit in its practical short-term development *dominated* by the relative importance of finance capital, nevertheless remains *determined* by the developments in the primary revaluation circuit of capitalist production.[14] The credit-induced explosion of fictitious capital threatens to collapse as soon as it becomes apparent that the debtors will never realize the profits or wages necessary to service their loans—and the crisis brings the dramatic divergence between profits and productive investments, which had built up since the 1980s and escalated after 2000 (Foster and Magdoff 2009, 133), to the surface.

In the short run, the reoccurring accumulation cycle plays an important role in the long-term evolution of capitalism in that the boom opens up spaces for expansion and experimenting, while the bust as a kind of stress test eliminates the ineffective outcomes of this experimentation.[15] Accordingly, the cyclical 'minor' crises that shook the finance-dominated regime of accumulation before 2006 were usually connected to either the opening of new markets into the realm of the accumulation regime, such as the crises in East Asia in 1997, Russia in 1998, and Argentina in 1999, or the developing of new economic sectors for capital accumulation, such as the collapse of the bubble of the so-called New Economy in 2000—albeit demonstrating the inherent instability of capitalist accumulation, they also in a sense bore witness to its aggressive dynamism. It is an important observation for understanding the specific character of the Great Recession that in this important aspect the development after 2001 and the crisis of 2007 was different: The credit-induced boom in real estate and the inflation in financial assets were not facilitating any notable expansion into new markets or productive sectors (Candeias 2011).[16] This indicates that the Great Recession is not to be understood as a minor crisis but indicates the point of exhaustion of an accumulation regime, whose immanent contradictions have become more and more difficult to process and contain:

Already in 2002 the Enquete-Commission of the German Bundestag found that the real interest rates in almost all industrial countries had been exceeding the growth rates of the respective economy for almost all periods since the early 1980s (Deutscher Bundestag 2002, 69ff.), suggesting a long-term growing disparity between the amount of fictitious capital circulating and the actual value realized. Especially investment banks had used their assets with enormous leverage, a leverage which was inversed when panic set in in 2008: after they had leveraged every Dollar they actually had to their disposal by 1:24, the average investment bank now "had to sell 24 Dollar worth of assets for every Dollar they lost in the subprime-market."[17]

To sum up this brief description of the logics of the development from the crisis of Fordism to the Great Recession: 'Neoliberalization' as a tendency in regulatory transformation that answered to the crisis of Fordism (Brenner et al. 2010, 329) with its combination of accumulation by dispossession, both by the pressure to commodify ever more realms of social life and by expanding into new geographical spaces (Harvey 2009, also 2007, 431–42), wage suppression, and the high degree of creativity in innovation of financial instruments to circumvent or profit from the remaining barriers to commodification and capital circulation, was only temporarily and partially successful in reversing or even just halting the falling rate of profit it inherited from Fordism. It did so via a reduction of the *faux frais* (Marx), an increase in the rate of exploitation (both through the intensification and the extension of worktime while wages were stagnating), and through the opening of new markets.

Using a distinction developed to differentiate Fordism from the earlier period of classical Imperialism, one could also say that while Fordism was basically driven by intensive accumulation, the finance-dominated regime of accumulation is based largely on extensive capital accumulation (Vroey 1984, 47ff.). It is neither able to solve the problem of over-accumulation nor to establish a new productive base—microelectronics and computerization did never assume the same 'locomotive function' that the auto-industry had played for Northern Atlantic Fordism. Consequently, the rates of profit in Western Europe and in Northern America did not even get close to the level of the 1950s and 1960s at the absolute height of the finance-dominated accumulation regime in the 'Roaring Nineties' (Brenner 2006).[18]

It would follow from this that the best comparison to the Great Recession is indeed, as the labelling implies, the Great Depression. And, accordingly, if over-accumulation of capital and the resulting pressure on profits are really the moving force behind this crisis, then overcoming it would necessarily involve a massive devaluation of capital and/or the shift to new economic sectors for capital to be profitably invested in. An economically and socially sustainable revitalization of capitalist accumulation most probably would require a combination of the two, as was the case when the New Deal in the USA combined the devaluation of excess capital through high taxation with heavy investments in the social and material infrastructure.

This was not a fringe position in the debate on the necessary political measures to deal with the crisis: A number of intellectuals and policy advisors well beyond the usual suspects have argued for quite some time now that the only possible and sustainable solution to the current conundrum would be a "Green New Deal" (GND). In 2011 the United Nations Environment Programme called for a transition to a "green" capitalist economy that supposedly would be able to address both the lack of chances to profitably invest in the productive sectors of the economy and the imbalances of wealth (UNEP 2011). Already in 2009, the OECD had released a "Declaration on Green Growth" assuming that a "greening" of the economy would bolster innovation and avoid future crises (OECD 2011). Economists politically and theoretically as far apart as Thomas Friedman and Paul Krugman have called the US administration to "green the bailout" that reacted to the crisis (Krugman 2010; Friedman 2008).

In the beginning, Barack Obama seemed to openly embrace these plans. In a speech before both houses of congress in early 2009, he promised heavy investment in US infrastructure, a reindustrialization program, and a shift away from fossil-fuel-based growth to sustainable, green technologies (Goldenberg 2009). However, substantial redistributive policy measures did not materialize. After the unprecedented state interventionism of the bailouts, the credo of the economic measures seemed to be first and foremost the restabilization of the current mode of accumulation.

2.3 Class Relations and Capital Interests in the Crisis

One important explanatory factor for this interesting non-transformation is pointed out by political scientist Ingmar Solty: He explains that, no matter if whether one considers Obama's political will for structural changes in this situation to be authentic or not, there simply existed no social force able to effectively push for these reforms against the will of relevant factions of the capitalist class (Solty 2013a). This is a trace worth following because it relates closely to the aforementioned third regard in which the understanding of the political economic dynamic behind the crisis is important for understanding the protests that arose in its wake: the way in which it shaped political economic lines of conflict that provided a resonating body for the protests. This following section will therefore sketch out (since a more detailed analysis would exceed the limits of this background chapter) the different classes'—and especially the different capital factions'—mobilized interests in the first phase of the acute crisis.

The presidential election of 2008 can serve as a kind of natural experiment on the interests of different classes in the economic crisis. It took place only three months after the bankruptcy of the Lehman Brothers. This made the economic crisis the dominating topic of the last stretch of the presidential campaigns of Barack Obama and John McCain, and most voters reported that economic issues were very important for their voting decision (Pew Research Center 2008). Furthermore, the very detailed and easily accessible statistical data not only on the demographic patterning of the electoral choice but also on the contributions of different economic sectors to the respective campaigns allows both a good first estimate of different classes' relation to the different presidential candidates and also different economic sectors' 'investment' in the political economic agendas associated with their campaigns. A look at the demographic patterning of voting behavior as well as at the different donors that contributed to their campaigns therefore provides an interesting window into the political economic conflicts or tensions of US society in the first months of the crisis, which, as will turn out, in many respects already prefigured the increasing polarization of the political landscape that later also gave rise or at least shaped both the TP and Occupy Wall Street (OWS) (Fig. 2.1).

With regard to income groups' voting behavior in 2008, one can identify one very clear tendency: The Pew Research Center and the New York Times Exit Poll both report that households from the lower half of the income distribution—which means households with an annual income of less than $50,000—disproportionately voted for Obama (60% vs. 38%). Between $50,000 and $100,000, the outcome is evenly split, while above $100,000, the voters were slightly more inclined to vote for McCain

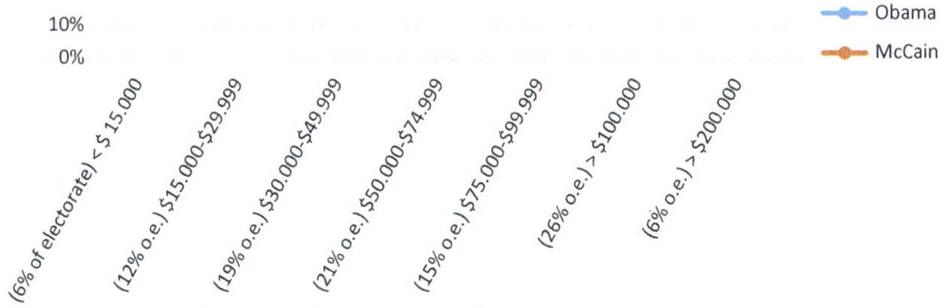

Fig. 2.1 Presidential Election Results in 2008 by Income Class (Data from New York Times "National Exit Polls Table")

(49% vs. 50%) (Pew Research Center 2008). Interestingly though, according to exit poll data published by the New York Times, Obama fared slightly better in the income group of those that earned between $75,000 and $100,000 (51% vs. 48%) and even more so among those that earned more than $200,000 annually (52% to 46%). This means that while the lower half of the income distribution voted overwhelmingly for the Democratic candidate (which has been traditionally the case in the decades before, with the share increasing unambiguously since 1992), the upper half was almost evenly divided, even though the distribution there seems to be somewhat patterned, and the richest 5% of the population again tended to vote Democratic. Mainly, the last observation sets this election apart from the previous ones—not only that in earlier elections the richest 5% tended to vote Republican, they also were tending much more clearly to one side. In 2004, for example, the numbers had been reversed and were less ambiguous, with 63% of these households voting for Bush and only 35% for Kerry.

It is not surprising that the lower half of the income distribution, whose members were impacted worst by the economic recession, overwhelmingly voted for the candidate that promised "change". Accordingly, those that deemed their economic situation to have been worse in 2008 than it had been previously had overwhelmingly voted for Obama (71% vs. 28%) (New York Times 2008). Even among the 'white' voters, which disproportionately voted for McCain (55% vs. 43%), the income group that was most inclined to vote for Obama was that of those earning less than $50,000 (47% vs. 51%) (Pew Research Center 2008). However, the data also shows that while poorer people tended to vote for Obama, the simple inversion is not true—the upper half of society did not clearly vote for McCain.

What is very interesting are the lines along which the different factions of the upper half of the income contribution tended to fall into one camp or the other: Obama clearly won among those working in professional occupations and among those with a graduate degree (both: 58% vs. 40%) (Teixeira 2010, 21 f.; New York Times 2008). He also narrowly won among those with a college degree (50% vs. 48%) and clearly among those that lived in urban areas (New York Times 2008). If we take all these indicators together, we can conclude that the group that was most likely to vote for McCain is to be sought among those that earn relatively high incomes but only have relatively low educational degrees, while Obama's support came from those that realized relatively low incomes and/or had relatively high educational degrees—hinting to two social classes which will turn out to be the decisive parts of the constituency of the TP and

OWS, respectively, namely, the so-called classical petty bourgeoisie and the so-called new petty bourgeoisie.

A look at the different employers of the donors to the different presidential campaigns does indicate a similar split between the two petty bourgeoisies[19]: Among the top 20 employers whose employees donated to Obama's campaign are four Ivy League universities (the University of California is the employer whose employees gave the largest sum to the campaign) and four software and entertainment companies. The top four contributors to McCain's campaign are banks, while he also received many donations from people employed in the US Army or the Ministry of Defense. The differences in support from universities and high-tech companies on one side and the Military thus very likely reflect the identified pattern of the general voting behavior, namely, that people with graduate degrees rather voted for Obama and those to whom national security deemed the central political question tended to vote for McCain (Pew Research Center 2008).

Additionally, the fact that four new technology companies are among top 20 employers of supporters of Obama, while not a single one is among the top 20 employers of supporters for McCain, is already a first hint at the fault line between the different capital factions. The image of this fault line becomes more clear-cut if one considers the data that the Center for Responsive Politics provides on the so-called bundlers. Bundlers are donors who, after reaching the limit for possible personal contributions to a candidate's campaign, reach out to others, who would also like to donate and bundle their contributions into one donation. This is the single largest source of money donated to the candidates—and both candidates received about the same amount of donations from this type of donor (McCain: $75,750,000; Obama: $76,250,000) (Opensecrets.org 2009a, b).

Both presidential candidates got the biggest amount of money from companies from the so-called "FIRE" sector (finance, insurance, and real estate) and from large law firms. With regard to the other sectors, however, there are clear differences: Obama received more than $28 million in donations from companies in communication/electronics (McCain less than five million), while McCain received at least 2.55 million from energy companies and 2.3 million from construction companies (Obama: 600 k and 1.05 million, respectively). The total of donations (PACs and individual contributions alike) to McCain from oil and gas companies was more than $2.5 million, while Obama did not even receive a million worth of donations from this sector (Opensecrets.org 2013b, d).

All this indicates two things that will be important for the further course of my argument: (i) First, it appears that the so-called middle class is split into two camps. As will become clear in the next chapter, this split in important regards already prefigures the political polarization that gave rise to the TP and OWS. (ii) Second, and this relates to the crisis diagnosis outlined in Sect. 2.2, the factions of capital are similarly split: Obama's campaign in 2008 was associated with interests in education and high-tech industries, and, if one furthermore considers that a contribution to McCain's campaign is very likely also a contribution against Obama's campaign, a move away from fossil-fuel-intensive industries.[20] McCain on the other hand was supported by oil and gas industries and favored by companies active in construction. This indicates a confrontation between industries that fits the expectations one would have from the diagnosis of a Green New Deal being one possible solution to the crisis: The profiteers of a shift in the productive cores toward a 'green economy' are donating to Obama's campaign, while the possible losers of such a development donate to McCain's campaign.[21] The confrontation between the different industries as it is documented in the different donor profiles of the political parties only grew fiercer in the years that followed (Opensecrets.org 2015, 2013a, c, e), contributing to the rising political polarization which in turn contributed to the political gridlock that hindered substantial reform.

2.4 The First-Cut Theory of the Crisis-Protests: The Interregnum and Its Hot Topics

It might seem as if all this is wandered far off from the protests under scrutiny in this book. It however not only provides important background information on the larger societal conflicts and dynamics in which the protests unfolded, as was argued in the introduction of this chapter. Furthermore, the findings of this chapter can already help to understand some peculiarities of the protests—even if only in a very abstract and underdetermined manner.

The Great Recession brought to the fore long-term crisis tendencies in the accumulation regime(s) of Northern Atlantic Capitalism. The finance-dominated accumulation regime was not able to generate the profit and growth rates sufficient to stabilize the midterm reproduction of itself and its ecologically dependent co-regimes. After the bursting of the dotcom bubble at the turn of the millennium, no new productive sectors had been developed that balanced the falling of the profits in these societies. Instead, the financial sector mainly in the USA accelerated the production of fictitious capital. For some time the US economy did effectively function as the world's "consumer of the last resort" (Catte et al. 2011, 788), but only to the expense of the inflation of a bubble which began to be corrected violently in the Great Recession.

This structural crisis did not lead to a political economic transformation. Instead, the dominant strategy was the continuation of the respective mode of regulation. This more-of-the-same approach was armored with multi-scalar and diverse debt-ceilings and austerity rounds in the USA that shield the economic policies against contention from the electorate. Even before the austerity turn of the federal government, spending restrictions have been enforced mainly on the state and the local level. In fact, the job loss in public sector employment on the local level during and after the Great Recession was so severe compared to earlier recessions that the Yale economists Polak and Schott spoke of "America's Hidden Austerity Program" (2012). This "austerity by gridlock" (Williamson 2013) is further strangling demand at home, which is in turn balanced by a "beggar thy neighbor" policy in which the USA attempt to stimulate growth by increasing their international competitiveness (and thereby their net exports) through wage suppression.[22] As a result, growth returned, but it remained (almost) jobless for years, while stagnant or falling wages kept inequality rising (Rattner 2014; OECD 2014; Tankersley 2013).[23]

The apparent non-transformation of the US economy rests on specific 'relations of force' (Poulantzas) between the different social classes and especially between different capital factions. The labor movement was not able (or willing) to fundamentally challenge the predominant mode of regulation. However, the lower social classes overwhelmingly sympathized with the Obama campaign's promise of "change". With regard to the different capital factions' interest in the USA, the analysis of the different sources of private donations to the presidential candidates suggested a split between two camps, on the one hand, the supporters of a shift of the productive or 'locomotive' sector toward high-tech and 'green' technologies, and, on the other hand, those industries that opposed such a shift, the latter of which concentrated their support on the Republican candidate McCain. The result of this confrontation was political deadlock.

A number of critical sociologists and political scientists have addressed the resulting social situation, this persevering at the critical juncture, as an

"Interregnum" in the Gramscian sense (e.g., Solty 2013b; Bauman 2012; Candeias 2011; Röttger 2009). This concept, originally developed by Gramsci in reference to interwar Europe, refers to a period in which the old order is apparently dying, yet, the new one "cannot be born" because the ruling classes effectively do not have the power to solve the crisis, but only to prevent it from being solved at their expense. This leads to "all sorts of morbid symptoms" (Gramsci 1991, 354), since the existing mode of regulation lost its integrative force to build social hegemony and instead has to rely on direct domination of the social classes that splinter off the dominating block, since the existing social order is not able to fulfill the implicit promises that had hitherto granted these classes' loyalty. In the absence of alternative projects, however, this disappointment rather takes the form of undirected anger, frustration, or chiliastic hopes.

As will be discussed especially in Sect. 5.4, this diagnosis is indeed a good starting point for thinking about the specificities of the protests as 'crisis-protests'. What was discussed in this chapter, however, already helps us to understand a little better why the protests under scrutiny found such a strong social resonance for their respective topics at the specific time of their emergence. Some commentators have puzzled over why the first popular mobilization against the politics of crisis in the USA was the right-wing TP. From the story just told, this makes perfect sense. Large parts of the progressive factions from the unions up to left-wing democrats had supported the presidential race of Obama and were still hoping for a major policy shift in early 2009. Exactly this shift, however, was fiercely opposed by factions of the capitalist class that saw their position in the economic field endangered: It is therefore no surprise that the TP sprung up exactly when Keynesian redistributive measures were under consideration in the Obama administration.[24] The TP's early focusing on what they discussed as "fiscal responsibility" (resisting any redistributive measures) and the delegitimizing of the administration which limited its capacity to impose reforms both aptly served this purpose. The mobilization against Obamacare, which became the central campaigning point of the nationwide TP organizations, was where both these projects intersected: In the eyes of the TP supporters, it came to symbolize both a redistributive effort unfairly privileging those deemed undeserving and served to delegitimize reforms of the federal government more generally as totalitarian.[25]

Many observers have pointed out the important role of financiers from the extractive, chemical, and the financial industries in "test marketing" and "bankrolling" the TP early on (e.g., Rich 2010; Lo 2012). A late trace of the impact that the think tanks and lobbying groups funded by these industries had on the perception of the crisis policies is maybe the anger with which some of my TP interviewees reacted to the mentioning of the word "sustainable" alone: They interpreted the term as hinting to a secret plan to transform the whole of the US economy into a totalitarian, planned economy under the auspices of the United Nations. In a similar vein, the quick demise of the TP after the Republican victory in the 2010 midterm elections, which rendered any plans for ground-breaking reforms by the administration (if they ever really existed) impossible, seems plausible: The grassroots mobilization simply lost its important blocking function which instead was from now on exerted by congress itself—especially by the so-called TP candidates which long outlived the TP as an actual protest mobilization.

OWS, on the other hand, exploded onto the scene after this blockade against any redistributive effort became obvious with the debt-ceiling crisis in 2011. It was not only the inspiration of the mass demonstrations in Southern Europe and Northern Africa, it was also the apparent closure of any chance for political change by established means that triggered the broad social support for OWS. Slogans like "Banks got bailed out, we got sold out" and "the system isn't broken, it's fixed" capture this disappointed anger at the fact that the promised (however vaguely defined) change seemed to just have disappeared from the agenda. While the TP represents a faction that splintered off the dominating block because they felt threatened by its transformation, the OWS represented those that splintered off because they found the promised transformation, which many of them had supported, not taking place. It is not stretching speculation too far to suspect that the refusal to formulate any demands on the side of OWS was at least partially caused by the experience that those governing did not even seem to be able to fulfill their own demands.[26]

To sketch out the fault lines along which the tensions of the processing of the socioeconomic crisis built up in this sense helps to understand why exactly those lines of conflict along which the protests were articulated became heated at this specific social and historical conjuncture. It is, however, only a small part of the story. Obviously, nobody would claim that the TP was, on the ground, primarily composed of large-scale stockowners of oil and finance enterprises. Some might argue that those on the streets were merely deceived by behind-the-scenes financiers and ideologues, but this would mean to deny the authentic element of the passionate grassroots activism by thousands of people who felt that this was their struggle.

OWS' peculiar protest-practices and socio-demographic composition is also only very insufficiently explained by pointing out the disappointment of Obama's former supporters.

In other words, while this short sketch helps to understand the overdetermination of the protests as occurring around central lines of social conflict, the development of the concrete protest-practices is still strongly underdetermined at this level of analysis. What is missing therefore is a more nuanced understanding of who these protestors actually were and to what developments they were exposed to in the lead up to the protests. In delineating the class-generational units that can be identified as the core constituencies of the protest mobilization and in situating them in the more concrete context of social conflicts around the mobilizations, the next chapter therefore sets out to fill this gap in the research literature and, furthermore, prepares the ground for the following systematic reconstruction of the socio-specific interpretative dispositions that shaped these classes' articulation of discontent as critique as protest.

Notes

1. In the last 30 years, the Regulation Approach developed and differentiated into a multiplicity of 'schools' partially in conflict with each other. In the following, I will concentrate on what I consider to be consensual at least to the Marxist (as opposed to the neo-institutionalist) branches of 'the' Regulation Approach. (For an overview on the development of the Regulation Approach, cf. Becker 2013; Jessop 2001a, b).
2. Glyn et al. were able to demonstrate that the *profit squeeze,* a remarkably fast and consistent falling of the average rate of profit that triggered this crisis, occurred, almost simultaneously, in Germany, Japan, the USA, and the UK (cf. Glyn et al. 1988).
3. The rising organic composition refers to the increasing amount of capital per labor-unit used in the production process. This (in tendency) rising prominence of constant capital per unit of variable capital is one of the driving forces of the falling rate of profit, since only the latter has the ability to produce surplus value (Marx 1974, 3: 222 f.).
4. As Jessop highlights, the very translation of the term "regulation" from French to English might be a source of confusion in that regard, since the intuitive understanding of the English term is much closer to the French term "réglementation", which denotes the much smaller scope of social institutions of economic regulations in the narrow sense (Jessop 2001b).

5. (For a similar criticism of the implicitly liberal or "pluralist" assumptions of social movement theory, see Skocpol 1980.)
6. In this sense, Wallerstein remarks with regard to class struggle in times of structural crisis: "But when the system is far from equilibrium (…) small social mobilizations can have very great repercussions (…). We might also call it the moment when political agency prevails over structural determinism. (…But) neither (…) is there a small group at the top calling all the shots (…) the chaos of the structural crisis is reflected in the relatively disordered configuration." (Wallerstein 2010, 141).
7. Mayer and Roth polemically remark that the Resource Mobilization approach is a "theory of social movements (…that) might more adequately be called theory of mobilization." (Mayer and Roth 1995, 300; see also Cox and Flesher-Fominaya 2013) Francis Fox Piven and Richard A. Cloward make a very similar observation with regard to classical social movement theory to understand protests and resistance of the subaltern in formally democratic societies: "Whatever the intellectual source of error, the effect of equating movements with movement organizations – and thus requiring that protests have a leader, a constitution, a legislative program, or at least a banner before they are recognized as such – is to divert attention from many forms of political unrest (…) Having decided by definitional fiat that nothing political has occurred, nothing has to be explained, at least not in the terms of political protest. And having contrived in this way not to recognize protest or to study it, we cannot ask certain rather obvious and important questions about it" (Piven and Cloward 1979, 5).
8. This is not to say, however, that some aspects of Financialization are not dysfunctional for the overall stability—one prominent example being the infamous high-frequency trading—since Financialization does not follow a central plan, but rather amounts to a chance find that emerges from the anarchy of the world market, it is no wonder that different actors try to capitalize on it also in destructive ways.
9. The reader familiar with world system theory and Braudel's theory of long waves of capitalist development will notice that this part of the argument is well consistent with the observation that capitalism periodically underwent a process of Financialization during the shift from an old center of capitalist accumulation to a new center of capitalist accumulation, but avoids the assumption of inevitability sometimes simmering through the description of this observation (cf. Silver und Arrighi 2011).
10. Stockhammer shows that the household debt as a percentage of the disposable income has grown all over the EU and in the USA between 1995 and 2005 (Stockhammer 2007, 10).
11. Considering the astronomic rise in the 'wages' for top-level management positions which took place during the same time, these numbers might in

fact be an understatement of the development that the actual wage share in a Marxian sense was subjected to in both countries. Altvater provides slightly different numbers based on the data of the IMF: A fall from 67% to 62% in the USA and from 74% to 63% in continental Europe. However, the trend and the result are comparable (Altvater 2008, 496).

12. Some have therefore argued that Financialization in fact is slowing down overall capital accumulation rather than facilitating it (e.g., Stockhammer 2000).
13. It should be noted that this finance-dominated accumulation regime is not a homogenous world market-spanning arrangement. Yet, it is neither one among a set of equally important "varieties of capitalism". As Jessop highlights, the world market as an integrated, uneven totality is to be thought of as variegated and hierarchized. The finance-dominated accumulation regime is, based on the central importance of the US economy for the world market, the ecologically dominant element in this variegated totality—in a nutshell, this specific regime "is a problem-*maker* for the others rather than a problem-*taker*", defining relatively small corridors for maneuver for the other regimes (Jessop 2014).
14. This differentiation between dominating and determining aspects of the finance-dominated accumulation regime was, to my knowledge, first developed by Sablowski: It relies on Althusser's theory of materialist dialectics, which had argued that, for example, in medieval Europe, Catholicism can well be considered the dominant social force, albeit its ultimate functioning was, like all social relations, determined by the logics of the Feudalist mode of production. In a more illustrative language, Altvater differentiates between the 'hardware' of capitalist production that has increasing troubles to keep up with the development of its financial 'software': Albeit most of the time we only *see* the processing of the latter, this is nevertheless ultimately determined by the constraints of the former (Sablowski 2011, 41; Altvater 2008; Althusser 1969).
15. As David Harvey argued convincingly, the credit sector plays a central role in giving a dynamic to the upswing of the accumulation cycle, in that it at least temporarily eases the tension between productive forces and social relations and opens up a space for experimentation with new forms and technologies of production, marketing, and consumption of goods. However, as the expected profits priced into the expansion of credit fail to realize, the fictitious capital cannot be converted into real capital and the overall credit contracts rapidly—ironing out many erratic and superfluous creations that were only feasible because the plethora of fictitious capital was desperately seeking for chances for investment (Harvey 2007, 324–29). This also fits with the results of a study by the two Harvard economists Reinhart and Rogoff, who compared the crisis of 2007 with crises in

"industrial" countries since the 1970s. They point out that another typical feature of the buildup of a crisis is an inverted V-shape of the development of real growth in the years before the crisis. After the crisis, economic growth accelerates and then slows down, while the amount of fictitious capital keeps expanding at an accelerating pace, a reoccurring pattern of emancipation of the creation of fictitious capital from the actual economic productive prospects before a crisis. They even argue that the increase in housing prices before the bust was not above the average of that experienced by other countries that experienced banking crises (Reinhart and Rogoff 2008; see also Marx 1974, 3: 523).

16. Even Thomas Friedman made a similar observation already in 2008, namely, that the post 2001-boom, other than the railroad-boom in the late nineteenth and the dotcom-boom in the late twentieth centuries, had not lead to the establishment of any useful infrastructure to survive the bursting of the bubble (Friedman 2008).
17. Barry Eichengreen, 'die Parallelen zur Asienkrise' FAZ, 27.09.08, cited in: Haug (2008, 284) (translation N.K.).
18. Non-Marxist economists also have pointed out a development that seems to underscore this hypothesis: The so-called Solow-Paradox, a phenomenon originally observed in the late 1980s, refers to the fact that the highly capital-intensive computerization of production did not yield the expected increases in productivity, the growth of which in fact slowed down instead (Hoffmann 2015; Acemoglu et al. 2014). The productivity paradox was named after Solow for his famous quip: "you can see the computer age everywhere but in the productivity statistics" (Solow 1997). In a Marxist theoretical framework, this slowing down of productivity growth would in fact show the declining rate of profit due to an increase in the organic composition of capital rather than a declining growth of use-value-output.
19. The Center for Responsive Politics, through its webpage OpenSecrets.org, systematizes and makes available these data on donations to presidential campaigns: Donors to presidential candidates that donate more than $200 have to reveal their employer, which allows the Center for Responsive Politics to code and accumulate the donations so that the organizations that are connected to the largest total of donations to the respective candidate can be identified (Opensecrets.org 2013f, g).
20. This was also reflected in how the voters of the respective candidates thought about the issue of "offshore drilling", which was hotly debated during the presidential race: "McCain won by a large margin among voters who support offshore drilling (59–39% for Obama)" (Pew Research Center 2008).
21. What remains unclear is the role of the financial sector. It spread its donations almost evenly among the two frontrunners, which could either mean that they did not expect substantial regulatory and redistributive measures

from either of the candidates or that they wanted to make sure that both candidates remembered them well after the election, no matter what their plans had been before.

22. A sharp criticism of the supposed shortsightedness of these policies was formulated by Keynesian economist Krugman in early 2011 (Krugman 2011).
23. Since 2012, the unemployment rate in the USA began to decline, but this was accompanied by a decrease of the working population in the overall US population (cf. The Economist 2015).
24. This was analyzed with great clarity by Keynesian economist Paul Krugman at the time (Krugman 2009).
25. For the interpretative dispositions of the TP's core constituency that these projects were able to resonate with, see Sect. 5.1 "The Tea Party: Disappointment Without Disillusionment".
26. In 2009, Obama himself stated that his administration "is the only thing between (the large financial institutions) and the pitchforks" (Barack Obama, cited in: Javers 2009).

Bibliography

Acemoglu, Daron, David Autor, David Dorn, Gordon H. Hanson, and Brendan Price. 2014. *Return of the Solow Paradox? IT, Productivity, and Employment in U.S. Manufacturing*. Working Paper 19837. National Bureau of Economic Research. http://www.nber.org/papers/w19837. Accessed 29 Oct 2017.

Aglietta, Michel. 2000. *A Theory of Capitalist Regulation. The US Experience*. London/New York: Verso.

Althusser, Louis. 1969. On the Materialist Dialectic. In *For Marx*, 161–218. London/New York: Verso.

Altvater, Elmar. 2008. Die Finanzkrise – mehr als ein Weltmarktsungewitter. *Das Argument* 278: 490–504.

Barker, Colin. 2013. Class Struggle and Social Movements. In *Marxism and Social Movements*, ed. Colin Barker, Laurence Cox, John Krinsky, and Alf Gunvald Nilsen, 39–61. Leiden: Brill.

Bauman, Zygmunt. 2012. Times of interregnum. *Ethics & Global Politics*, Nr. 5 (1): 49–56.

Becker, Joachim. 2013. Regulationstheorie: Ursprünge und Entwicklungstendenzen. In *Fit für die Krise? Perspektiven der Regulationstheorie*, ed. Roland Atzmüller, Joachim Becker, Ulrich Brand, Lukas Oberndorfer, Vanessa Redak, and Thomas Sablowski, 24–56. Münster: Westfälisches Dampfboot.

Boyer, Robert. 2000. Is a Finance-Led Growth Regime a Viable Alternative to Fordism? A Preliminary Analysis. *Economy and Society* 29 (1): 111–145.

Brenner, Robert. 2006. *The Economics of Global Turbulence*. London/New York: Verso.

Brenner, Neil, Jamie Peck, and Nik Theodore. 2010. After Neoliberalization? *Globalizations* 7 (3): 327–345.

Bundestag, Deutscher. 2002. *Schlussbericht der Enquete Kommission 'Globalisierung der Weltwirtschaft – Herausforderungen und Antworten*. Drucksache 14/9200. Bonn: Deutscher Bundestag, 14. Wahlperiode. http://dip21.bundestag.de/dip21/btd/14/092/1409200.pdf. Accessed 29 Oct 2017.

Candeias, Mario. 2011. Interregnum – Molekulare Verdichtung und organische Krise. In *VielfachKrise Im finanzmarktdominierten Kapitalismus*, ed. Alex Demirović, Julia Dück, Florian Becker, and Pauline Bader, 45–61. Hamburg: VSA.

Catte, Pietro, Pietro Cova, Patrizio Pagano, and Ignazio Visco. 2011. The Role of Macroeconomic Policies in the Global Crisis. *Journal of Policy Modeling* 33 (6): 787–803.

Cox, Laurence, and Cristina Flesher Fominaya. 2013. European Social Movements and Social Theory: A Richer Narrative? In *Understanding European Movements: New Social Movements. Global Justice Struggles, Anti-Austerity Protests*, ed. Cristina Flesher Fominaya and Laurence Cox, 7–29. London/New York: Routledge.

De Vroey, Michel. 1984. A Regulation Approach Interpretation of Contemporary Crisis. *Capital & Class* 8 (2): 45–66.

Demirović, Alex, and Thomas Sablowski. 2013. Finanzmarktdominierte Akkumulation und die Krise in Europa. In *Fit für die Krise? Perspektiven der Regulationstheorie*, ed. Roland Atzmüller, Joachim Becker, Ulrich Brand, Lukas Oberndorfer, Vanessa Redak, and Thomas Sablowski, 187–238. Münster: Westfälisches Dampfboot.

Foster, John Bellamy, and Fred Magdoff. 2009. *The Great Financial Crisis: Causes and Consequences*. New York: Monthly Review Press.

Foster, James E., and Michael C. Wolfson. 2009. Polarization and the Decline of the Middle Class: Canada and the U.S. *The Journal of Economic Inequality* 8 (2): 247–273.

Friedman, Thomas L. 2008. Green the Bailout. *The New York Times*, September 28. http://www.nytimes.com/2008/09/28/opinion/28friedman.html. Accessed 29 Oct 2017.

Glyn, Andrew, Alan Hughes, Alan Liepietz, and Ajit Singh. 1988. *The Rise and Fall of the Golden Age*. 43. WIDER Working Papers. Helsinki: World Institute for Development Economics Research of the United Nations University. https://www.wider.unu.edu/publication/rise-and-fall-golden-age. Accessed 29 Oct 2010.

Goldenberg, Suzanne. 2009. Obama Focuses on Development of Green Economy in Speech Before Joint Session of Congress. *The Guardian*, February 25.

http://www.theguardian.com/world/2009/feb/25/barack-obama-green-economy-environment. Accessed 20 Nov 2017.

Gramsci, Antonio. 1991. 3. Heft. In *2.-3. Heft*, ed. Wolfgang Fritz Haug, vol. 2, 327–448. Gefängnishefte. Hamburg: Argument.

Harvey, David. 2007. *The Limits to Capital*. London/New York: Verso.

———. 2009. The 'New' Imperialism: Accumulation by Dispossession. *Socialist Register* 40.

Haug, Wolfgang Fritz. 2008. Editorial I: Die Krise denken. *Das Argument* 278: 483–489.

Hirsch, Joachim, and Roland Roth. 1986. *Das neue Gesicht des Kapitalismus*. Hamburg: VSA.

Hoffmann, Catherine. 2015. Ein großer Irrtum. *sueddeutsche.de*, May 31. http://www.sueddeutsche.de/wirtschaft/produktivitaet-ein-grosser-irrtum-1.2498761. Accessed 29 Oct 2017.

Javers, Eamon. 2009. Inside Obama's Bank CEOs Meeting. *POLITICO*, April 3. http://www.politico.com/news/stories/0409/20871.html. Accessed 29 Oct 2017.

Jessop, Bob. 2001a. Introduction. In *Regulationist Perspectives on Fordism and Post-Fordism*, ed. Bob Jessop, vol. 3, xxv–xliii. Cheltenham/Northampton: Edward Elgar.

———. 2001b. Series Preface. In *The Parisian Regulation School*, vol. 1, ix–xxiii. Cheltenham/Northampton: Edward Elgar.

———. 2014. Capitalist Diversity and Variety: Variegation, the World Market, Compossibility and Ecological Dominance. *Capital & Class* 38 (1): 45–58.

Krugman, Paul. 2009. Tea Parties Forever. *The New York Times*, April 13. http://www.nytimes.com/2009/04/13/opinion/13krugman.html. Accessed 29 Oct 2017.

———. 2010. Building a Green Economy. *New York Times*, October 4. http://www.nytimes.com/2010/04/11/magazine/11Economy-t.html. Accessed 29 Oct 2017.

———. 2011. The Competition Myth. *The New York Times*, January 23. http://www.nytimes.com/2011/01/24/opinion/24krugman.html. Accessed 29 Oct 2017.

Lapavitsas, Costas. 2013. *Profiting Without Producing: How Finance Exploits Us All*. London/New York: Verso.

Lipietz, Alain. 1998. Kette, Schuss und Regulation: ein Werkzeug für die Sozialwissenschaften. In *Nach dem Ende des 'Goldenen Zeitalters. Regulation und Transformation kapitalistischer Gesellschaften*, ed. Hans-Peter Krebs, vol. 255, 77–115. Berlin: Argument.

Lo, Clarence Y.H. 2012. Astroturf Versus Grass Roots: Scenes from Early Tea Party Mobilization. In *Steep. The Precipitous Rise of the Tea Party*, ed. Christine Trost and Lawrence Rosenthal, 98–129. Berkeley: University of California Press.

Marx, Karl. 1974. *Das Kapital.* Vol. 3, MEW 25. Berlin: Dietz.
Mayer, Margit, and Roland Roth. 1995. New Social Movements and the Transformation to Post-Fordist Society. In *Cultural Politics and Social Movements*, ed. Marcy Darnovsky, Barbara Epstein, and Richard Flacks, 299–319. Philadelphia: Temple University Press.
McNally, David. 2009. Von der Finanzkrise zur Weltwirtschaftskrise (2. Teil). *Das Argument* 281: 471–478.
New York Times. 2008. National Exit Polls Table. http://elections.nytimes.com/2008/results/president/national-exit-polls.html. Accessed 29 Oct 2017.
OECD. 2011. Towards Green Growth: A Summary for Policy Makers. http://www.oecd.org/greengrowth/48012345.pdf. Accessed 29 Oct 2017.
———. 2014. Income Inequality. In *Society at a Glance 2014: OECD Social Indicators.* Paris: OECD Publishing.
Opensecrets.org. 2009a. Bundlers, Barack Obama. http://www.opensecrets.org/pres08/bundlers.php?id=N00009638. Accessed 29 Oct 2017.
———. 2009b. Bundlers, John McCain. http://www.opensecrets.org/pres08/bundlers.php?id=N00006424. Accessed 29 Oct 2017.
———. 2013a. Democratic Party, Top Industries 2010 Cycle. https://www.opensecrets.org/parties/indus.php?cycle=2010&cmte=DPC. Accessed 29 Oct 2017.
———. 2013b. Presidential Candidate Comparison: Sector Totals, 2008 Cycle. http://www.opensecrets.org/pres08/sectorallc.php?cycle=2008. Accessed 29 Oct 2017.
———. 2013c. Presidential Candidates: Contributions by Sector, 2012 Cycle. https://www.opensecrets.org/pres12/sectorall.php?cycle=2012. Accessed 29 Oct 2017.
———. 2013d. Presidential Candidates: Selected Industry Totals, 2008 Cycle. http://www.opensecrets.org/pres08/select.php?ind=E01. Accessed 29 Oct 2017.
———. 2013e. Republican Party, Top Industries 2010 Cycle. https://www.opensecrets.org/parties/indus.php?cycle=2010&cmte=RPC. Accessed 29 Oct 2017.
———. 2013f. Top Contributors to Barack Obama, 2008 Cycle. http://www.opensecrets.org/pres08/contrib.php?cycle=2008&cid=N00009638. Accessed 29 Oct 2017.
———. 2013g. Top Contributors to John McCain, 2008 Cycle. http://www.opensecrets.org/pres08/contrib.php?cycle=2008&cid=N00006424. Accessed 29 Oct 2017.
———. 2015. Top Industries/Interest Groups 2014 Overview. https://www.opensecrets.org/overview/industries.php. Accessed 29 Oct 2017.
Panitch, Leo, and Sam Gindin. 2010. Capitalist Crisis and the Crisis This Time. In *The Crisis This Time*, ed. Leo Panitch, Greg Albo, and Vivek Chibber, 1–20. London/New York/Halifax: Merlin Press.

Pew Research Center. 2008. Inside Obama's Sweeping Victory. http://www.pewresearch.org/2008/11/05/inside-obamas-sweeping-victory/. Accessed 29 Oct 2017.

Piven, Frances Fox, and Richard A. Cloward. 1979. *Poor People's Movements: Why They Succeed, How They Fail*. New York: Vintage Books.

Polak, Ben, and Peter K. Schott. 2012. America's Hidden Austerity Program. New York Times Blogs. *Economix: Explaining the Science of Everyday Life* (blog). http://economix.blogs.nytimes.com/2012/06/11/americas-hidden-austerity-program/. Accessed 29 Oct 2017.

Radice, Hugo. 2010. Confronting the Crisis: A Class Analysis. In *The Crisis This Time*, ed. Leo Panitch, Greg Albo, and Vivek Chibber, 21–43. London/New York/Halifax: Merlin Press.

Rattner, Steven. 2014. Inequality, Unbelievably, Gets Worse. *The New York Times*, November 16. http://www.nytimes.com/2014/11/17/opinion/inequality-unbelievably-gets-worse.html. Accessed 29 Oct 2017.

Reinhart, Carmen M., and Kenneth S. Rogoff. 2008. *Is the 2007 U.S. Sub-Prime Financial Crisis So Different? An International Historical Comparison*. Working Paper 13761. National Bureau of Economic Research. http://www.nber.org/papers/w13761. Accessed 29 Oct 2017.

Rich, Frank. 2010. The Billionaires Bankrolling the Tea Party. *The New York Times*, August 28, http://www.nytimes.com/2010/08/29/opinion/29rich.html. Accessed 29 Oct 2017.

Roth, Roland, and Dieter Rucht. 2008. Einleitung. In *Die sozialen Bewegungen in Deutschland seit 1945: Ein Handbuch*, 9–36. Frankfurt am Main: Campus.

Röttger, Bernd. 2009. Krisen des Kapitalismus – historische Perspektiven. *Das Argument* 283: 758–766.

Sablowski, Thomas. 2011. Die jüngste Weltwirtschaftskrise und die Krisentheorien. In *VielfachKrise Im finanzmarktdominierten Kapitalismus*, ed. Alex Demirovic, Julia Dück, Florian Becker, and Pauline Bader, 29–44. Hamburg: VSA.

Sablowski, Thomas, and Sabah Alnasseri. 2001. Auf dem Weg zu einem finanzgetriebenen Akkumulationsregime? In *Ein neuer Kapitalismus?* ed. Mario Candeias and Frank Deppe, 131–149. Hamburg: VSA.

Silver, Beverly J., and Giovanni Arrighi. 2011. Das Ende des langen 20. Jahrhunderts. In *VielfachKrise Im finanzmarktdominierten Kapitalismus*, ed. Alex Demirovic, Julia Dück, Florian Becker, and Pauline Bader, 211–228. Hamburg: VSA.

Skocpol, Theda. 1980. Political Response to Capitalist Crisis: Neo-Marxist Theories of the State and the Case of the New Deal. *Politics & Society* 10 (2): 155–201.

Solow, Robert M. 1997. We'd Better Watch Out: Review of Cohen, Stephen S. and Zysman, John: Manufacturing Matters, New York 1997. *New York Times Book Review*, December 7.

Solty, Ingar. 2013a. Einleitung: Die Innen-Außen-Dialektik des American Empire in der globalen Krise. In *Die USA unter Obama: Charismatische Herrschaft, soziale Bewegungen und imperiale Politik in der globalen Krise*, 15–71. Hamburg: Argument.

———. 2013b. The Crisis Interregnum: Considerations on the Political Articulation of the Global Crisis. From the New Right-Wing Populism to the Occupy Movement. *Studies in Political Economy* 91: 85–112.

Stockhammer, Engelbert. 2000. *Financialization and the Slowdown of Accumulation*. Working Papers Series: Growth and Employment in Europe: Sustainability and Competitiveness. Wirtschaftsuniversität Wien. http://epub.wu.ac.at/366/1/document.pdf. Accessed 29 Oct 2017.

Stockhammer, Engelbert. 2007. *Some Stylized Facts on the Finance-Dominated Accumulation Regime* (Workingpaper Series). Political Economy Research Institute, University of Massachussettes, Amherst.

Tankersley, Jim. 2013. Jobless Recoveries Are Here to Stay, Economists Say, but It's a Mystery Why. *The Washington Post*, September 19. http://www.washingtonpost.com/business/economy/jobless-recoveries-are-here-to-stay-economists-say-but-its-a-mystery-why/2013/09/19/6034bcb4-20c7-11e3-966c-9c4293c47ebe_story.html. Accessed 29 Oct 2017.

Teixeira, Ruy. 2010. Demographic Change and the Future of the Parties. https://www.americanprogressaction.org/wp-content/uploads/issues/2010/06/pdf/voter_demographics.pdf. Accessed 29 Oct 2017.

The Economist. 2015. An Incorrect Dial? *The Economist*, August 5. http://www.economist.com/blogs/freeexchange/2015/05/americas-unemployment-rate. Accessed 29 Oct 2017.

UNEP. 2011. Towards a Green Economy: Pathways to Sustainable Development and Poverty Eradication. A Synthesis for Policy Makers. http://www.unep.org/greeneconomy/Portals/88/documents/ger/GER_synthesis_en.pdf. Accessed 29 Oct 2017.

Wallerstein, Immanuel. 2010. Structural Crises. *New Left Review* 62: 133–142.

Williamson, Vanessa. 2013. The Tea Party and the Shift to, Austerity by Gridlock' in the United States. http://scholar.harvard.edu/files/williamson/files/investment_or_austerity_in_the_united_states_williamson_apsa.pdf. Accessed 29 Oct 2017.

CHAPTER 3

The Demographics of the Mobilized: The Core Constituency of the Protests

As Piven and Cloward remark in *Poor People's Movements*, albeit in the context of a protest-clientele quite different from the one I discuss below, "(…) people experience deprivation and oppression within a concrete setting, not as the end product of large and abstract processes, and it is the concrete experience that molds their discontent into specific grievances against specific targets" (Piven and Cloward 1979, 20). This chapter seeks to identify and understand these "concrete experiences" as socially specific—more precisely as class-specific—expositions to the crisis. On the one hand, a class-specific analysis is appropriate because the probable events—through and in which people 'encountered' the crisis—are unevenly distributed in social space. On the other hand, different social groups were subjected to these events and dynamics in the context of different sets of real and anticipated objective life chances that had hitherto (consciously and non-consciously) structured their biographical trajectories. It is therefore crucial to understand who took part in the mobilizations, since this allows us to retrospectively single out experiences common to or at least homologous between relevant parts of the respective mobilization and to discuss how these experiences contributed to the form and content of the protest.

To understand the specific experiences and expectations that define the groups that joined the respective mobilization (and what differentiates a group from another), it is important to leave behind common sense

N. C. Kumkar, *The Tea Party, Occupy Wall Street, and the Great Recession*, Critical Political Theory and Radical Practice,
https://doi.org/10.1007/978-3-319-73688-4_3

concepts such as the 'middle class', a category often invoked in commentaries on the social composition of both the Tea Party and Occupy Wall Street (e.g., Milkman et al. 2013, 16; Skocpol and Williamson 2012, 12). This category indeed connects neatly to both the ideological self-perception of many of the mobilizations' participants and to public discourse about the political and economic crisis as one of social polarization and the "shrinking of the middle class". However, as a contingent gradational sequencing of the continuum of different income levels, the catchall category of 'middle class' does not necessarily capture common realms of experience that result from a shared position in society as a *structure* in the proper sense of the term.[1] In other words, the category of the middle class only very superficially allows the socially specific experience of the developments of society to be grasped, even if—in a constructivist sense—it contributes to shaping how developments are socially negotiated and perceived.

This is not to say that such income-based categories cannot provide expression to certain mechanisms. Groups of people exposed to particular developments might very well cluster in certain income ranges as, for example, perhaps best illustrated through one of the most popular slogans of OWS: "we are the 99%". It powerfully symbolized one effect of the culmination of different dynamics, namely, the skewing of revenue streams more and more toward the top centile of the distribution. Furthermore, the slogan provides expression to the lack of agency the rest of the population has in shaping the political or economic life of the nation. Granted, as a slogan, it necessarily condenses and therefore simplifies. At the same time, however, its moralizing force can also obscure an understanding of the politico-economic determinants of the development it decries. The concrete changes in distributional patterns due to the historic low of the wage share which in turn helped to stabilize the rate of profits and set the stage for skyrocketing capital gains in some sectors then tended to disappear behind a smoke screen of debates on 'privilege', which 'unfairly' make some people richer than they 'ought to be'.

The range of possible biographical experiences and expectations of individuals are, to an important degree, determined by the economic capital at their disposal. However, their concrete form and content is also determined by objective life chances that accompany a certain position in the overall social division (and governance) of labor and by a socially specific "ethos" or habitus meaning the complex of cultural and moral patterns and horizons that orient one's engagement with these chances.[2] To understand how and why life chances and socially specific ethos are relevant, consider the examples of Marco and Max. Both Marco and Max are around 30 years old and able to dispose of almost the same income; thus, they are members of the same birth cohort and statistical income class. Marco, however, is the nephew and employee of the owner of a small plumbing business in southern Connecticut. He served in the US Air Force for half a decade before 2009 and now is supposedly not able to take over his uncle's business because he lacks an official license to do so.[3] Marco is thus subject to a different development of his life chances and will most probably experience and interpret the somewhat similar situation of a biographical blockade differently than a young photographer living in NYC who has to work three clerical jobs (to juggle her expenses) and who, through an internship, still hopes to find employment in her original field of study 'later'.

To grasp these specific positions, this chapter therefore takes as its conceptual starting point not the category of the 'income class' but rather the category of *class in the Marxian sense* of the term.[4] This concept seeks to capture the systematic culmination of certain effects of the social structure on and around certain positions in this structure. By capturing positionality in the overall structure of revenue streams resulting from the dynamic circuit of capital reproduction, this concept highlights individual and group socioeconomic reproduction. The class structure of capitalist societies is understood as the result of complex mediations ultimately rooted in the dialectics of the value form and the exploitation of labor at the heart of capitalist commodity production. The two basic classes that define the dynamics of the capitalist class society are therefore the bourgeoisie and the proletariat—those who own the means of production and appropriate the surplus product of those who do not own the means of production and therefore have to sell their labor power.[5]

This is not to deny the existence of other classes. However, they also need to be understood in their relation to the basic structures of capitalist societies and the antagonism between capital and labor—no matter whether they are historically rooted in other modes of production, such as crafts(wo)men or the peasantry, or if they only evolved within capitalism. Especially important for this book are two intermediate classes or contradictory class positions: the *classical petty bourgeoisie* and the *new petty bourgeoisie*.[6] The *classical petty bourgeoisie* is defined by its members' ownership of means of production, which exempts them from being forced to sell their labor power to others, but which does not suffice to allow them to live from the appropriation of other people's surplus product. For small shop owners and crafts(wo)men, their economic base has secularly eroded through the process of capitalist accumulation (cf. Hagelstange 1988). This general downward trend was only punctuated by short upswings in the 1980s (cf. Steinmetz and Wright 1989), when deregulation, wage depression, and the subsequent rise in service sector activity led to an increase in self-employment; in the late 1990s, corresponding with the boom of the so-called New Economy; and the early 2000s, during a credit-induced boom in construction and finance activity (cf. Hipple 2004, 2010). None of these upswings were able to balance the secular decline of this class' relative size. The Bureau of Labor Statistics reports that the share of unincorporated self-employment in the overall workforce in the USA was 7% in 2009. In 1967, before the onset of the crisis of Fordism, and the wage suppression and economic liberalization that came with it, this share was still 9.7% (Hipple 2010, 19). In fact, already in 1948, just as postwar expansion was gaining momentum, their numbers had dropped to 19.8% (Hipple 2004, 14)—down from more than half the US population at the beginning of the twentieth century (Braverman 1974, 403–10).

The *new petty bourgeoisie*, on the other hand, consists of salaried employees, who, 'capitalizing' on their knowledge, enjoy relatively high levels of autonomy in their work and sometimes power over the organization of the production process themselves. The rise of this class is associated with the increasing differentiation and complexity of capitalist societies and their administration since WWII, suggesting a secular expansion of this class as, for example, indicated by the rising share of people with higher-education degrees in most countries. The restructuring of production processes and the relative decline in public spending for welfare programs and the educational sector—key sectors of employment for this class—accompanied the transition to the finance-dominated accumulation regime. In combination with the devaluating effect of the overall 'inflation' in degrees in higher education, this culminated in a massive devaluation of their cultural capital. Thus, especially in the USA, the boundaries between the new petty bourgeoisie and the proletariat are increasingly blurred (cf. Ehrenreich and Ehrenreich 2013).

In contrast to the classical petty bourgeoisie, members of this class tend to possess no or very little economic capital. They might formally work independently as 'freelancers'—however, even as freelancers, they usually do not own the actual means of production but rather offer skills-based services to those that do. Belonging in the category of the "incorporated self-employed", their growing numbers since the 1980s partially explain the stabilization of the overall number of the self-employed in the USA (Hipple 2010). Referring to Marx's differentiation between the formal and the real subsumption of labor under capital, it can be inferred that their 'self-employment' is a merely formal independence from capital, while they remain real subsumed under it in the process of production (cf. Marx 1969, 531–41).

At the core of these two classes' respective strategies for status preservation are two different kinds of capital—economic and cultural capital. Both forms of capital are accumulated (dead) labor—in the case of the petty bourgeoisie, mostly one's own labor or labor transferred from one's family—and function as capital only insofar as they allow the appropriation of the product of (living) labor. Cultural capital—no matter if incorporated as knowledge or skills, or institutionalized in the form of educational degrees—is dependent on its social recognition and ultimately its transferability into economic gain in order to function as capital. To have little cultural capital therefore does not mean that one is 'uneducated' or, even less so, that one is not 'talented', but merely that one lacks social recognition and rewards for being 'educated', 'intelligent', or 'talented' (Bourdieu 1983). Therefore, although educational degrees are perhaps the best available statistical indicator to measure cultural capital, they provide only a very rough picture. As an aggregate statistic, the complex hierarchies between degrees in different fields of study and different schools—as well as the context in which they are (or aren't) actualized as capital—are factored out. Thus, when considered, education as cultural capital must always be contextualized through regarding the changing social meaning of these degrees (cf. Bourdieu 1994, 251–76).

Together, these concepts of class and capital allow us to model the experience of precariousness and loss of status that members of both classes experienced in the last decades and especially since the Great Recession. They also provide insight into the different mechanisms and pathways through which the threat of 'declassing' and the economic policies addressing the economic crisis are experienced. Someone whose social reproduction depends first and foremost on his/her economic capital—for example, someone running a small construction company—will be far more responsive to fears of economic redistribution than someone whose social reproduction depends mainly on cultural capital. Likewise, the devaluation of cultural capital that accompanies austerity measures through drastic cuts to the relative share of the social wealth spent on education and public funding of the cultural sector will more broadly frighten the latter, rather than the prior.[7]

Focusing on social classes to understand the different socioeconomic background of the crisis experience underlying the protest mobilizations also allows us to break with methodological individualism and differentiate between the proximate cause and the underlying reasons for joining a mobilization. Of course, the individual 'triggering' experiences that ultimately tipped the scales for a particular person to decide to become an active participant in the mobilizations are often very different and contingent. In the TP, for example, I spoke to recent veterans who felt their service to the common good did not receive enough recognition, to a temporarily unemployed banker, to retirees looking for a meaningful activity, and to a republican who yearned for a repetition of the great success of a "support our troops" rally she organized during the third Gulf War. A too strong focus on these individual features, however, fails to explain either the broad support that the movement initially had in certain segments of the US population or why participants considered especially *this* movement to be a meaningful and appropriate mobilization to become engaged in, as the aforementioned motives would explain joining almost any social movement (or other social activities). As Chaps. 4 and 5 will discuss, the participants find themselves socially predisposed to connect to each other beyond these contingent and diverse precipitating factors that brought them to join the protests.

Of course, the protest mobilizations are not to be understood as the unmediated expression of the experience and 'objective interests' of one (and only one) clearly discernible social class. Instead, it will be assumed in the following that the mobilizations are not to be understood so much as class movements but rather as "mediated expressions" of class struggle (Barker 2013, 47). The relation of a protest mobilization's aims to the class relations of the whole of society is often rather ambivalent and subject to hidden and open contention. Regarding the demographics of the mobilized, this means that it would be a futile endeavor to try to identify only one social class responsible for carrying out the protest, but that members of different social classes can be identified as supporting it. This could be, and sometimes has been (e.g., Hirsch and Roth 1986, 219), read as indicating that class is not an adequate lens for examining and understanding the form and content of protests. The empirically observable social heterogeneity is, however, not arbitrary but in itself systematically socially structured. While members of different social classes recognize themselves in what they perceive to be the mobilization's 'message', this identification is grounded in these groups' socio-specific backgrounds of experience.

In her Bourdieu-inspired analysis of the events of May 1968, Gilcher-Holtey demonstrated that, in contrast to what is indicated in many descriptions of these events, it was not only young disappointed students and academics that formed the movement in more or less accidental conjuncture with the unions. Instead, the rhetoric of 'autogestion',[8] in which the students articulated their conflict within the very institutions they at the same time relied on, resonated very well with certain parts of the young working class in France, who found themselves in a homologous conflict within strict institutions that were no longer able to deliver the accustomed status security (Gilcher-Holtey 2001).

Furthermore, in the structured whole of different social classes participating in protests, it is also possible to identify (at least in the mobilizations under scrutiny here) a certain social class from which the movements' "core constituency" is recruited. *Core constituency* is used here to designate the *leading class-generational unit* of the movement (Mannheim 1964; Rosenhek and Shalev 2014). The attribute *leading* neither signifies that this group in the mobilization necessarily encompasses the largest number of participants nor that the institutional leadership is necessarily recruited from its ranks (cf. Poulantzas 1973, esp. 34ff.). *Leading* rather refers to the socio-demographic group whose 'style' and interests are dominant in shaping the practice of the movement.

Class-generational unit is used here in the sense of Mannheim's classical concept. Its purpose is to capture the specificity of the experienced environment—a *conjunctive realm of experience*, in Mannheim's terminology (1997)—that unites certain groups who are defined by living through a specific set of events, which defines them as a generational unit, and by experiencing these events from a similar socio-biographic perspective, which is determined by their shared class background.

The identification of the core constituency is grounded in a dialectical interplay between the available surveys, the results of the habitus reconstruction, and the relation of the reconstructed habitus of the different groups to the overall movement practices. This means that although the identification of the core constituency is grounded in empirical observations, it is ultimately a theoretically informed construction that has to prove its analytic value through the explanatory power of the models developed with its help.

In the following, I will use the available data from surveys and my own observations to delineate the class-generational units that form the core constituencies of the respective protest mobilizations and their *corridors of experience* or the large socio-tectonic shifts that affected these class-generational units. For the moment, this analysis is conceptualized independently from the question whether and to what extent the mobilized constituency itself perceived these developments as relevant, as understanding this factor would presuppose a reconstruction of the group's interpretative predispositions.

This move aims to prepare the ground for a more complex modeling of the unfolding of the mobilization in the larger socio-political context of their emergence. It remains a rough and abstract sketch not only because the material that such a delineation can rely on does not allow for more concretion—the number of available surveys is rather small and measured variables often are not easily translated back into the conceptual framework of this study—but also because it is, as stated in the introduction, a secondary approximation that will become more fine-grained and concrete with the habitus analysis in Chap. 5.

3.1 The Tea Party's Core Constituency: The Darkening Horizon of the Classical Petty Bourgeoisie

Compared to OWS, the TP as a mass mobilization proved relatively long-lived. The supporting organizations had a high level of institutionalization, which contributed to the comparatively solid database that allows for a delineation of its core constituency. A nationwide, representative CBS/New York Times telephone poll conducted in early 2010 included a question asking if the respondents considered themselves TP supporters (New York Times 2010). This survey served as the main source of quantitative data on which the comprehensive TP monograph by Skocpol and Williamson relied (2012) and also serves as the main referent for the following sketch of the TP's socio-demographic composition. Ekins, a research fellow at the right-wing libertarian Cato Institute, also published an interesting analysis of the results of the CBS/NYT survey and compared these results to those from three other surveys. The three surveys she used in her comparison were another representative, nationwide telephone poll conducted by *The Washington Post*, the Kaiser Family Foundation, and Harvard University in October 2010 that also featured a question about TP support, a survey conducted by the Cato Institute with the participants of their Tea Party Convention in Virginia in October

2010 and one conducted by Politico and Target Point at a Tea Party Rally in Washington DC in April 2010 (Ekins 2011; Edison Research 2010; The Washington Post, Kaiser Family Foundation, and Harvard University 2010). Furthermore, a research team of Cho et al. collected a study relying on an extensive list of Tea Party events that were mobilized via the internet platforms of the movement and “meetup.org” during and after the midterm election season of 2010, which provides a window into the geographic patterns of TP activities (Cho et al. 2012).

All these surveys, of course, have their methodological limitations. The exact meaning of ‘support’ in the phone surveys, for example, is left undefined, and the Cato Tea Party convention most probably addressed a specific subset of TP activists rather than a representative sample. Together, however, they nevertheless allow for identifying a number of demographic specificities of the mobilized constituency of the TP. All surveys report that the overwhelming majority of the TP supporters self-identify as “Caucasian” (89% according to the CBS-survey), that they are on average older than the general US population, and that men are overrepresented among them. The majority of the TP supporters belong to the upper third of the US income distribution, and the surveys conducted directly at the TP events indicate that the mobilized constituency of the TP even had a significantly higher annual disposable income than those that self-identified as “supporters” of the TP (e.g., while the CBS poll found a fifth of the TP supporters to belong to the highest income quintile, the Cato survey found 41% of its respondents belonging to this group).[9]

The same is true for education. TP supporters on average have higher educational degrees than the general US population, and the active participants in the events are again even more educated than the average TP supporter. However, given the strong correlation between income level and educational degrees in the USA, these two variables have to be seen in context. While TP supporters are “wealthier and more educated” (Zernike and Thee-Brenan 2010) when compared to the total US population, their educational level is below the average of their respective income group, even if we consider that their overall age cohort has a lower percentage of holders of higher educational degrees.[10]

The mobilized constituency of the TP therefore generates relatively high amounts of revenue with comparatively low levels of cultural capital.[11] In the context of the class typology used here, this suggests that a substantial portion belongs to the classical petty bourgeoisie. While it is not possible to estimate the portion that belong to the bourgeoisie proper, since that would require information on their overall wealth and income from capital gains, which is not available, my observations suggest the classic bourgeois group is rather small or even negligible. Although the surveys unfortunately do not provide detailed information on the professional status of the TP supporters needed to substantiate this claim, both the Cato survey and the Politico survey find that the percentage of self-reported small business owners among the active TP members is more than three and a half times higher than among the general US population (26[12]/29% as compared to 7% [Hipple 2010]).[13] Indeed, Skocpol and Williamson's observations point in the same direction as my observations on TP meetings and events: "(T)he plurality seemed to be small business owners, often in fields like construction, remodeling, or repair (…). A fair number of others worked in technology, insurance, or real estate (…) only a relatively small portion of Tea Party participants were employed in the public sector – with the exception of the military" (Skocpol and Williamson 2012, 23 f.).

It is maybe worth noting that the demographic composition of those belonging to the category of the 'self-employed'—a category which might be the best-fitting proxy for classical petty bourgeoisie in the data provided by the Bureau of Labor Statistics—is demographically very similar to the TP profile just sketched out. They too tend to be overwhelmingly identified as "white" (86.9% of all unincorporated self-employed are listed as "non-Hispanic white", compared to 89% "Caucasians" among the TP supporters in the CBS poll), are older, and have a significantly higher income than the average US population (Hipple 2010). These observations indicate that being a "small business owner" might in fact be the subgroup of the US population most overly represented among TP activists as well as the group whose demographic composition most closely resembles that of the TP.[14]

The classical petty bourgeoisie finds itself in a specific, contradictory position in relation to what Bourdieu calls the 'field of power'. Its (relatively) high endowment with economic capital (partially) aligns the classical petty bourgeoisie with the ruling class, as they are both 'buyers' rather than 'sellers' of labor power. Its comparatively low endowment with cultural capital (vis-à-vis others with comparable social status), however, on the whole, excludes its members from actively participating in public debate about the future of society at large.

This contradictory position can help explain many aspects of TP supporters' experience of crisis, such as their feeling of being dominated by a 'liberal elite'. However, it also clarifies a common misconception of the TP in the eyes of many academic and non-academic observers alike, namely, that the TP is recruited from the "lower middle class" (see, e.g., Lundskow 2012; Langman 2011) which seems odd, given that all available surveys suggest that members of the highest third of the income distribution are strongly overrepresented among TP activists. The inner rationality of this socio-optical illusion is that it expresses differences in endowments of cultural capital between the participants in the rallies and their (*new* petty bourgeois) observers from media and academia. These commentators are accustomed to pre-reflexively evaluating social status via cultural capital, since cultural capital is what determines their own social status, and therefore almost automatically perceive the TP activists to be 'below them'.

My own observations at TP meetings, events, and protests also indicate that the active group participating in what can be called 'proper' social movement praxis, such as attending meetings, rallying, and petitioning, is relatively homogenous in terms of social class. In the TP meetings and events I observed, the classical petty bourgeoisie was the most numerically significant fraction, especially if one includes retirees from this class. Another, smaller fraction was employed in the financial, insurance, or energy industry. In Bourdieu's terminology, this group can be seen as part of the executive petty bourgeoisie—they too dispose of relatively little cultural capital but also of comparatively less economic capital than the classical petty bourgeoisie (Bourdieu 1994, 549–55). The last group I was furthermore able to identify is that of the aspiring working class, who perceived their status ascendancy as being primarily blocked by unjust government regulation. All three groups, however, are unified by the figure of the 'small business owner'. He is the common point of reference in all of their biographical trajectories—be it as their aspired to, their past, or their present socioeconomic status.

Geographically, at least two patterns can be identified: Using the data of the CBS/NYT poll, Ekins shows that the TP supporters seem to be concentrated mostly in the US South, which Skocpol and Williamson also suggest.[15] The latter, however, furthermore convincingly argue that this might to a large extent be the result of typical internal migration patterns in the USA, wherein older, wealthier people disproportionately tend to move to the South when they retire (Skocpol and Williamson 2012, 24). In other words, rather than understanding the TP as a 'Southern phenomenon', one might more plausibly assume that the South attracts demographics that are also prone to support the TP. The mapping of the nationwide distribution of TP protest events and gatherings around the mobilization peak of the midterm election in 2010 by Cho et al. furthermore shows that, despite over-representation in the South, the TP was active in all regions of the USA. Thus, while "support" (which is a very unspecific term) for the TP parallels the general distribution of conservative voting behavior, actual TP activism might have a more complicated relationship to its geographical surroundings,[16] preventing the pinpointing of a clearly regionalized pattern of TP activism.

A statistical analysis of the smaller-scale geographic pattern of TP activism by Cho et al. produced seemingly contradictory findings on the relation between the impact of the crisis and TP activism in counties across the USA. On the one hand, they identify a clear correlation between the rate of housing foreclosures and the level of TP activism. The top 50 counties[17] with the highest foreclosure rates saw about a sixth of the total TP events in the period observed, indicating a clear connection between being exposed to the economic crisis and joining the TP. On the other hand, they found that the 50 counties that experienced the highest peaks in unemployment in this period barely saw *any* TP protest events or gatherings. This finding fits well with the fact that only 14% of the TP respondents in the CBS/NYT poll reported that the crisis has brought them (or even their family) economic hardship. Regarding the geographic dispersion of the protests, these two findings also both fit a clear pattern. The study shows a concentration of TP activism in suburban and rural rather than in urban areas, which reflects both the higher concentration of foreclosures in the former and the higher concentration of unemployment in the latter.

The paradox of the relation/non-relation between exposure to economic crisis and the inclination to support the TP in a given county is dissolved if some of the socio-political developments to which its core constituency had been exposed in the decades leading up to the emergence of the TP are considered. Against the backdrop of the secular decline of the classical petty bourgeoisie, the occupational groups that Skocpol and Williamson especially identified as the recruitment pool of the TP were among the few that directly benefited from the policies of the FED and the Bush administration after the bursting of the dotcom bubble. The owners of small businesses profited from the historically low wage levels, while aggregate demand for their services and goods was kept up by the loose monetary policies of the FED and the expansion of credit. Especially the credit-induced boom in the housing sector catered to those who ran businesses in construction, remodeling, or repair—an important sector of self-employment especially for those with comparatively low cultural capital. Inflation in asset prices not only boosted private pension funds, which especially those with relatively high monetary wealth invested in, but also brought with it numerous business opportunities for those offering services in finance, insurance, or real estate.

In all these industries—construction, real estate, and finance—profits in the Great Recession contracted both very notably and stronger than in most other sectors (United States Census Bureau 2012). On the asset side, when mounting foreclosures rates hit their neighborhoods in 2007–2009, it devaluated the very same assets that secured the debts of exactly those age cohorts[18] that tended to support the TP. Thus, what many in the TP experienced was not so much a direct decline of the standard of living, but an eclipsing of the future economic prospects and a crumbling of one's safety assets.

It is in this light that a number of apparent paradoxes, such as the one just cited, can be understood. TP activities that are concentrated in areas with high foreclosure rates are not a direct expression of the hardship of losing one's house, but rather are the mediated effect of the loss of property values and the corresponding plummeting demand for a series of activities that the businesses of TP activists are disproportionately engaged in. The apparent contradiction between exceptionally bleak expectations for both the future of the economy in general and one's own economic future in particular and simultaneously judging one's own current economic situation as "fairly good" (New York Times 2010) also has a rational core. It is the reasonable (if perhaps not conscious) expectation that small entrepreneurs are very likely to be the first to fall victim in the "fight of hostile brothers" (Marx 1974, 263)—a state into which market competition transforms in times of crisis—especially in rapidly contracting sectors of the economy. Similarly, the disproportionate number of TP activists who blame the Obama administration rather than the Bush administration for the bad state of the economy in 2009 and expect that the stimulus package by the Obama administration will not help the economy to recover (New York Times 2010) has to be understood in this context. The Bush administration's policies had, at least in the short run, in fact shielded these sectors against the overall decline of petty bourgeois self-employment until an accelerated decline set in after 2007, while Obama's stimulus package was mostly geared toward other sectors of the economy.

3.2 Occupy Wall Street's Core Constituency: The Biographically Blocked, Aspiring New Petty Bourgeoisie

Given the broad media coverage and the attention that OWS received in parts of the academia, it is somewhat surprising how scanty empirical knowledge of the demographics of OWS actually is. Nationwide telephone surveys on support for the movement do exist, but reveal little more than the fact that there had initially been a wider support for OWS than there had been for the TP (35%–40% vs. 20%–30%, depending on the poll) and that those supporting it were on average younger and more left-leaning than those opposing the goals of OWS (Montopoli 2011; Pew Research Center 2011). The most thorough and scientifically solid survey was conducted by a team around Milkman et al. with participants in the large OWS-initiated May Day rally in NYC in spring 2012 (2013). Interesting insights into the early composition of the mobilization are provided by a series of surveys conducted via one important website of OWS in the Fall of 2011 by Cordero-Guzman (2011) who was kind enough to allow me to use the first two waves of his survey, conducted in the week before October 2 and 21, respectively, for secondary analysis.[19] Representative data on the nationwide demographic composition of the movement comparable to that provided for the TP and including a control group of non-supporters are missing. Nonetheless, a number of specificities that contrast clearly to those identified for the TP can be identified even on this basis:

Just as in the TP, the participants in OWS disproportionately self-identified as "white" (63% in Milkman et al.'s, and even 76% in Cordero-Guzman's study[20]), and men were slightly over-represented. OWS' constituency is clearly younger than that of the TP. Although the survey by Milkman et al. found only 40% of those actively involved in OWS to be "under 30 years old" (even though this already is an overrepresentation compared to NYC's population), the data of Cordero-Guzman shows that the largest single group of active participants in the occupation was between 25 and 35 years old (30.9%) and roughly 50% to be below 35 years—which seems coherent with my own observations. It is also plausible to assume that the overall sample of Milkman et al. is older on average than a representative sample of OWS participants would be, given the high number of older unionized workers that presumably take part in May Day activities. The majority of participants in OWS already finished at least a college education (over 64% in the Cordero-Guzman survey, and

80% in Milkman et al., compared to 34% of NYC's population), indicating that most were at the beginning of their working lives rather than students. Indeed, according to the data by Cordero-Guzman, the largest group of participants (44.5%) was working full time at the time of the survey. This could be interpreted as contradicting the expectations of the "biographical availability" theorem (Beyerlein and Bergstrand 2013; originally McAdam 1986), which would lead one to expect an over-representation of those that are still in education compared to those who already entered the labor market (the TP activists, whose children often moved out some time ago, are in that sense more 'typical').

The majority of the participants were endowed with comparatively high amounts of cultural capital, with more than 90% (in both surveys) of them having completed some college, a college degree, a graduate degree or being currently enrolled in college or university, putting them well above the average of both the population of NYC and even the highest income quartile of their birth cohort of the USA in general (Bailey and Dynarski 2011, 25 f.). The findings on the income of the participants diverge sharply between the two surveys: Cordero-Guzman's data places almost two-thirds of the OWS supporters in the bottom half of the US income distribution, and the single largest subgroup of all educational groups even in the lowest quintile, while Milkman et al. place most active participants in OWS in the middle three income quintiles of the US income distribution and well above the average of NYC's population.[21] Both studies, however, find them to be on average clearly income-poorer than the TP supporters, which must be understood at least partially in the context of their younger age.

The study by Milkman et al. furthermore shows a high percentage of participants working in education, arts, and the entertainment industries (33%), and comparatively few in management, business, finance (4.2% compared to 12.4% of the population of NYC), sales, office work, and service (16.9% compared to 43.8% of the population of NYC). All this indicates that the class-generational unit that forms the social basis of OWS is to be sought primarily in the youth segment of what is called the 'new petty bourgeoisie'. The new petty bourgeoisie is different from the classical or 'old' petty bourgeoisie in that its members are salaried employees that do not legally own means of production, but are, due to their specialized knowledge (cultural capital), expected (and expecting) to be able to find relatively high-prestige and high-paying work in the non-productive (in a Marxian sense) sectors of the economy or, due to their knowledge of production processes, are de facto in control of means of production. The intergenerational reproduction of this class does not so much rely on economic capital as it does on cultural capital—investment in education is therefore this class' key strategy for status inheritance and improvement.

Like the classical petty bourgeoisie, the new petty bourgeoisie finds itself in a contradictory position vis-à-vis the field of power—however, the contradictory position is symmetrically inverse: The classical petty bourgeoisie is a buyer, or at least not a seller, of labor power, but is excluded from the conversations on the management of society. The new petty bourgeoisie is a seller of labor power and therefore is positioned homologically to the proletariat in the economic field proper. However, through its cultural capital, it is aligned with the ruling class in that its social status stems from the degree to which it is able to participate in the discourse on the management of society.

Fittingly, OWS has a very high percentage of participants that went to or still attend "elite colleges and universities".[22] Nevertheless, the study of Cordero-Guzman found 13.5% of those that answered the full survey to be unemployed at the moment, while the survey of Milkman et al. found that 36.6% of those interviewed under 30 had lost a job in the last five years. These numbers are much higher than those one can find in surveys on the TP. This is not surprising, since young people were hit disproportionately by unemployment during the Great Recession (Tseng et al. 2013). Even if these numbers are not extraordinarily high compared with the rest of their birth cohort, they nevertheless indicate a problem in the intergenerational class reproduction of the new petty bourgeoisie, which in the last decades suffered relatively less in periods of labor market contraction (Shierholz et al. 2014).

Studies that would allow for comparing the geographical patterns of the larger Occupy mobilization to that of the TP are unfortunately missing. However, a study of the geographical distribution of early Occupy activities in California based on the respective groups' Facebook presence conducted by a research team at the University of California Riverside indicates that they were more highly concentrated in urban areas and in towns with at least four-year colleges and a democratic voting majority. Interestingly, the rate of foreclosures was not in any way significantly correlated with Occupy activities, while the rate of unemployment seemed to be even negatively correlated (Curran et al. 2013).

Paul Mason and, following him, also Milkman et al. and others, have identified the core constituency of OWS as being represented by the ideal type of the "graduate without a future" (Mason 2013; Milkman et al. 2013; Milkman 2014). I will translate this finding, which is supported by my own observations, into the class analytically more fruitful figure of the *proletarianized youth of the new petty bourgeoisie*. This highlights the main effect of the crisis that this group was subjected to prior to the protest mobilization: the devaluation of accumulated cultural capital.

Cultural capital functions as capital only insofar as it functions as a claim to social recognition and is potentially transferable into economic capital. It is not an intrinsic quality of knowledge or skill but instead the potential social exchange value of that knowledge. The expansion of higher education therefore exerted an inflationary pressure onto the value of this very education: The share of those with at least a college degree in the overall population has expanded continuously since WWII from 4.6% of the US population over 25 years old in 1940 to 32% in 2013 (United States Census Bureau 2014). At the same time, returns on investments in higher education declined. The price of educational degrees rose sharply (the average cost of a university education rose from 23% of the median annual income in 2001 to 35% in 2010), while the median expected income to be earned with a degree stayed the same since 1979 after adjusting for inflation (The Economist 2012). This is indeed a very significant relative loss in this group's share of the social product per person, considering that the overall material wealth of the USA as measured in inflation-adjusted GDP per capita has increased by an annual rate of circa 2% over that same period, meaning it almost doubled (OECD 2016). The fact that the number of enrolled students nevertheless increased over this period might not be least of all due to the fact that the wages of those who only hold a high school diploma actually decreased in that same period of time (The Economist 2012).

With the Great Recession, this creeping devaluation took on shock-like qualities. The contracting labor market not only further depressed wages paid in the aspired occupations, it also drastically reduced the numbers of positions available. Often highly indebted,[23] many graduates found themselves either unemployed or working several small jobs that did not even nominally require a degree in higher education (Vedder et al. 2013). Student loans, an important part of the debt held by the age group of the core constituency,[24] present an especially heavy burden on the debtor's future: Only very few (and typically low-paid) occupational groups can qualify for income-based repayment plans; most others must repay their debt within 10 years after finishing their degree. A default on the loan severely impacts credit scores, which in turn brings with it a whole array of consequences—from difficulties obtaining further credit, to renting an apartment, or even impacting the a chance to find a job—which exerts high pressure on remittance even when barely feasible. One effect of the weak labor market during the Great Recession has been that the rate of student loans defaults has reached its highest value since 1995 (cf. Dayen 2014). And regardless if they turn out to be impossible to repay, these loans remain binding even after a debtor declares bankruptcy (cf. Dynarski 2014). No wonder that intellectuals involved in OWS characterized these loans as "mortgaging the future" (Ross 2013). However, even if under-employment and unemployment turn out to be a mere biographical 'bump' in the career trajectory of this class-generational unit, this episode will most likely dampen the income prospects for the rest of their lives, as econometric analysis has shown (e.g., Gregg and Tominey 2005).

The usage of the term *proletarianization*, however, may raise some eye-brows, since the just described core constituency is not exactly what is often imagined as 'proletarian'. Nonetheless, it is used here in a sense quite close to the original Marxist meaning of the term. It designates the dispossession of means of production that accompanies both the com-modification/privatization of commons and the devaluation of those means of production still held by small producers, which leaves those thereby expropriated with nothing to sell but their bare labor power. As such proletarianization is a process rather than a state, and it acquires its meaning through its relation to the whole of the material reproduction of class society. This process encompasses both a growing precariousness of social existence as well as a declining standard of living, but is nevertheless not reducible to these factors.

In this sense, 'knowledge' can only be considered cultural capital and the basis of a distinct class position of the new petty bourgeoisie, insofar as it functions as a claim to a part of the surplus product. In this case, eco-nomic devaluation therefore produces a de facto shift in class position, even if the incorporated and objectified knowledge held by the respective subjects remain unchanged. The devaluation neither necessarily impacts the concrete usefulness of knowledge in the labor process nor alters its function as a cultural marker of distinction vis-à-vis certain social groups (although both most likely coincide with devaluation), to prevent this knowledge from functioning as capital. In fact, the relative independence and the potentially differing pace of these three processes—devaluation, the loss of concrete usefulness, and the diminishment of its social prestige, which is rooted in the double nature of knowledge as both exchange and use value (social prestige is a kind of use value *qua* exchange value)—provides the basis for an escalation of the contradictions inherent in the class position of the new petty bourgeoisie. For example, although de facto in a proletarian position, employed in deskilled labor processes, and poorly paid, these people might still perceive their position (and be perceived by others) as 'privileged'—an ideological interpretation that gains credence because, indeed, they are not subject to being deprived of basic social recognition, as is the case for many marginalized groups in the working class.

Although degree devaluation without doubt affected broad segments of this generation of students in the USA, the Great Recession presented an especially hard break for the young and aspiring new petty bourgeoisie that primarily depends on educational titles to secure its reproduction as a class. Possession of a degree is expected to function as a claim to a certain social status not obtainable through the direct inheritance of economic capital. Mason describes this as the experience of a sudden shift of the "projected life-arc from an upward curve to a downward one"(Mason 2013, 67). A better metaphor, however, is perhaps that of objectively losing the vanishing point anticipated of a life trajectory, which finds its subjective correlate in a feeling of a loss of future, which is documented in countless stories told on the already mentioned "we are the 99%" Tumblr blog, but also in slogans such as "Banks got bailed out, we got sold out", or "I awoke in a sweat from the American Dream".

The class-generational dimension can perhaps best be illustrated through "Old Economy Steve", an internet phenomenon that was extremely popular in 2012/13. The meme depicts the face of a young man, photographed in his late teens in the 1970s, bearing different statements as captions (Roose and Becket 2013). These statements usually contrast parents' harsh criticism of their college-age offspring in view of the OWS cohorts' experience of their current post-graduation prospects, implying that the parent generation's prospects were much rosier than that of their children. Examples are "Becomes homeowner at 22 – thinks his son's generation has it easy because they can afford $200 smartphones",[25] or "'In my first job, I only made 15k' – in 1979, that was the equivalent of 47k" and the simple, resigned "Graduates college, doesn't move back with his parents",[26] which highlights how the difficult labor market also poses problems for youth seeking to emancipate themselves from their parents. Indeed, to add insult to injury, the widespread phenomenon of young adults having to move back in with their parents due to unemployment has already brought about a sobriquet for this unfortunate segment of the so-called millennial generation: the "boomerang kids" (cf. Davidson 2014).

Of course, conflict in different generations' interpretation of social developments and events is nothing new in social movements—examples being the conflicts over cultural liberalization associated with the student movements in Western Europe, the USA, and across large parts of the world in the late 1960s and 1970s. In the USA, however, OWS might represent the first time that this conflict is playing out before the background of an actual decline in living standards from one generation to the next[27] and, in the case of the children of the new petty bourgeoisie, the conflict is aggravated by a loss of status relative to the rest of society that comes with the devaluation of cultural capital as their most important asset. The devaluation at the core of this class-generational unit's experience of crisis does not necessarily contradict the finding that OWS activities were negatively correlated with the rate of unemployment in a given area. Unemployment and foreclosure still are far more widespread among the working classes and therefore are concentrated in working class neighborhoods rather than in college towns.

To explain the actual protest-praxis of OWS, however, a narrow focus only on the delineated core constituency would be insufficient. Wherever OWS' protest events took place, and especially where they established a more permanent presence via the occupation of public space, Occupy attracted the members of other class-generational units outside the core constituency who had impacted the trajectory of the movement's mobilization in its first year.[28] While the core constituency's concentration in certain areas explains where the protests occurred, the protest in turn proved attractive beyond this socio-demographic group.

Drawing on news coverage, my own observations, and accounts of my interviewees, the following image of OWS NYC can be rendered[29]: One group, very vocal from the very beginning, is the class-generational unit of the seasoned activist from the Alter Globalization Movements (AGM). Usually already in their late-thirties to early-forties, this group is also recruited from the new petty bourgeoisie, but, different from their younger counterparts in the core constituency, experienced less significant loss or precariousness of their social status during the crisis. Employed in the cultural, the educational, or NGO sector of the economy, they were drawn to OWS mostly as a new and promising political project that continued their earlier engagement in other movements and protests. Prominent examples are Marina Sitrin and David Graeber, both of whom are broadly published activist-academics with roots in the AGM. This group played an important role in shaping the 'practical ethics' of the occupation. They introduced concepts like the GA and communication tools such as the (in)famous hand signals,[30] as well as corresponding political rationalizations of their collective practices, such as "horizontalism" or "small-a anarchism".[31] However, all of the members of this group to whom I spoke spent significantly less time and energy on and in the Occupation itself than the members of the core constituency did.

The anti-institutional rhetoric of OWS and the ethics of practical care resonated strongly with the marginalized parts of NYC's population, especially the homeless and, albeit to a lesser degree, the young "precariat" from the outer Boroughs: coming from a social background in which the state and its institutions are largely experienced as absent or repressive, they found the decision to pose no demands to the state and the refusal to collaborate with any political institution or party compelling[32] and the supply of self organized healthcare and food in the camps provided a practical incentive to join. And lastly, the unionized working class, despite its organizational structures having great difficulties in connecting to the practices in the park, nevertheless, supported OWS at several decisive moments in its early trajectory. Thus, as a social group, OWS was relatively less homogenous than the mobilized TP participants, which is one of the reasons why it was so difficult to sustain this alliance after the occupied park—the tangible interface to project one's affinities on—disappeared.[33]

3.3 The Second-Cut Theory of Crisis-Protests: Objective Class Position and 'Being-Subjected-to' the Crisis

Through developing a more nuanced understanding of the socioeconomic and politico-economic developments that the constituencies of the protest were subjected to in the years before, during, and after the Great Recession, this chapter is another important step in the untangling and reconstructing of the complex mediation of the dynamics of the economic crisis and the protests that occurred in its wake (Table 3.1).

Table 3.1 Core constituencies and corridors of experience

	The Tea Party	*Occupy Wall Str.*
Core constituency	Classical petty bourgeoisie and administrative petty bourgeoisie, >45 years old	Proletarianized/biographically blocked youth of the new petty bourgeoisie, 25–35 years old
Trajectory	Shock-like devaluation of economic capital, insecurity about future wealth	Creeping devaluation of cultural capital, accelerated in 2007/2008

As the table shows, it is possible to identify a number of similarities and dissimilarities between the class-generational units forming the core constituencies of the protests and between their trajectories through social space in the years around the Great Recession. OWS' core constituency is recruited from the new petty bourgeoisie. It was confronted with an escalation of the creeping devaluation of its members' cultural capital—a process long underway—that increasingly blurred the distinction between them and the administrative bourgeoisie or what we could call the "service proletariat" (Bahl and Staab 2010).

The TP's core constituency is recruited from a very different class-generational unit—mostly from the older cohorts of the classical petty bourgeoisie. However, what they have in common with OWS' core constituency is the 'being-subjected' to an acute biographical crisis—2008 for them, as for OWS' core constituency, meant a sudden darkening of their economic horizon. This might explain why the growth of the two mobilizations was so explosive in character. The TP core constituency, however, was on average much older than that of OWS. Together with the fact that in their case the darkening of the economic horizon was not connected to acute socioeconomic hardship provides a plausible explanation for why the protest-practices of the TP took a less life-changing form and had a more 'conservative' character in general. The identification of the different class-generational units and the crisis dynamics they were subjected to finally also help us understand some peculiarities of the socio-geographical patterning of the protest: OWS was concentrated in large cities and university towns because that is where its core constituency lives. Likewise, the classical petty bourgeoisie tends to live and was hit hard particularly in suburban boomtowns where they owned real estate or made a living in construction or by selling real estate.

However, the translation and transformation of 'being-subjected-to' certain socioeconomic dynamics into protest as a social practice requires a more concrete reconstruction, particularly regarding how this 'being-subjected-to' was actually perceived as a 'lived experience of' the crisis. This is why the next two chapters turn toward the conceptualization and reconstruction of the mediation between social dynamic and subjective perception and especially of the class-specific habitus as the structuring principle of this mediation.

Notes

1. A structure in this sense is a totality of relations of difference in which the elements gain their meaning through their positionality within the whole, rather than through any inherent qualities of the elements themselves or of isolated 'interactions' between those elements (cf. Bourdieu 2007, 42–74).
2. See Sect. 4.1 "The Category of the Habitus: Structures *Do* Come down to the Streets".
3. Throughout this book, all names of interviewees are anonymized and their personal data (occupation, place of residence, etc.) is altered to protect their anonymity.
4. Marx and Engels use "class" very differently and often in a very broad sense throughout their writings, as it was common in the nineteenth century (cf. Dahrendorf 1959, 4). Thus, for example, in his writings on the living conditions of the English working class, Engels refers to the bourgeoisie as the 'middle class', following the historically older terminology according to which this class is located between the aristocracy and the peasantry (Engels 1962, 250ff.). Marx and Engels explain in the Communist Manifesto that in developed capitalism the number of classes tends to be reduced to just two opposing "camps"—the capitalist and the proletariat (Marx and Engels 1960, 462). On other occasions, Marx draws a detailed picture of a multiplicity of conflicting classes (e.g. Marx 1960). "Class in a Marxian sense" is therefore rather a reference to a class-analytical tradition that formed in opposition to, and dialogue with, other conceptions of class (cf. Wright 2000).
5. Exactly this dialectic gets lost in Weberian and other 'resource-based' conceptions of class. "'Class situation' is (...) 'Market situation'" (Weber 2001, "'Klassenlage' ist 'Marktlage'", translation N.K.) reifies and dehistoricizes the market as the central coordinating instance of capitalist economies and veils the exploitation of one class by another through both classes' relation to the market.

6. This basic typology of social classes in advanced capitalism (bourgeoisie, proletariat, classical petty bourgeoisie, new petty bourgeoisie) in some variant is common to most Marxist analyses of the class structure since the 1970s (cf. Burris 1999). It is also used by Bourdieu in various instances, even though he (to the best of my knowledge) never explains the genesis of this class typology or connects this typology to the Marxian assumption of the basic conflict between capital and labor, thereby replicating his ambivalence toward Marxian arguments (Burawoy 2012).
7. It might even give the first a sense of satisfaction since it 'does justice' to the humiliations (s)he experienced in school—which result in a disdain against everything that is connected to 'legitimate' culture, which in my interviews and discussions with TP activists was very often portrayed as 'elitist', 'detached', and giving rise to "educated idiots" (TPG3, "Tipping Point". See Sect. 5.1.2).
8. The term could be translated both to 'autonomy' and 'self-governance' and thereby throws a bridge between the left-communist idea of a council-democracy and the student movement's ideal of 'self-realization'.
9. This difference might also partially be explained by the interviewing situation. Cf. fn. 21.
10. The highest income quartile of the birth cohort of 1961–64 had a college completion ratio of 36%, the second of 17% (Bailey and Dynarski 2011). Even the relatively educated sample of the Cato survey, which had placed 41% of its respondents in the highest quintile (so that we may assume at least a good 50% are in the highest quartile), only reported a college-completion rate of 23%.
11. Unfortunately, the surveys do not provide information on the capital stock of the respondents, so that this conclusion is mediated by the proposition that the income, which cannot be explained by the cultural capital disposed of, has to be generated by gains on economic capital.
12. The Cato survey listed the answer 'being a small business owner' not as a response to a question for socioeconomic status/employment, but as an answer to the question for motives to join the TP. It is not clear to me if this has systematically impacted the resulting numbers, especially since they are roughly comparable to those of the Politico survey (Ekins 2011, 56).
13. Even if we include the incorporated self-employed, which are usually subsumed under regular employees, the total share is still below 11%. And this is only the ratio of all those working, while the TP surveys also asked unemployed and retired participants, who, according to the CBS/NYT poll, make up almost 50% of the TP supporters. As the anecdotal observations by Skocpol and Williamson, as well as my own, suggest, the small business owners make up the most important subgroup of those in the TP

that are currently neither unemployed nor retired, and most retirees had been small business owners themselves.

14. Unfortunately, the suspicion following from this claim, namely, that being a "small business owner" might be the strongest predictor for TP activism, cannot be tested statistically since the only available large survey that also included non-TP supporters as a potential control group (the aforementioned CBS poll) did not include a question on self-employment.
15. Interestingly, another poll by the Washington Post and the Pew Research Center confirms this result, but finds OWS support also to be slightly over-represented in the South, a phenomenon that seems to defeat most rationalizations that follow the common sense distribution of political leanings across the geography of the USA (Cohen 2011).
16. An anecdotal evidence for this might be the important initial role that TP activists played in the campaign for Chris Christie's election as governor of New Jersey, a traditionally "blue" state—even though as a relatively 'moderate' conservative, he lost the support of the TP very soon after his election.
17. The study analyzed data from 3141 counties in total, which means these 50 counties represent less than a 1/60 of the overall sample.
18. The decline in the median household wealth from 2005 to 2011 is to a large part due to the decline in the real estate prices (Gottschalck et al. 2012).
19. The numbers cited in the following are drawn from this secondary analysis rather than from Cordero-Guzman's own published results: In his presentations of the result, Cordero-Guzman analyzed the demographic composition of those that reported that they 'support' OWS. Since his survey however included a question on participation as well, I was able to filter out those that took part in the protests themselves. Especially the wave conducted before October 2 was interesting in that regard since it preceded the nationwide spread of Occupy and therefore is a unique window into the demographic composition of those that took part in the events in Zuccotti Park. Since, however, the differences between the demographics of the participants in the two waves did not seem significant, I will in the following only refer to the second wave, which had a larger number of participants. For tables summarizing the findings of the secondary analysis, see Appendix 2: Results of the Secondary Analysis of Hector Cordero-Guzman's Survey on Occupywallst.org
20. Albeit this discrepancy is definitely lower than in the TP, this stands in stark contrast to the overall population of NYC, which is majority 'non-white'. Just as in the TP, however, these numbers also might have to be read in the context of the class composition of the movement: If, as this book argues, the movement in its practices reflects and speaks to the dispositional struc-

ture of the youth of the new petty bourgeoisie, then this overrepresentation is again a little less pronounced (as 'whites' still are a bigger group in this class, especially among students that attend high-ranking colleges and universities, which are overrepresented in OWS). However, the overrepresentation of 'whites' was frequently problematized in interviews and group discussions with OWS participants.

21. There are a variety of possible explanations for this dramatic divergence. One might be connected to the interviewing situation itself, since the large demonstration in May probably mobilized a clientele that sympathized with OWS, but found itself in less 'severe' living conditions and therefore was not among those who were active in really taking part in the mobilization as the all-encompassing endeavor that the occupation became for many early occupiers (82.8% of those interviewed by Milkman et al. visited the camp at some point, but only 10.3% reported that they lived in it). Another might be an effect of the interview as a social setting. If it is true that in the USA the social desirability effect tends to cause people to overstate their incomes, as Jacob et al. suggest, then the social pressure of the face-to-face interviewing situation in the survey by Milkman et al. might have furthered this tendency compared to the anonymity of the online survey (cf. Jacob et al. 2013, 157). These factors indicate that the numbers of Cordero-Guzman might be closer to the 'true' values for those present in the park, even if they probably are a slight underestimation.
22. "(…) among those with a four-year degree, 28% had attended top-ranked colleges for their undergraduate degrees; among those currently in college or graduate school, 19% were enrolled in top-ranked colleges or universities". Milkman et al. (2013) identify schools as "top-ranked colleges and universities" if they belong in the top 50 of the US news and world report (top 25 for liberal arts colleges).
23. Numbers are unfortunately largely missing: The study by Milkman et al. found that over 50% of those under 30 taking part in the protest held more than $1000 in student loans, but did not inquire if people have higher student loans. However, since the average student debt in New York was $27,478 in 2015, and since, nationwide, graduate students (who were overrepresented in OWS) have student debts that are about four times as high as those of undergraduate students, the real numbers are most probably much higher. The burden as which this is perceived by the participants might be reflected in the high prominence that the topic of student debt had in the mobilization early on (Mitchell 2015; Marcus and Roberts 2015).
24. The median unsecured household debt without credit card debt (which means mainly medical bills and student loans) of households 35 years or younger was $13,000 in 2011 (cf. Vornovytsky et al. 2011).

25. http://ak-hdl.buzzfed.com/static/enhanced/webdr02/2013/5/25/19/grid-cell-9730-1369522814-3.jpg (accessed 16.04.2016).
26. http://cdn.theatlantic.com/static/mt/assets/business/Old_Economy_Steve.png. (accessed 16.04.2016).
27. As measured in inter-generational inflation-adjusted net household wealth and income (cf. Howe 2014; Pereira 2011).
28. For the socio-spatial dynamics of the park that made this possible and for the habitual dynamic underlying this, see Chap. 7.
29. The relative numerical importance of these groups is hard to define, since the available surveys do largely leave out some of these groups: Cordero-Guzman's survey most probably did not reach the classical working class, since they only joined the protest later on, and both the survey of Milkman et al. (since it was conducted at a rally rather that at the occupation itself) and the one by Cordero-Guzman (since it was conducted online) most probably underestimate the numbers of homeless active in OWS.
30. OWS used a set of hand signals to communicate nonverbally during the assemblies which was explained at the beginning of every meeting (Klein 2011; Occupy Together 2011).
31. Sitrin published a book in which she discusses 'horizontalism' as a political praxis she experienced during the uprising in Argentina 2001. Graeber has written extensively on how he intervened in early discussions in OWS (cf. Graeber 2013; Sitrin 2006).
32. For the analysis of this group's habitual processing of OWS "politics", see Sect. 7.3 "Class Alliances and Internal Conflict: Other Experiences of OWS".
33. See Sect 7.4 "Summary: "That's Not a Solution"".

Bibliography

Bahl, Friederike, and Philipp Staab. 2010. Das Dienstleistungsproletariat. Theorie auf kaltem Entzug. *Mittelweg* 36 (19): 66–93.

Bailey, Martha J., and Susan M. Dynarski. 2011. *Gains and Gaps: Changing Inequality in U.S. College Entry and Completion*. Working Paper 17633. National Bureau of Economic Research. http://www.nber.org/papers/w17633. Accessed 29 Oct 2017.

Barker, Colin. 2013. Class Struggle and Social Movements. In *Marxism and Social Movements*, ed. Colin Barker, Laurence Cox, John Krinsky, and Alf Gunvald Nilsen, 39–61. Leiden: BRILL.

Beyerlein, Kraig, and Kelly Bergstrand. 2013. Biographical Availability. In *The Wiley-Blackwell Encyclopedia of Social and Political Movements*. Blackwell. http://onlinelibrary.wiley.com/doi/10.1002/9780470674871.wbespm012/abstract. Accessed 29 Oct 2017.

Bourdieu, Pierre. 1983. Ökonomisches Kapital, kulturelles Kapital, soziales Kapital. In *Soziale Ungleichheiten*, ed. Reinhard Kreckel, 183–198. Göttingen: Schwartz.

———. 1994. *Die feinen Unterschiede: Kritik der gesellschaftlichen Urteilskraft.* Frankfurt am Main: Suhrkamp.

———. 2007. *Zur Soziologie der symbolischen Formen.* Frankfurt am Main: Suhrkamp.

Braverman, Harry. 1974. *Labor and Monopoly Capital: The Degradation of Work in the Twentieth Century.* New York/London: Monthly Review Press.

Burawoy, Michael. 2012. Gramsci Meets Bourdieu. In *Conversations with Bourdieu. The Johannesburg Moment*, ed. Michael Burawoy and Karl von Holdt, 51–67. Johannesburg: Wits University Press.

Burris, Val. 1999. Class Structure and Political Ideology. *Critical Sociology* 25: 308–332.

Cho, Wendy K. Tam, James G. Gimpel, and Daron R. Shaw. 2012. The Tea Party Movement and the Geography of Collective Action. *Quarterly Journal of Political Science* 7: 105–133.

Cohen, Jon. 2011. A Movement of One's Own – Tea Party Is Red, and OWS Is Blue. *The Washington Post – Blogs,* October 25. http://www.washingtonpost.com/blogs/behind-the-numbers/post/a-movement-of-ones-own--tea-party-is-red-and-ows-is-blue/2011/10/24/gIQA1UEODM_blog.html. Accessed 29 October 2017.

Cordero-Guzman, Hector R. 2011. *Main Stream Support for a Mainstream Movement – The 99% Movement Comes From and Looks Like the 99%.* Working Paper. New York: School of Public Affairs, Baruch College Ph.D. Programs in Sociology and Urban Education City University of New York. http://occupywallst.org/media/pdf/OWS-profile1-10-18-11-sent-v2-HRCG.pdf. Accessed 29 Oct 2017.

Curran, Michaela, Elisabeth A. G. Schwarz, and Christopher Chase-Dunn. 2013. *The Occupy Movement in California.* IROWS Working Paper. http://irows.ucr.edu/papers/irows74/irows74.htm. Accessed 29 Oct 2017.

Dahrendorf, Ralf. 1959. *Class and Class Conflict in Industrial Society.* Stanford: Stanford University.

Davidson, Adam. 2014. It's Official: The Boomerang Kids Won't Leave. *The New York Times,* June 20. http://www.nytimes.com/2014/06/22/magazine/its-official-the-boomerang-kids-wont-leave.html. Accessed 29 Oct 2017.

Dayen, David. 2014. The Crisis of Student Loans Is Real, No Matter What Pundits Tell You. *The Guardian,* June 26. http://www.theguardian.com/money/2014/jun/26/student-debt-selective-statistics-crisis-misleading-data. Accessed 29 Oct 2017.

Dynarski, Susan. 2014. Remember the Problems with Mortgage Defaults? They're Coming Back with Student Loans. *The New York Times,* June 12. http://www.

nytimes.com/2014/06/13/upshot/student-loan-woes-echo-mortgage-crisis.html. Accessed 29 Oct 2017.

Edison Research. 2010. Politico/TargetPoint Poll Topline Results. Conducted April 15, 2010 at the Washington, DC. *Tax Day Tea Party*. http://www.targetpointconsulting.com/system/uploads/19/original/Tea_Party_Exit_Poll_Topline_FINAL.pdf?1271676755. Accessed 29 Oct 2017.

Ehrenreich, John, and Barbara Ehrenreich. 2013. *Background Notes for Death of a Yuppie Dream*. New York: Rosa-Luxemburg-Stiftung. http://www.rosaluxnyc.org/en/backgroundnotes1/. Accessed 29 Oct 2017.

Ekins, Emily E. 2011. *The Character and Economic Morality of the Tea Party Movement*. https://www.researchgate.net/publication/228161071_The_Character_and_Economic_Morality_of_the_Tea_Party_Movement. Accessed 29 Oct 2017.

Engels, Friedrich. 1962. Die Lage der arbeitenden Klasse in England. Nach eigner Anschauung und authentischen Quellen. In *MEW 2*, 229–506. Berlin: Dietz.

Gilcher-Holtey, Ingrid. 2001. 'Kritische Ereignisse' und 'Kritischer Moment'. Pierre Bourdieus Modell der Vermittlung von Ereignis und Struktur. In *Struktur und Ereignis*, ed. Andreas Suter and Manfred Hettling, 120–137. Göttingen: Vandenhoeck & Ruprecht.

Gottschalck, Alfred, Marina Vornovytsky, and Adam Smith. 2012. Household Wealth in the US: 2000 to 2011. United States Census Bureau. https://www.census.gov/content/dam/Census/library/working-papers/2014/demo/wealth-highlights-2011-revised-7-3-14.pdf. Accessed 29 Oct 2017.

Graeber, David. 2013. *The Democracy Project: A History, a Crisis, a Movement*. New York: Spiegel and Grau.

Gregg, Paul, and Emma Tominey. 2005. The Wage Scar from Male Youth Unemployment. *Labour Economics* 12 (4): 487–509.

Hagelstange, Thomas. 1988. Niedergang oder Renaissance der Selbständigen? Statistische Daten zur Entwicklung in der EG und in Nordamerika. *Zeitschrift für Soziologie* 17 (2): 143–151.

Hipple, Steven F. 2004. Self-Employment in the United States: An Update. *Monthly Labor Review*, July 13–24.

———. 2010. Self-Employment in the United States. *Monthly Labor Review*, September, p. 16–32.

Hirsch, Joachim, and Roland Roth. 1986. *Das neue Gesicht des Kapitalismus*. Hamburg: VSA.

Howe, Neil. 2014. Are You Born to Be Better Off Than Your Parents? (Part 1 of 'Generations in Pursuit of the American Dream'). *Forbes*, July 16. http://www.forbes.com/sites/neilhowe/2014/07/16/part-1-generations-in-pursuit-of-the-american-dream/. Accessed 29 Oct 2017.

Jacob, Rüdiger, Andreas Heinz, and Jean Philippe Décieux. 2013. *Umfrage: Einführung in die Methoden der Umfrageforschung*. München: Oldenbourg.

Klein, Alex. 2011. Jazz Hands and Waggling Fingers: How Occupy Wall Street Makes Decisions. *Daily Intelligencer/New York Magazine*, December 10. http://nymag.com/daily/intelligencer/2011/10/occupy_wall_street_hand_gestur.html. Accessed 29 Oct 2017.

Langman, Lauren. 2011. Cycles of Contention: The Rise and Fall of the Tea Party. *Critical Sociology* 38 (4): 469–494.

Lundskow, George. 2012. Authoritarianism and Destructiveness in the Tea Party Movement. *Critical Sociology* 38 (4): 529–547.

Mannheim, Karl. 1964. Das Problem der Generationen. In *Wissenssoziologie: Auswahl aus dem Werk*, 509–565. Berlin: Luchterhand.

———. 1997. A Sociological Theory of Culture and Its Knowability (Conjunctive and Communicative Thinking). In *Structures of Thinking*, 141–288. London/New York: Routledge.

Marcus, Jon, and Daniel Roberts. 2015. The Real Student Debt Problem. *Time*. http://time.com/3544912/graduate-school-loans-debt/. Accessed 29 Oct 2017.

Marx, Karl. 1960. Der achtzehnte Brumaire des Louis Bonaparte. In *MEW* 8: 111–207. Berlin: Dietz.

———. 1969. *Das Kapital 1*. MEW 23. Berlin: Dietz.

———. 1974. *Das Kapital 2*. MEW 24. Berlin: Dietz.

Marx, Karl, and Friedrich Engels. 1960. Manifest der kommunistischen Partei. In *MEW* 4: 459–93. Berlin: Dietz.

Mason, Paul. 2013. *Why It's Still Kicking Off Everywhere*. London/New York: Verso.

McAdam, Doug. 1986. Recruitment to High-Risk Activism: The Case of the Freedom Summer. *American Journal of Sociology* 96 (1): 64–90.

Milkman, Ruth. 2014. Millennial Movements: Occupy Wall Street and the Dreamers. *Dissent* 61 (3): 55–59.

Milkman, Ruth, Stephanie Luce, and Penny Lewis. 2013. *Changing the Subject: A Bottom-Up Account of Occupy Wall Street in New York City*. New York: Joseph S. Murphy Institute for Worker Education and Labor Studies. https://www.documentcloud.org/documents/562862-changing-the-subject-2.html. Accessed 29 Oct 2017.

Mitchell, Josh. 2015. The Average Student Debt Load in D.C. Is a Whopping $40,885. *WSJ Blogs – Real Time Economics*, March 10. http://blogs.wsj.com/economics/2015/03/10/the-average-student-debt-load-in-d-c-is-a-whopping-40885/. Accessed 29 Oct 2017.

Montopoli, Brian. 2011. Poll: 43 Percent Agree with Views of 'Occupy Wall Street.' http://www.cbsnews.com/news/poll-43-percent-agree-with-views-of-occupy-wall-street/. Accessed 29 Oct 2017.

New York Times. 2010. *Polling the Tea Party*. New York: New York Times/CBS News Poll. http://www.nytimes.com/interactive/2010/04/14/us/politics/20100414-tea-party-poll-graphic.html. Accessed 29 Oct 2017.

Occupy Together. 2011. Hand Signals. Occuprint. http://occuprint.org/Posters/HandSignals. Accessed 29 Oct 2017.

OECD. 2016. *Quarterly National Accounts: Quarterly Growth Rates of Real GDP*. https://stats.oecd.org/index.aspx?queryid=350#. Accessed 29 Oct 2017.

Pereira, Eva. 2011. Wealth Inequality Between Young and Old Generations Reaches Record High. *Forbes*, August. http://www.forbes.com/sites/eva-pereira/2011/11/08/wealth-inequality-between-young-and-old-generations-reaches-record-high/. Accessed 29 Oct 2017.

Pew Research Center. 2011. Pew Research Center October 20–23, 2011 Omnibus Final Topline. http://www.people-press.org/2011/10/23/october-20-23-2011-weekly-survey/. Accessed 29 Oct 2017.

Piven, Frances Fox, and Richard A. Cloward. 1979. *Poor People's Movements: Why They Succeed, How They Fail*. New York: Vintage Books.

Poulantzas, Nicos. 1973. *Zum Marxistischen Klassenbegriff*. Berlin: Merve.

Roose, Kevin, and Stefan Becket. 2013. Meet the Real-Life 'Old Economy Steve.' *Daily Intelligencer*. http://nymag.com/daily/intelligencer/2013/05/meet-the-real-life-old-economy-steve.html. Accessed 29 Oct 2017.

Rosenhek, Zeev, and Michael Shalev. 2014. The Political Economy of Israel's 'Social Justice' Protests: A Class and Generational Analysis. *Contemporary Social Science* 9 (1): 31–48.

Ross, Andrew. 2013. Mortgaging the Future: Student Debt in the Age of Austerity. *New Labor Forum* 22 (1): 23–28.

Shierholz, Heidi, Alyssa Davis, and Will Kimball. 2014. *The Class of 2014: The Weak Economy Is Idling Too Many Young Graduates*. EPI Briefing Paper. Washington, DC: Economic Policy Institute. http://s2.epi.org/files/2014/Classof2014FINAL.pdf. Accessed 29 Oct 2017.

Sitrin, Marina. 2006. *Horizontalism: Voices of Popular Power in Argentina*. Edinburgh/Oakland: AK Press.

Skocpol, Theda, and Vanessa Williamson. 2012. *The Tea Party and the Remaking of Republican Conservatism*. Oxford: Oxford University Press.

Steinmetz, George, and Erik Olin Wright. 1989. The Fall and Rise of the Petty Bourgeoisie: Changing Patterns of Self-Employment in the Postwar Unite States. *American Journal of Sociology* 94: 973–1018.

The Economist. 2012. Not What It Used to Be. *The Economist*, December. http://www.economist.com/news/united-states/21567373-american-universities-represent-declining-value-money-their-students-not-what-it. Accessed 29 Oct 2017.

The Washington Post, Kaiser Family Foundation, and Harvard University. 2010. *Role of Government Survey*. http://www.washingtonpost.com/wp-srv/special/politics/Post-Kaiser-Harvard-Role-of-Government-2010.pdf. Accessed 29 Oct 2017.

Tseng, Terence, Mark Esposito, and Jorgo Chatzimarkakis. 2013. Youth Unemployment After the Financial Crisis: 'Quo Vadimus'? *The World Financial Review*. http://www.worldfinancialreview.com/?p=3622. Accessed 29 Oct2017.

United States Census Bureau. 2012. Table 793. Corporate Profits Before Taxes by Industry: 2000 to 2009. In *Statistical Abstract 2012*. United States Census Bureau. http://www.census.gov/prod/2011pubs/12statab/business.pdf. Accessed 29 Oct 2017.

———. 2014. Educational Attainment CPS Historical Tables. 2014. https://www.census.gov/hhes/socdemo/education/data/cps/historical/index.html. Accessed 29 Oct 2017.

Vedder, Richard, Christopher Denhart, and Jonathan Robe. 2013. *Why Are Recent College Graduates Underemployed? University Enrollments and Labor-Market Realities*. Policy Paper. Center for College Affordability and Productivity. http://centerforcollegeaffordability.org/uploads/Underemployed%20Report%202.pdf. Accessed 29 Oct 2017.

Vornovytsky, Marina, Alfred Gottschalck, and Adam Smith. 2011. Household Debt in the US: 2000 to 2011. United States Census Bureau. https://www.census.gov/content/dam/Census/library/working-papers/2011/demo/debt-highlights-2011.pdf. Accessed 29 Oct 2017.

Weber, Max. 2001. ‚Klassen' ‚Stände' und ‚Parteien'. In *Wirtschaft und Gesellschaft: Gemeinschaften*, 248–72. Tübingen: J.C.B. Mohr.

Wright, Erik Olin. 2000. *Class Counts: Comparative Studies in Class Analysis*. Cambridge: Cambridge University Press.

Zernike, Kate, and Megan Thee-Brenan. 2010. Poll Finds Tea Party Backers Wealthier and More Educated. *The New York Times*, April 14, sec. U.S./Politics. http://www.nytimes.com/2010/04/15/us/politics/15poll.html. Accessed 29 Oct 2017.

CHAPTER 4

Theoretical and Methodological Considerations: Habitus and Habitus Reconstruction

The two previous chapters focused on the causes and socially structured articulations of the crisis dynamics encountered by the constituencies of the protests. What thereby was largely factored out from the equation is the way in (and degree to) which this *being-exposed-to* was perceived and lived through as a *meaningful experience of* by these very constituencies, as well as how they translated and articulated their discontent into critique as protest. In short, still lacking in our analysis is the perceptive and behavioral mediation of the contradictions within the social structure through the specific perspective of the defining actors of the protest mobilizations. This next step allows us to more comprehensively reconstruct the relation between the crisis and the protest. As Bourdieu wrote apropos the seeming arbitrariness of precipitating events vis-à-vis their social impact: "one should not say (…) that a historical event triggered a behavior, but that it had a triggering effect because a habitus effectible by this event lent this potency to it". This approach goes a step beyond *attribution theory*, which also highlights the importance of the meaning attributed to a certain event to understand someone's reaction to it, by insisting that different actors are *socio-biographically predisposed* to attribute certain meanings to certain events (Bourdieu 2001, 190 f. translation N.K.).[1] Inquiring into the habitus therefore not only asks for the interpretation as a given, but for the rootedness of the basic structure of this interpretation in the socio-spatial position and trajectory of the respective subject.

N. C. Kumkar, *The Tea Party, Occupy Wall Street, and the Great Recession*, Critical Political Theory and Radical Practice,
https://doi.org/10.1007/978-3-319-73688-4_4

Before Chap. 5, "Experiencing the Crisis: Results of the Habitus Reconstruction", can present the results of the habitus reconstruction for the core constituencies of the protest mobilizations, this chapter prepares the ground in two ways. In Sect. 4.1, the category of the habitus and its potential for providing an understanding of the protest mobilizations will be discussed. Section 4.2 then presents some methodological considerations on how habitus can be reconstructed from the empirical material at hand by using the so-called documentary method and briefly outlines the basic structure of the process of interpretation.

4.1 The Category of the Habitus: Structures *Do* Come Down to the Streets

"*Les structures ne descendent pas dans la rue*"—structures do not come down to the streets—was a slogan of the student movement in France in 1968. This was a criticism of the structuralist current in French academia, which was considered to be too deterministic and detached to understand the 'agency' driving social conflict. Even if this criticism of classical structuralism may very well be justified, it is the wager of my critical reconstruction of the relation between the Great Recession and the protest-practices that critical reconstructions of concrete protest-practices, nonetheless, cannot accept the thus implied dichotomy of structure and agency. Instead, structure and agency must be understood as facets of a dialectical relation between subjectivized and objectivized history that unfolds in practice. In other words, if the structure does not 'reach down' to the street, this is because it has not been reconstructed with a sufficient degree of concretion. In this sense, Bourdieu's concept of the *habitus*—as the structure mediating a subject's relation to its environment—is the kind of structure that *does* come down to the streets.

Habitus describes a socially specific set of dispositions guiding a subject's perceptions and actions. These dispositions allow actors to pre-reflexively make sense of their world ("understanding" as opposed to "interpreting" in the terminology of Mannheim) and react to it without reflexively weighing all the objectively available choices. One can try to understand this embodied and incorporated knowledge as the "feeling for the game", which allows a well-trained player to anticipate and react to the development of the game (s)he is playing—for example, when lifting one's foot to hit a ball that was just kicked by another player—at a pace *and* with a precision that would be impossible if it were undertaken as the result of conscious calculation (cf. Bourdieu 1987, 122). In much the same way, the accounts of some of my interviewees on their first contact with the mobilizations reflected a pre-conscious attraction to the mobilization, which was documented in phrases like "it just resonated with me".

This complex of dispositions is biographically formed as sedimented life history and functions as one "generative grammar" (Bourdieu 1974, 143). This grammar allows for improvising solutions to new situations according to a set of 'rules' (or rather structured affinities and differentiations) that proved to be efficient in other contexts. The concept bears a certain family resemblance to other socio-phenomenological concepts, such as Schütz's "unquestioned assumed",[2] Berger and Luckman's "typificatory schemes" constituted by routine (Berger and Luckmann 1991, 56–59), and Goffman's "primary frameworks" (Goffman 1974, 21ff.). It, however, adds another twist: Bourdieu (in a Durkheimian fashion) insists that these schemes of classification mirror and complement the social structure they arise from (Bourdieu 2001, 220). The habitus in other words not only structures the subject's perception of the environment, it, as a result of its genesis, is also socially structured itself.

Those objectively classified into the same category by the social structure tend to share the same schemes of classification for dealing with this very structure (Bourdieu 1994, esp. 177ff.). Close proximity in social space greatly increases the likelihood of the incorporation of similar interpretative and behavioral predispositions resulting from shared defining experiences. In the terminology of Bourdieu, the habitus of a given social class is not necessarily homogenous, but it is certainly homologous. This means that decisive structural features are similar enough across the different cases to make them both appear as—and, in their mutual recognition, function as—individual variations on a shared theme (Bourdieu 1987, 112 f.).

The process of incorporating these structures is always ongoing and can be thought of as resulting in a hierarchically layered complex of structures, in which the already incorporated structures determine what structures can potentially be incorporated next, while the next structure specifies the practical meaning of the earlier structure (Bourdieu 1979, 188). In the liminal case of a total fit between the habitus and the field in which it unfolds, this history stays hidden, since the actor behaves as if (s)he has chosen the most appropriate, viable strategy after having reviewed and processed all available information. Accordance to the rules and objective chances of a given field is, however, most effective not as the result of any form of detectable censorship or conscious calculation but of having incorporated them to the degree that interests do not even have to be brought into accordance to the rules, because, in form and content, interests are practically coherent with the rules and objective chances (cf. Bourdieu 1988a, 9).

As an example, one can take the example of a successful, aspiring social scientist. A specific upbringing in a highly educated and politically engaged family made her cherish the pleasures of solving intellectual riddles and pushing aside questions of their purpose or necessity while also being rewarded for showing compassion toward those she considered to be 'weaker'. In school this behavior was rewarded as talent and ambition, because she, in contrast to her more 'vulgar' classmates, studied for the sake of learning and did not question every new task in math class by asking its practical value. Finally, at the very prestigious university from which she eventually received her PhD, she again stood out because she eagerly followed and exceeded the obligatory curriculum without caring too much (or too directly) about career opportunities, for example, gladly attending office hours to continue discussions with her professor, instead of asking for grading modalities.

This, however, does not necessarily mean that she does not seek social recognition, power, or wealth, but rather that her dispositions harmonize so neatly with the structure of the field in which she is positioned that the very strategies she non-consciously adopts to reach these aims are in perfect accordance with the field's rules of conduct and her own opportunities in that field. Her honest, subjective lack of direct interest in a career might actually function as her objective lead vis-à-vis competitors who in their 'drivenness' appear less 'scientific'. Even in this liminal case of a perfect fit, however, what prepared her for the practices in this field is a trajectory through different social environments, such as the family, school, and most probably some volunteer work or campus activism. This also makes it difficult to speak of the habitus as 'belonging' to a certain field. It is a practical unity of structures shaped by different fields, consisting of a system of oppositions, orientations, and symbolizations that allow the 'analogic' logic of praxis to unfold. It is clear enough to make 'sense' of—and in—praxis, but not too rigid to allow for strategic action when confronted with situations in different social settings (Bourdieu 1979, 157 f.).

Practically, the habitus' role in processing the world can be modeled in two ways. On the one hand, it can be imagined as a system of limits and limitations. Arising from the disappointments of the past, the actor only considers certain 'imaginable' social choices and excludes a whole range of virtually present alternatives visible to a different observer of the same situation. In this sense, Bourdieu speaks of the social process of (social) aging as an ongoing "mourning work", an inner detachment from more and more 'objectively' possible turns of the social trajectory and objects of desire (Bourdieu 1994, 189 f.). On the other hand, among the choices perceived as available, it works as a practical taxonomy of attraction and repulsion via analogy. Very rough and general structures of dichotomies—"a (...) matrix of common-places" (Bourdieu 1994, 730 f.)—that hierarchize, for example, 'refined' over 'crude', 'high' over 'low', 'spiritual' over 'material', and so on, are processed into complex patterns of 'taste', defining which of the available options the actor feels drawn to or repelled by. Together these two can result in a kind of *amor fati*—a love for one's fate. Intuitive "sense for one's place" (Bourdieu 1994, 734ff.), on the one hand, provides a knowing of 'what's not for those like us' and, on the other hand, also a feeling for what can be strived for, giving one's life trajectory a sense of purpose and accomplishment. Attachment to certain objects is likewise structured by an anticipated future, a vanishing point giving meaning to the present (Bourdieu 2001, 267–74; but also Berlant 2011, esp. 23ff.).

In stable social surroundings, this habitually patterned orientation in social space tends to be constantly reinforced by the environment. Those striving for more than they can reasonably expect are treated as 'wannabes', while those who settle for a station considered 'too low' are seen as 'slackers'. The genesis and stabilization of the habitus is, at least in Bourdieu's later writings, conceptualized in a manner that bears strong affinities with psychoanalytical theory. Constant striving for social recognition leads to attaching desires or *illusio* to (social) objects in a way that renders oneself desirable to the generalized other (Bourdieu 2001, esp. 210–214; Steinmetz 2006).

Although often misinterpreted in an intentionalist manner, as if a subject consistently consciously strives to be 'different' from others, the function of the habitus should instead be understood as a marker and a decipherer of social difference. In fact, those that too obviously strive for distinction are often perceived as and punished for being pretentious. Indeed, the proper functioning of the habitus is displayed when the appropriate behavior comes 'naturally' to the specific social subject, because of genuine interest and a sense of investment in the respective social game.

Two criticisms of the concept of the habitus that are often raised are that the relation of the habitus to its surroundings is practically tautological and/or is affirmative—or, as Burawoy formulates with malicious wit, by uniting the two accusations in his political criticism of Bourdieu:

> Since we have no way of measuring 'disposition' or 'habitus' independent of behaviour, the argument is simply tautological – immigrants and women are submissive because of their habitus of submission as demonstrated by their submissiveness. (Burawoy 2012, 188)

The scientific dimension of this problem, the difficulty of differentiating the disposition from the enactment, or the *modus operandi* from the *opus operatum*, in Bourdieu's terminology (Bourdieu 1979, 209), is basically a methodological one and will be addressed below in the "4.2 Methods II: Habitus Reconstruction and Documentary Method". The underlying political critique, however, must be briefly taken up here, since it encapsulates a very common misreading of the concept of the habitus as designating a purely conservative force, designed to explain why nothing ever changes and why the dominated are always complicit with their domination. This misreading stems from the fact that the broadly read and adapted works by Bourdieu seem mainly to be concerned with the liminal case of a perfect fit of mental and social structures (Wacquant 2004; see, e.g., Bourdieu 1994, 204). In many other writings, however, he provides a much less determinist perspective that is concerned exactly with the question of conflict and symbolic revolutions—be it through actors finding themselves displaced from the fields they were socialized in or be it through social space itself being radically altered (Bourdieu 2001, 206 f.).[3] Even in less dramatic situations, constant incremental change and the dynamics of social space nevertheless constantly place explosives at the point where habitus and social structure interact in perception and practices (Gebauer and Krais 2002, 76).[4]

Beyond a simple opposition of "freedom and determinacy", or "individual and society" (Bourdieu 1987, 103), the concept of habitus therefore demands a search for sources of dynamism and change in the immanent contradictions of a structure folding back onto itself through looking at the perceptions and behaviors of those involved in its reproduction. As "socialized subjectivity" (Bourdieu and Wacquant 1996, 157), the habitus is the locus in which the "structure governs the praxis" (Bourdieu 1987, 251), yet it also guarantees the *relative* independence of the praxis from its immediate social context (Bourdieu 1987, 105). How the dual character of the habitus, which encapsulates contradictions as well as potentials for reflecting on and transforming one's social position, also structures and limits this very potential for reflection and change might be illustrated, again, by referring to the successful social scientist already mentioned above. Now holding a postdoc position at a very prestigious university in NYC, Erica[5] heard of OWS from a colleague, a young professor at an Ivy League university, and decided to visit the occupation at Zuccotti Park, because it sounded "very interesting." Already her way of feeling attracted can be read as a document of a habitus primarily geared toward the accumulation of cultural capital. Other interviewees not established in the academic field talked about it as being "important", thereby displaying a direct investment in what they perceived as the mobilization's task rather than the distanced, curious position of Erica. In her encounter with the movement, however, she was confronted with a social surrounding that challenged this disposition and apparently rendered problematic her experience of the relation between herself and what was going on in the park:

> I mean, the first thing that I would say, was that, it was, I mean, (deletion) I was like, DISgusted. With myself. Honestly, I, I didn't, I never considered myself that type of person, I never thought of myself as somebody who, like, (2) sort of exist, I mean, not that I sort of idealized myself, but I didn't understand the extent to which I have really internalized these ideas sort of like teacher-student, or, you know, anyways. So that was just, that was an incredible learning experience for me. And very helpful. But the things I got involved in down there were, I got involved, almost full time, while we were actually still in the park, um, in this (working group) called the think-tank. (Erica_OWS)

This sequence is telling in at least two regards. On the one hand, it shows that in the situation she is confronted with, the reward she expected—admiration and social recognition as a critical scientist—was withheld, allowing her to take a critical stance toward the unconscious social supplement of this role, namely, acting as a "teacher" to others. On the other hand, it also shows that this questioning itself remains structured by the very same habitual structure it challenges. Not only does she reinterpret the 'shock' first and foremost as a "learning experience," after deciding to get involved, she chose the think tank working group as the focus of her activities—probably the closest she could get to a university seminar setting in Zuccotti Park.[6] The habitus and its interaction with the dynamics of its social surroundings thereby becomes *both* a base and a limit for the articulation of discontent as critique. Thus, reconstructing the habitus of the protests' core constituencies and contrasting it with the social settings and dynamics in which it is deployed and shaped helps to further explain the particular development of the protest mobilizations.

4.2 Methods II: Habitus Reconstruction and Documentary Method

In reconstructing the habitus of the mobilizations' respective core constituency, this study uses the so-called documentary method as developed by Bohnsack and others, building on Mannheim's sociology of knowledge, and Garfinkel's ethnomethodology. A methodological framework designed to systematically reconstruct habitus, its epistemological foundations are very similar to the ones that Bourdieu also relied on in the development of the concept itself (Meuser 2007), namely, the aforementioned sociology of knowledge, but also Panofsky's writings on the habitus in art history (cf. Bourdieu 2007). In studies that employ the concept of habitus, it is usually 'constructed' (Matthiesen 1989)—meaning that it is developed apart from the actual empirical material and then checked for its explanatory power. While this way of employing habitus has indeed produced fascinating studies and insights, it nevertheless makes it difficult to defend the concept from accusations of being tautological, as demonstrated, for example, in Burawoy's biting critique discussed in the last part of this chapter.

The documentary method's epistemological foundations differ from those often implicitly invoked in other schools of qualitative social research. As its terminology might appear counterintuitive, I will briefly introduce its methodology, focusing on those aspects that are guiding the concrete method of interpretation. The following short summary of some core concepts, however, is intended primarily to serve as a brief glossary to orient the reader rather than as an actual introduction into methodology and method, since an actual discussion of the details and niceties of the documentary method and its relation to the theory of practice would far exceed the limitations of this short subchapter—and they are also far more convincingly laid out elsewhere.[7] Those interested in a more detailed illustration of the method's employment will find an exemplary interpretation of a passage of a group discussion with Tea Party activists in Appendix 3.

Flick, Kardoff, and Steinke (2004, 6) categorize the research perspectives of qualitative social science into three broad categories. The first perspective, under which they subsume phenomenology and symbolic interactionism, aims at obtaining access to the subjective perspective or experiences of those observed and interviewed. The second 'constructivist' perspective is more concerned with describing the social construction of situations. The documentary method falls under the third category, which designates approaches that aim at a hermeneutic analysis of underlying structures, and therefore at a reality which, albeit actualized in discourse and concrete social interactions, nevertheless, is to be differentiated from it. This also requires a methodological toolkit different from theoretical coding, content, or discourse analysis, which are the most broadly used methods in approaches subsumed under the first two categories.

The first central differentiation guiding the reconstruction of a group's shared habitus from their discourse is between the *formulating* and the *reflecting interpretation*. These different and subsequent steps of analysis aim at different layers of the discourses' reality, namely, that of its *communicative* and its *conjunctive* content. The first is the explicit information circulating in the discourse of the group, 'what they want to say to each other' (or to the interviewer). The first step in analyzing transcribed protocols of interviews and group discussions—the formulating interpretation—is translating explicit content into the researcher's own language. Even if this explicit, communicative content is not unambiguous, a thorough reading of the transcripts alongside the knowledge accumulated in the course of the research on the group and sometimes in discussion of the respective sequences in my analysis group allowed me to paraphrase it in a manner that renders it pragmatically unproblematic for the purposes of this study.[8]

The reflecting interpretation, in contrast, aims at identifying what implicitly allows the group to understand, as opposed to interpret, each other. The basic idea is that the group's discourse consists of explicit propositions, which, in order to be 'meaningful' beyond their pure factual content, actualize or *document* latent orienting patterns always-already shared by the respective group.[9] Thus, the reflecting interpretation, summed up in this chapter, does not follow the individual strands of the group discussions and instead seemingly removes passages from their context. Its main focus is neither the individuals' story nor the rich content of what is said, but rather how the respective social group—defined by its shared conjunctive space of experience and therefore transgressing the boundaries of the concrete group of individuals present in the group—is collectively actualized or "documented" in these passages.

These collectively shared patterns orienting the group's discourse can be identified both because they reappear as *homologous patterns* across elaborations on different topics in one discussion and across different discussions, and because they are *sedimented* in the *metaphorical repertoire* of the group. If, for example, a participant of a TP group discussion uses the allegory of 'standing in line' to describe his frustration leading to his engagement in the TP, this allegory provides a key for identifying a reappearing pattern in other interviews and discussions with members of the same social group.[10] Especially fruitful for the identification of these patterns are the *opening passages* in which the group collectively 'makes sense' of the discussion impulse, since these passages allow for reconstructing the movement of 'synchronizing', in which the group 'feels out' on which level they are understanding each other. Even more important are what Bohnsack calls *focusing metaphors*—passages of high emotional and metaphorical density in which the group or the interviewee 'homes in' on centers of shared experience and interpretation. In these passages, the group is heavily engaged, often 'speaks as one', finishes each other's sentences, and the like (whereby engagement is not necessarily synonymous with volume, even though this quite often was the case). These passages were identified based on the formulating interpretation, and subjected to another, 'fine' or detailed formulating interpretation to prepare the subsequent step of *reflecting interpretation:*

The basic structure of the habitus, as documented in the discourse of the group and therefore as reconstructible through reflecting interpretation, is the *orienting frame*, which must be differentiated from the *orienting scheme*. The latter is what is explicated as rationalizations of actions and interpretations by the groups—in Alfred Schütz's terminology, it consists of 'in-order-to-motives', in contrast to 'because motives' (Schütz 1981, 123)—and is located on the level of communicative knowledge. The framing approach in social movement studies is mostly concerned with orienting schemes, since its main emphasis is on the question of persuading participants, not on the pre-reflexive understanding that grounds these acts of persuasion (cf. Benford 1997; Snow et al. 1986). In contrast, in the documentary method, the orienting frame is understood as not explicated but documented—it is that which can be reconstructed as orienting or guiding the actions and interpretations of the group and also how orienting schemes are deployed. In other words, *orienting schemes are figures of rationalization of actions and interpretation that in their practical logic are determined by orienting frames.* Both are occasionally summed up to in the general terms *orienting pattern* or *orienting figure* that designate orienting schemes as well as orienting frames.

For example, in the sequence cited on pp. 130 f., after a euphoric description of the fun and fulfilling experiences that participants in OWS had in the park, M states that they were also able to "improve the country by getting people to do something about the corruption", thereby employing an orientation scheme 'corruption is bad for the country and people should feel responsible to do something about it'. However, the very subordinate and disconnected character of this statement in regard to the preceding propositions also documents that this scheme does not itself actualize elements connected to the orienting frame guiding the previous emotionally dense description, but merely serves as the ex-post rationalization of actions she is afraid might otherwise appear as 'selfish'.

Located on the level of conjunctive knowledge and 'because-motives', the orienting frame is fundamentally structured by the order of repulsion and attraction as which the habitus is traceable in the subject's interaction with its environment. In the discourse of the group, this can be reconstructed as the pairing of *negative and positive horizons* structuring the collective activity of elaborating on sets of propositions, which is reconstructed through fine-sequential analysis. These horizons are usually not made explicit but appear in metaphorical forms, and, especially in times of crisis of the respective habitus' relation to its environment, the group might problematize only one horizon via their propositions, leaving the other horizon implicit.

In addition to an orienting frame spanned between two horizons, a final element in reconstructing how the habitus is documented in the respective group's discourse is the *potential for enactment* of the orientation given by the orienting frame. Does the group experience attraction and repulsion as something they can meaningfully act upon, or is it merely something they have to endure? In short, *the habitus articulates itself in the discourse as orienting frames spanned between a negative and a positive horizon, and which are invested with a certain potential for enactment.*

The *twofold comparison* is a central tool for identifying and validating the orienting frames considered to be crucial for understanding a respective socio-demographic collective's habitus' relation to crisis and protest.

The aim is, on the one hand, to distinguish the respective group's habitus from patterns that are, in fact, displayed across groups and might be considered broadly or even universally shared.[11] On the other hand, the habitus must be differentiated from patterns or structural features that could be considered individual. Such patterns resonate with those identified in the accounts and exchanges of members in the same group but nevertheless are irreducible to them.[12] The latter is done by *intra-group comparison* between the different interviews and discussions (and the different passages of these interviews and discussions) of a given mobilization's core constituency, while the prior is done via *inter-group comparison*, comparing the orienting frames reconstructed for the respective mobilizations.

This part of the reconstruction is called *immanent reconstruction* because it aims at distilling the immanent logic of the empirical material. The next synthetic step is *socio-genetic reconstruction*: The group-specific orienting frames are attributed to their respective realms of experience. These are identified either through their actualization in the interactions themselves or through inter-group comparisons that help to identify certain biographical circumstances as group specific (Bohnsack 2007).[13]

Notes

1. Attribution theory, especially the concepts developed by Kelley, is an important part of the epistemological foundations of the framing approach in social movement studies (e.g., Snow and Benford 1992, 137 f.). While framing approaches usually ask for the connection of a certain frame to the broader set of beliefs and ideology of a given society to explain the frame's resonance with society, I will argue in the following that the category of the habitus urges one to ask for the socio-biographically specific disposition of social groups to resonate with a certain framing of events.
2. "Das fraglos Gegebene" (translation N.K.) (Schütz 1981, 199).
3. Bourdieus study on the troubles of homeowners from the working and petty bourgeois classes (1998), for example, describes the suffering that is caused by the geographical displacement of the habitus that results from moving to the suburbs. *Homo Academicus* (1988b) analyzes the tensions that result from the inflation of educational titles and the corresponding loss of status of academics as one of the preconditions of the events of May 1968, and especially his early writings on Algeria (2010) document how the concept of the habitus was originally developed by Bourdieu to understand the inner conflicts of those that live in a rapidly transforming social environment.

4. In her study on "Act Up's Fight against Aids", Deborah Gould draws an intricate picture of the contradictory habitus that those at the margins of society find themselves equipped with. Their internalization of both the stigma society attached to them and the very structure of desire corresponding to this stigmatized position results in painful conflict that, however, also opens up potentials of resilience (Gould 2009).
5. The biography of Erica before she first went to OWS was only briefly touched upon in our interview, so that the story presented above should rather be read as a thought experiment on what a possible and plausible genesis of her habitus could look like—this is also the reason why I decided not to address her by her 'name' earlier.
6. This quote and its interpretation here are both to be understood as merely illustrative. In fact, one should be very careful with accepting the kind of self-objectification offered by Erica here, since self-objectification can produce the false impression of transparency while, often non-consciously, covering up hidden conflicts. This effect is even more dangerous the closer the interviewer (or interpreter) and the interviewee are in regard to their socio-biographical position—which is, in this case, almost a perfect fit, since a postdoc in the social sciences is interviewed by a doctoral student in the very same field (cf. Bourdieu 2002, 788 f.). In this case, one of the latent conflicts may be the tension between her and others involved in the mobilization, resulting from the fact that Erica's alleged "learning experience" also remained a source of profit in the academic field. This ability to profit from OWS outside of OWS is one of the sources of multifaceted tensions between the veteran-activist-academics such as Erica and other social classes involved in OWS.
7. The following summary is based on Bohnsack (2012, 2010, 1989). (For a short English introduction, see: Bohnsack 2013a, 2004; for a thorough *methodological* discussion of the affinities between the Documentary Method and Bourdieu's theory of practice, see: Bohnsack 2013b.
8. When I referred to information gained by interviews in the last chapters, I mostly referred to information gained in this step of analysis.
9. This in many regards resembles the differentiation between 'manifest' and 'latent' structures of meaning, as it is at the core of the methodology of objective hermeneutics—another reconstructive methodology which was also used for the purpose of habitus reconstruction (Oevermann 2005; Wernet 1997). For a discussion of the methodological differences between objective hermeneutics and the documentary method, see Bohnsack (2010, 69–81).
10. See Sect. 5.1, "The Tea Party: Disappointment Without Disillusionment".
11. Examples for such a pattern is the frame of "individual rights" that has been identified as being universally adaptable in the USA by previous

research, or the fact that *all* my interviews documented an orientating frame that was marked by the opposition of "big" (business, labor, government) and "small" (homeowners, business, 'men', grassroots initiatives), in which the first was perceived as hostile and foreign, while the latter was designated a point of sympathy and identification.

12. Of course these patterns are not "individual" in the sense of lacking reference to some sort of conjunctive realm of experience—indeed, I do very much doubt that one can meaningfully speak of an individual orientation frame or habitus—but rather refer to potential lines of conjunctive communities that do not correspond to those that served as the basis of interviewee recruitment and comparison.
13. Most of the time, however, it is a mixture between the two, in which the topic is explicitly present in some interactions, and further research and comparison reveals it to be present across a large portion of the group. Max, an activist in OWS, for example, was almost the only one explicitly referring to her working multiple jobs to make ends meet, which nevertheless turned out to be a very common feature of OWS participants, even if they did not explicitly talk about it.

Bibliography

Benford, Robert D. 1997. An Insider's Critique of the Social Movement Framing Perspective. *Sociological Inquiry* 67 (4): 409–430.

Berger, Peter L., and Thomas Luckmann. 1991. *The Social Construction of Reality: A Treatise in the Sociology of Knowledge*. London/New York: Penguin Books.

Berlant, Lauren. 2011. *Cruel Optimism*. Durham: Duke University Press.

Bohnsack, Ralf. 1989. *Generation, Milieu Und Geschlecht*. Biographie und Gesellschaft. Opladen: Leske + Budrich.

———. 2004. Group Discussion and Focus Group. In *A Companion to Qualitative Research*, ed. Uwe Flick, Ernst von Kardoff, and Ines Steinke, 214–221. London/Thousand Oaks/New Delhi: Sage.

———. 2007. Typenbildung, Generalisierung und komparative Analyse: Grundprinzipien der Dokumentarischen Methode. In *Die Dokumentarische Methode und ihre Forschungspraxis*, ed. Ralf Bohnsack, Iris Nentwig-Gesemann, and Arnd-Michael Nohl, 225–253. Wiesbaden: VS Verlag für Sozialwissenschaften.

———. 2010. *Rekonstruktive Sozialforschung*. Opladen/Farmington Hills: Barbara Budrich.

———. 2012. Orientierungsschemata, Orientierungsrahmen und Habitus. Elementare Kategorien der Dokumentarischen Methode mit Beispielen aus der Bildungsmilieuforschung. In *Qualitative Bildungs- und Arbeitsmarktforschung*, ed. Karin Schittenhelm, 119–153. Wiesbaden: Springer.

———. 2013a. Documentary Method. In *SAGE Handbook of Qualitative Data Analysis*, ed. Uwe Flick, 217–233. London/Thousand Oaks/New Delhi: SAGE.

———. 2013b. Dokumentarische Methode und die Logik der Praxis. In *Pierre Bourdieus Konzeption des Habitus: Grundlagen, Zugänge, Forschungsperspektiven*, ed. Alexander Lenger, Christian Schneickert, and Florian Schumacher, 175–200. Wiesbaden: Springer.

Bourdieu, Pierre. 1974. Der Habitus als Vermittlung zwischen Struktur und Praxis. In *Zur Soziologie der Symbolischen Formen*, 125–158. Frankfurt am Main: Suhrkamp.

———. 1979. *Entwurf einer Theorie der Praxis auf der ethnologischen Grundlage der kabylischen Gesellschaft*. Frankfurt am Main: Suhrkamp.

———. 1987. *Sozialer Sinn: Kritik der theoretischen Vernunft*. Frankfurt am Main: Suhrkamp.

———. 1988a. *Die politische Ontologie Martin Heideggers*. Frankfurt am Main: Suhrkamp.

———. 1988b. *Homo Academicus*. Stanford: Stanford University Press.

———. 1994. *Die feinen Unterschiede: Kritik der gesellschaftlichen Urteilskraft*. Frankfurt am Main: Suhrkamp.

———. 1998. *Der Einzige und sein Eigenheim*. Hamburg: VSA.

———. 2001. *Meditationen: zur Kritik der scholastischen Vernunft*. Frankfurt am Main: Suhrkamp.

———. 2002. Verstehen. In *Das Elend der Welt – Zeugnisse und Diagnosen alltäglichen Leidens an der Gesellschaft*, ed. Alain Accardo, Balazs Gabrielle, Stephane Beaud, Emmanuel Bourdieu, Pierre Bourdieu, Sylvain Broccolichi, and Patrick Champagne, 779–822. Konstanz: UVK.

———. 2007. *Zur Soziologie der symbolischen Formen*. Frankfurt am Main: Suhrkamp.

———. 2010. *Algerische Skizzen*. Berlin: Suhrkamp.

Bourdieu, Pierre, and Loïc J.D. Wacquant. 1996. Die Ziele der reflexiven Soziologie: Chicago-Seminar, Winter 1987. In *Reflexive Anthropologie*, 95–249. Frankfurt am Main: Suhrkamp.

Burawoy, Michael. 2012. Manufacturing Dissent. Burawoy Meets Bourdieu. In *Conversations with Bourdieu. The Johannesburg Moment*, ed. Michael Burawoy and Karl von Holdt, 175–198. Johannesburg: Wits University Press.

Flick, Uwe, Ernst von Kardoff, and Ines Steinke. 2004. *A Companion to Qualitative Research*. London: SAGE.

Gebauer, Gunter, and Beate Krais. 2002. *Habitus*. Bielefeld: Transcript.

Goffman, Erving. 1974. *Frame Analysis: An Essay on the Organization of Experience*. Boston: Harvard University Press.

Gould, Deborah B. 2009. *Moving Politics. Emotions and ACT UP's Fight Against Aids*. Chicago/London: The University of Chicago Press.

Matthiesen, Ulf. 1989. 'Bourdieu' und 'Konopka'. Imaginäres Rendevouz zwischen Habituskonstruktion und Deutungsmusterkonstruktion. In *Klassenlage, Lebensstil und kulturelle Praxis. Theoretische und empirische Beiträge zur Auseinandersetzung mit Pierre Bourdieus Klassentheorie*, ed. Klaus Eder, 221–299. Frankfurt am Main: Suhrkamp.

Meuser, Michael. 2007. Repräsentation sozialer Strukturen im Wissen. Dokumentarische Methode und Habitusrekonstruktion. In *Die Dokumentarische Methode und ihre Forschungspraxis*, ed. Ralf Bohnsack, Iris Nentwig-Gesemann, and Arnd-Michael Nohl, 209–224. Wiesbaden: VS Verlag für Sozialwissenschaften.

Oevermann, Ulrich. 2005. *Klinische Soziologie auf der Basis der Methodologie der objektiven Hermeneutik: Manifest der objektiv hermeneutischen Sozialforschung*. http://publikationen.ub.uni-frankfurt.de/volltexte/2005/540/. Accessed 30 Oct 2017.

Schütz, Alfred. 1981. *Der sinnhafte Aufbau der sozialen Welt: Eine Einleitung in die verstehende Soziologie*. Frankfurt am Main: Suhrkamp.

Snow, David A., and Robert D. Benford. 1992. Master Frames and Cycles of Protest. In *Frontiers in Social Movement Theory*, ed. Aldon D. Morris and Carol McClurg Mueller, 133–155. New Haven/London: Yale University Press.

Snow, David A., E. Burke Rochford Jr., Steven K. Worden, and Robert D. Benford. 1986. Frame Alignment Processes, Micromobilization, and Movement Participation. *American Sociological Review* 51 (4): 464–481.

Steinmetz, George. 2006. Bourdieu's Disavowal of Lacan: Psychoanalytic Theory and the Concepts of 'Habitus' and 'Symbolic Capital. *Constellations* 13 (4): 445–464.

Wacquant, Loïc J.D. 2004. Following Pierre Bourdieu into the Field. *Ethnography* 5 (4): 387–414.

Wernet, Andreas. 1997. *Professioneller Habitus im Recht: Untersuchungen zur Professionalisierungsbedürftigkeit der Strafrechtspflege und zum Professionshabitus von Strafverteidigern*. Berlin: Edition Sigma.

CHAPTER 5

Experiencing the Crisis: Results of the Habitus Reconstruction

The reconstruction of the core constituencies' habitus is the very heart of the answer to the research question: *how can the lived experience of the Great Recession by the social classes that drove these mass protests be understood as shaping and informing their very protest-practice?* Or, the other way around: *how can the protests as a social practice be interpreted as a symptom of the socially specific lived experience of the socioeconomic crisis?*

The second chapter sketched out the political economic logic of the crisis dynamics that surfaced in the Great Recession. The third chapter identified the specific class-generational units that drove the protests and the way in which they were exposed to these crisis dynamics. These aspects already help to understand some peculiarities of the protest mobilization, as was argued in the first- and the second-cut theories of the crisis-protests. However, more importantly, they were preparing the ground for the habitus reconstruction. They allowed to identify the relevant socio-demographic groups among the protesters and provided a foil against which their perception of the crisis dynamics can be measured.

The reconstruction of the core constituencies' habitus serves to understand the socio-logics of how all this is translated into the lived experience of subjects and how the socially patterned lived experience of discontent is practically enacted and articulated as critique in the different protest-practices of the respective protest mobilization—for example, *how we can understand that the young, proletarianized aspirants of the new petty bourgeoisie considered*

N. C. Kumkar, *The Tea Party, Occupy Wall Street, and the Great Recession*, Critical Political Theory and Radical Practice,
https://doi.org/10.1007/978-3-319-73688-4_5

the protest-practice of Occupy Wall Street a plausible and attractive response to their socio-biographical situation.

To this end, this chapter will summarize and compare the findings of the interpretation of the interviews and group discussions I conducted with activists from the Tea Party's (TP) and Occupy Wall Street's (OWS) respective core constituencies. These reconstructions prove to be very fruitful for understanding the specificity of these mobilizations as crisis-protests: These protests are not only themselves reacting to a social situation that is structured by escalating crisis dynamics of global capitalism, they are in some sense *themselves* in crisis in that the very socio-biographical expectations that are oriented by and orienting their ethos have become unfeasible or at least precarious.

The reconstruction of their core constituencies' habitus reveals that their interpretations of the crisis and their articulation of critique and discontent are marked by strong contradictions. Their pre-reflexive orientation toward anticipated biographical trajectories finds itself at odds with the experienced reality of crisis. Yet, while the integration of the experience into the universe of the 'normal' fails, the habitus geared toward this universe of the normal continues to structure the interpretation of the events. This leads to sometimes painful conflicts in the perception and practice of protest that I labelled *disappointment without disillusionment* for the case of the TP (Sect. 5.1) and the *impossible exodus of prefigurative protest* for the case of OWS (Sect. 5.2). In a last, synthetic part (Sect. 5.3), the basic orienting patterns of the protests will be further accentuated via comparison and nuanced with the results of the analysis of another source, namely, the pictorial artwork used in two propaganda pamphlets handed to me by activists in OWS and the TP.

For the sake of readability, in the presentation of the results of the reconstruction of the habitus from both protests, I will not introduce single group discussions or interviews, but instead directly proceed to the respective core constituency's discourse on their protest mobilization as the 'case' which is to be analyzed across its multiple realizations in the different interactions.[1]

Since the reconstruction proceeded strictly from the material, theoretical references will be very scarce in this part of the book, and limited to cases in which they help to illustrate the structures or mechanisms presented as part of the interpretation rather than offering interpretations itself. Thus, the reference to Freud's theory of paranoia (p. 108) is not to be understood as offering an explanation for the observed, but rather as a description of a pattern that is in important aspects homologous to the one revealed by the interpretation. This at times might create a feeling of the interpretation ignoring the obvious or repeating commonplaces, especially since this chapter temporarily sets aside conclusions already drawn from the material in the previous chapters. Hopefully, this inconvenience is outweighed, however, by allowing the reader to get a better impression of how the reconstruction tried to remain systematically open to 'getting surprised' and to better estimate the validity and scope of the conclusions drawn from the material.

5.1 The Tea Party: Disappointment Without Disillusionment

In what follows, I will first discuss the common difficulty of the TP activists to agree on a starting point for their activism as the first 'riddle' that I encountered in the process of interpretation. While they all agree that there is an underlying reason for their common engagement, this very reason is not pinned down, but instead renegotiated at many occasions. In a similar vein, feelings of anger, fear, and sometimes aggression permeated much of the group's discourse, indicating that the respective propositions that were elaborated on in these passages resonated closely with the negative horizon orienting their experience of the crisis. However, this very negative horizon nevertheless is difficult to identify thematically.

First, I propose that this difficulty of agreeing on a starting point indicates the (relative) contingency of the protest-practices' precipitating or triggering event vis-à-vis the underlying strain or discontent. More importantly, these same passages also show that the underlying strain is not even necessarily reflexively and communicatively available to the activists, who, in their discourse, instead process it in a 'symptomatic', indirect way. This symptomatic processing of an underlying discontent in the groups' discourse is manifest in the 'split' between empirical events and the presupposition of an often vague and undefined underlying truth permeating the discourse. I label the homological element in these patterns of interpretation, the TP's *conspiratorial mode of interpretation*.

Second, the articulations of the underlying discontent and the perception of a 'split' reality is analyzed more closely through a metaphoric reoccurring in all TP discussions, namely, the idea that one was "standing in line" while everybody just "cut in". The interpretation of this metaphor and of two other reoccurring, interlinked motives, that of the suspended reward for one's work and suffering and that of a perceived vanishing of all natural and moral differences, together leads to the identification of the negative horizon orienting the TP's core constituency's experience of the crisis as being defined by a loss of orientation and of the wealth and status that functioned as their life trajectories' orienting end point, a fear which they experience as a diffuse aggression against them and the way things 'ought to be' (Sect. 5.1.1).

The following subsection explains how 'Barack Obama' as the *symbol of dangerous ambivalences* is so evocative for the fears that define the negative horizon of the TP's core constituency's orienting frame: As the USA's first African-American president, he blurs the difference between the 'top' and the 'bottom' of the social hierarchy, but also between the national 'inside' and the foreign 'outside' (Sect. 5.1.2). In the last subsection, the habitual dynamic structuring this interpretation of the crisis is summed up as the 'tragic' tension between an apocalyptic negative horizon of a loss of orientation and an almost indiscernible positive horizon invested with no potential for enactment, which stems from the dilemma that they feel hurt by the very same socio-symbolic order they built their claims on wealth and social recognition on, resulting in a dynamic which I labelled *disappointment while refusing to be disillusioned*. Finally, I will draw out some first connections between this habitual structure and the political practices of the groups I observed and the mobilization more generally (Sect. 5.1.3).

5.1.1 The Conspiracy Structure: The Crisis as 'Splitting' Reality

To illustrate the discourse-immanent logic of the observation which I labelled the 'split reality', let me turn to the transcription of the opening passage of a group discussion. It is chosen because it is particularly illustrative and dense. The central threads, however, were also reconstructed in the other group discussions with TP activists:

Interviewer: Why don't you just start by @telling me what brought you to the Tea Party?@ I mean, what, what happened
T: Ok I think-
L: We were, @.@
T: L, go ahead!
L: Obama got elected. And he immediately started doing things that was upsetting a lot of people. I mean, you know, we just felt our right were being taken away, and, ah
T: I, I
L: He had, ah, ahm, the congress, both houses were democratic, so, he pushed everything he wanted to get through, and we had no way of stopping him. And I think yeah, just all, those of us that didn't agree felt we had to do something.
S: well, wasn't it before though, with, right, before he was elected it started. And it started with the bail-outs. So that was really,
T: Bush.
L: Bush
S: yeah, that was really Bush
L: └ right ┘
S: And then, when we realized what was going on, wait, what are we bailing out people for, why are people being bailed out. Because to us, most of us it's like if you buy a house, and if you lose your house you lose your house, if your family wants to help you, that's different. But that started it off. And then, I remember my mom saying, this guy, who has no experience, is gonna run for president. I'm like what? And I saw his, I hate to say it, but his NAME, it sounded like a terrorist's name, so it got me upset! I was like that's weird, we have, like, you know, these it sounds like a terr-, like a name from the Middle East that would be like, is he American? You know, because it doesn't look like an American name at all-
L: He's not.
S: But @.@ well, we say he's not, so, well he's-
T: I, I think it started way, way, way before that.
(TPG3, Opening Passage)

Leaving aside the very rich manifest content of the passage, what is striking about the form of this passage is the collaborative movement of pushing the starting point further and further into the past. It is interesting to note that this almost seems to be a kind of competition about offering the earliest possible date: Even L, who originally suggests Obama's election, later on offers earlier events and developments.

Eventually, the group will bring up the year 1913 (the founding of the Federal Reserve Bank), while L even insists on the US civil war as the 'original sin' through which the perceived decay is to be understood. Both dates are of high symbolic importance in narratives of the US Libertarian Right. However, the group does not explicitly agree upon any of those suggested dates. Rather, what seems to be the decisive agreement is that it always happened *before*. This is also documented in the rest of this and in other group discussions, where candidates for the beginning of the decay that are named include the civil rights movement, 1968, or the "Frankfurt School". Some of these dates predate the birth of everybody in the group and all of them surely predate the beginning of their political activism. Yet, at the same time, the activists present themselves as not having been politically active or even 'aware' until fairly recently.

This documents an orienting pattern defined by a negative horizon which is, in the actors' own interpretation, decoupled from a contingent event that set the 'story' of the TP into motion. In other words, it implies a split between two kinds of starting points: In this story of the TP's emergence, the actual *precipitating event* becomes contingent and decoupled from the *true reason* to protest, which is the implicit negative horizon driving the protests as an articulation of discontent. The precipitating event takes the form of an 'awakening' to the realization that the own discontent has true reasons that are deeply embedded in an old yet hidden history operating on another level of reality than the manifest events.

Interestingly, while this seems to imply a greater 'solidity' ascribed to the hidden layers of reality as opposed to the triggering events, the latter are nevertheless agreed on, while the first ones are subject to discussion. If we reduce the group's discourse unfolding here to its explicit content, this seems to imply a paradox: The group agrees on empirically given events while disagreeing on how to interpret them, which seems to contradict the intuitive expectation that political agreement rests most importantly on shared interpretations (or 'framings') of empirical events.

However, this seeming disagreement, which never really tilts into conflict, documents a *homological structure* of interpretation that rests on the *split between the real and the apparent.* What holds the group's discourse together in these passages is not so much the common framing but the homology of their framings with regard to this specific structural characteristic, which will be described in more detail in the following. On the one hand, the shared joy of collaboratively searching for the deeper truth beyond the events that de facto brought them together and, on the other hand, the implicit assumption that the same discontent is driving this search. In the discussions of the other TP groups, this feature of the discovery of the 'split in reality' was also documented. In TPG2, for example, it crystallized in the metaphor of the "opening of the eyes" as what the participants described their turn to the TP. In a very similar vein, activists in the TPG3 refer to the TP as the ones who are "awake" and "looking behind the curtain", and in TPG1, an activist stated that they know of connections opaque to others because they are 'aware'.

This also allows to better understand the somewhat irritating triplet exchange in line 27–30: L's proposition that Barack Obama is not an American, which was an important topic in the early TP's discourse, is taken up and specified by S in a particular way. She seems to doubt the factual correctness of this claim, or at least is aware of the fact that most people outside of the TP (here represented by the interviewer to whom the laughter is directed) do not believe in it. However, not only does she not contradict L's proposition, she instead affirms it as a collectively shared statement of the group and thus assigns a somewhat ambivalent truth value to L's proposition, which is true as a group opinion, but not necessarily as a factual statement.

On the face of it, this surely is the attempt to deal with the communicative tension inherent in this situation, in which S tries to balance two factually contradicting claims (the one made by L and the other attributed to the interviewer). However, the strategy she chooses is feasible only because of the aforementioned shared conception of the 'split' reality: If Obama is in fact American or not is not of great importance, because it is a fitting symbol of the shared perception that there is something uncanny hiding underneath and that the understanding of this hidden reality is what allows to make sense of empirical reality, which is perceived as mere appearance. In fact, the speakers even seem to derive joy from the fact that the statement about Obama's citizenship might be factually false: The common 'stubborn' insistence on this fact also contributes to the constitution of the group as a 'community of believers'.

In his book on criminal literature, conspiracies, and paranoia in European modernity, Luc Boltanski outlines this as the basic structural conflict not only the detective and the spy novel but also conspiracy theories are processing (2013). On the one hand, there is "reality", understood as a meaningful ensemble of "what is going on", the stability and predictability of which is, from the late nineteenth century onward, mostly guaranteed by the nation state and its institutions. On the other hand, there is the seeming chaos of everything that is excluded by this reality, most prominently, the dynamics of global capitalism.[2] These repressed dynamics however reenter reality as "events"—nonsensical interruptions of what seemed to be going on—which means that the seeming predictability and security of reality is permanently threatened.

The work of the detective is to repair reality by uncovering the hidden causalities that led to an event and thereby reinscribe it into reality as something that 'makes sense'. The spy novel and the conspiracy theory on the other hand play (more or less joyfully) with the possibility that reality might, in the end, not make sense at all, but is in fact the mere appearance of the conspiracy as the 'real reality'. In this imagined universe, the "objective of the conspiracy is the *construction of reality*" (Boltanski 2013, 301, translation N.K., emphasis in original). It is in that sense I call this dimension of the TP activists' interpretational work with regard to the crisis 'conspirational'. The important advantage of this definition of conspiracy theories as compared to more 'substantive' definitions is that it brackets the factual correctness of the claims made by the theory and instead focuses on its form. This allows to understand the immanent logic of this theorizing in a way that is less pathologizing than 'substantial' conspiracy theory theories tend to be (at least implicitly) (cf. Hofstadter 2008).

To better understand why the TP activists rationalize their experience of the different dynamics of the crisis as a split in reality, one must examine closer what actual experiences (or better, what perceptional traces of these actual experiences) ground this conspiratorial coloring. To answer this question means to approach the precipitating events not as the arbitrary disturbances as which they are presented by the TP. Instead, I suppose that certain structural features of the experience of these events met the interpretational predispositions of the classical petty bourgeoisie in a way that made the fast and persistent spread of interpretations following the conspirational pattern possible. In other words, the habitual structure patterning the interpretation of the events itself contributes to the *contingent necessity*[3] of the spread of the mobilizations following these events. The riddle to be solved is therefore the elective structural affinity between the interpretative disposition and the interpreted event or between the implicit 'true reason' and the precipitating event.

The results of the interpretation of the focusing metaphor of TPG2 will help to shed light on this.[4] Following the reasoning of the group about their way to the TP, M offers a conclusion, summing up "what a Tea Party member is in a nutshell" (1). What is documented in this conclusion, which basically follows the structure of an argumentation (i.e., an ex-post rationalization or legitimization) for joining the TP, is the participants'[5] affective attachment to society and their own anticipated biographical trajectory:

M: Ah, the one thing I want to say, I guess to gather what a Tea Party member is in a nutshell? Um, picture yourself standing in, in line, um, to a movie, to, um, say anything. Sporting event. We're the person who has numerous times seen people cut in, cut in line, and just stood by and said, alright, it's not my problem, it's not my problem. You know, just. (..) Ah. We're, the Tea Party groups, are the ones that are finally saying, you know, enough is enough. You cut in line, this is not right, this is not, you are not playing by the rules. Whereas the left is the one that's saying, oh well, they, they are having a lawyer saying, they can cut the line because of X, Y, Z. We're the ones that are standing up for what's right, as for how our framework, ah, is. In this country. I guess, I don't know if that's a good analogy or not. But, that's who we are. We, we're, we finally had enough and we're standing up for what's right. (..) (TPG2, Standing in Line)

The centrality of this metaphor is discernible in its function as the symbolic conclusion of a very dense thematic passage, but also through its structural homology to other passages throughout all discussions and interviews with the TP: The instant described here, the one where one "finally" says "enough is enough" (5), refers to the same moment as the description of instances where one "opens one's eyes" in the logic of other descriptions and narrations on the same topic. This specific fable or metaphor however, is in important aspects different: While the other descriptions rationalize (and thereby excuse) why one was not 'active' before, namely, because one 'did not know better', this scenic description conveys that there was nevertheless already an uneasy 'feeling' culminating before.

This dynamic, other than the more or less arbitrary constellation of the 'opening of the eye', has a temporal and dramatically structured logic to it: The qualitative leap marking the 'opening of the eye' is to be understood as a certain moment in the escalation of developments, rather than only relying on a contingent precipitating event. Thus, the question become: What is the affective structure of this process that led to the TP? To what precisely did one "open one's eyes"?

At the very basis, what the speaker is confronted with is the permanent postponing of a reward he feels entitled to, which culminates in a point where he has "enough" (5).[6] It is interesting to note that this traumatic point—most probably the realization that there simply might not be any tickets left for the sporting event when one arrives at the cashier—remains implicit in this image. Only the rationalization of this experience, namely, that 'others' are getting something because they are cheating, and that is clearly evoking moral outrage about any sort of affirmative action, is made explicit. What is more interesting for the purpose of this chapter than this rationalization is the experience that lends itself to this rationalization, the implicit center of the scene thus described, which documents the negative horizon orienting the underlying experience: The perception that one has been duped about the reward one feels entitled to. The image of "standing in line" documents disappointment, yet at the same time the insistence on the reward and the very "line" itself. This already prefigures a pattern that will become more nuanced in the rest of this chapter, namely, that the peculiar combination of these two tendencies, ***disappointment without disillusionment***,[7] results in the outrage that is so clearly discernible in much of the TP's discourse and practice.

The central (and peculiar) importance of the foreclosure crisis for the emergence of the TP, as it was already sketched out in Sect. 3.1, can be understood more in depth via this interpretation of this metaphor: The decline in housing prices that many of the TP's constituency had experienced as a consequence of the foreclosure wave can be understood as a situation which, in its experience through the classical petty bourgeoisie, corresponds to this scenic draft of a reward that is felt to be unjustifiably kept away from the TP activists.[8] As the most important asset that people in the classical petty bourgeoisie typically own, the house is, especially in the USA, understood as a symbol of solidity and a self-reliant lifestyle, the very materialization of the 'American Dream'.[9] This means that the necessary abstinences in the form of mortgage payments that come with buying it (the "standing in line") are expected to lead, in the end, to a safe haven of independence and comfort which gives the sacrifices thus made a 'meaning'. The rising real estate prices over years seemed to validate that impression and were taken for granted—until both soaring mortgage payments and collapsing prices turned this haven into a potential trap,[10] especially in combination with loss of employment.

As in the metaphor above, however, this loss of security is almost never explicitly addressed in the accounts the TP members give of the years leading up to their involvement in the TP: P, a participant in the TPG2, is the only one explicitly mentioning the fact that the abandoned foreclosed houses in and the influx of poor people into her neighborhood is troubling her—and did so only in a follow-up interview. And T, a participant in TPG3, mentions the "two-punch situation" of fearing to lose his job right after he bought a house—the 'second punch' implicitly being the loss of real estate value to back up the mortgage. However, it is brought up indirectly via discussions on the topics of home ownership, foreclosure, and the policies (supposedly) implemented through the Homeowners Affordability and Stability Plan—even if seemingly as independent from one's own experiences. It is for the reason of this constant indirect discussion of the topic that the interpretation of these events as central for their experience of the crisis seemed initially plausible. It is further validated by the fact that the other explicitly negotiated metaphors that follow the logic of the 'standing in line' document a homological experience to the 'scene' of being indirectly impacted by the foreclosure crisis.

This symptomatic absence of this event from the accounts and its metaphoric and indirect reappearances have reasons beyond the central observation of Alfred Schütz that the reasons (as opposed to the purposes) of our actions are always difficult to point out in reflexive communication (Schütz 1981, esp. 129; Schütz and Luckmann 1984, 2:35). Rather, it is because of the very traumatic kernel of this experience: It not only touches the very substance of the self-narration of 'man forging his own destiny' but also points to the fetish character of the commodity itself as one cornerstone of structures of perception inherent to the social relations at the heart of capitalism. What is perceived as the innermost essence of a thing, the value of the house, reveals itself as being in fact a social relation and therefore reconnects the fate of the individual to forces of the social whole that are totally beyond her or his control (cf. Marx 1969, 85–98).

In this sense, the experience of the event fits like a key into the lock of the discontent of the classical petty bourgeoisie. As argued in Sect. 3.1, this class already had found its economic prospects darkening on all fronts—with the important exception of the economic sectors directly connected to the housing boom. For the TP activists, confronting the kernel of their experience of this event would therefore mean to call into question the very purpose of all the abstinences they went (and still go) through as a part of the lifestyle that is driven by a life and work ethos according to which every (wo)man is the forger of her/his own destiny and which is held together precisely by the promised security and relative wealth that is the vanishing point of the projected biographical trajectory.

As a result, the symbolization of this experience fails, and the way in which the discourse of the group processes this failing symbolization is effectively split in two: On the one hand, the topic "foreclosure" is thematically explicit not only in the discussion and interviews but also in leaflets distributed and talks hosted by the TP groups. One's own experience of the events as pointing to the negative horizon and the traumatic fears connected to the crisis, however, is absent in these propositions and is, instead, discussed in other contexts or in metaphors. The very traumatic nature of this negative horizon, the loss of biographical meaning that would result from the acceptance that the rewards one feels entitled to might not materialize, is maybe best captured in another sequence, earlier in this same passage of the discussion:

P: Yeah, and I, I think a little bit of it is a combination of, of, fear and an- anger. Because if you start shaking things like the rule of law and start creating new standards. If you wanna start saying that the constitution is a living, breathing document, and, and that there is no real foundation in it and you want to make new rules – then, what BINDS us? What, what, what is the measure of what can't be done if we don't want to follow the RULES. That means any politician or anybody can do anything they want and there is no consequence for it. And once THAT happens, (.) you know, its chaos. And nobody is then safe anymore. You're not safe from, your, your, your personal property, your family, you don't opp- you don't have any opportunity, to grow, I mean I think that was a big fear too, why you see, so many older people, who, who joined the Tea Party. Because (.) they're looking at all the things they built up. //M: mhm//all the securities that they thought were in place for their children and their grandchildren. And they're literally watching it disappear in front of their eyes.

M: yupp (.)

P: And then if, if, what are you living for, and what have all the things, you know, why, why did he serve his country, why do you have children, if, if, all those things you thought they could HAVE, they can't HAVE anymore! (.) (TPG2, "Standing in Line")

The escalating logic of this passage reveals the true kernel of the experience to be the insecurity of one's savings and assets, which culminates in the fear of a total loss of meaning of the biographical trajectory. Even if P herself is rather young, she senses the connection between the socio-biographical age and this fear as resulting from the abstinences and biographical 'investments' in the very social order one is now disappointed with.

The 'politicians' (just as the telling actant of the left's 'lawyers' in the passage before) already are to be considered secondary constructions for dealing with this trauma. The form of this is analogous to the paranoid structure as understood by Freud. Freud observed that what seems to be the 'illness' of the paranoiac is, in fact, her/his way of struggling with his 'illness': The mushrooming connections of everyone with everything in vast conspiracies that (s)he confronts us with is in fact an operation covering up the traumatic loss of attachment to her/his environment (Freud 1973a, 193). Similarly, what we encounter in this discourse is only the trace of the experience of panic triggered by a loss of perspective, which is perceived as external aggression, in the form of the rationalizations of it, the sinister and all-encompassing plan of the 'politicians'.

The rationalization that is offered by the TP'ers is usually presented as a variation of one (albeit often fuzzy and flexible) image. This image is structured by two intertwined but not necessarily interdependent logical patterns. The one is the mentioned conspiratorial logic, which has the function of supplementing what Boltanski calls the "lacking mass of causality" (Boltanski 2013, 266): It allows for an integrating of the impossible event into the reality of the activists without questioning the basic patterns structuring this reality.

The other pattern is defined by a channeling of the auto-aggression resulting from one's (now vain) abstinences away from oneself (and the traumatic scene of the loss) and onto others: The figure of the 'undeserving poor' which is a longstanding trope in the discourse of (not only) the US-American Right, functions as the screen onto which these aggressions are projected, as is easily discernible in both passages quoted above: In the first one (20–23), it is manifested as the anger that the welfare state supports people. In the second passage, this phenomenon is documented in the metaphor of a cutting-in-line. This metaphor documents the very structure of what is the object of aggression, namely, the idea that somebody might benefit without suffering for it. It is this pattern through which most of what has sometimes rightfully been called out as the racism of the TP filters into the discourse of the group—and in this tradition, the second passage also quite obviously attacks any form of *Affirmative Action* as contradicting "our framework" in "this country" (8).

Other, more concrete variants of the theme captured in the metaphor of 'standing in line' point into the same direction. For example, one activist in TPG1 explains that she has been a very careful spender all her life—"not buying every little gadget. This is, I think, my third phone"—and is now angry about the possibility of a government-funded pension system, which makes her doubt the value of her frugality. An activist in TPG3 tells that she is heating her house so little that her "kids are cold", because she is "saving energy", and now is upset that there is government assistance for those who are having difficulties to pay their electricity bills. In every one of these cases, frustration stemming from one's abstinences from pleasures is articulated as anger against those that are supposedly enjoying without hardship.

It is therefore no surprise that it is in this form that the foreclosure crisis appears in all three group discussions: as the critique of an unjust political response to it, in which irresponsibility gets rewarded and industriousness gets punished. In that sense the foreclosure crisis is also to be understood as the culminating point of a longer history of disappointment with one's own biographical trajectory. The classical petty bourgeoisie's ethos of frugality and self-reliance that was supposed to result in social upward mobility revealed itself as not really leading anywhere (anymore). The connection to the own experience is not thematically explicit, but nevertheless decipherable as soon as one focuses on the affective logic of these propositions and the documented orienting frame: *The 'undeserving poor' are the symmetrical inversion of the TP activists' self-perception. Where the latter had suffered without profiting, the former profit without suffering*, thereby becoming a metaphor documenting the negative horizon of a loss of social orientation: They should not be where they are, while one oneself is also in a sense 'lost'. No wonder they all could identify with Rick Santelli's outrage on the government not helping "those who carry the water instead of drink the water".

In the process of its communicative rationalization, the figure of the undeserving poor, the outcome of the transference of aggression, gets coupled with the conspiracies that capture the feeling of powerlessness by the activists and provide the causal links that help to make sense of what happens. As was not explicitly discussed until now, even though it also was discernible in most sequences cited, the collapse of the TP'ers hopes was also accompanied by frustrations about the missing recognition through the authorities—as discernible in complaints about the politicians doing 'what they want' (6) in the last passage, the 'left's lawyers' manipulating the countries 'framework' in the second-to-last passage (8) but, for example, also representatives that supposedly responded "arrogantly" to calls and letters. It is not a far stretch to suggest that the election of Barack Obama as the new president in 2008 and with it the end of George W. Bush's presidency contributed heavily to the crisis of the symbolic universe of the TP activists: Bush had, during his presidency, rhetorically over and over reemployed the trope of the 'simple American' that confronted the allegedly 'liberal elite'. For those that identified with this figure, the election of a progressive Democrat catered to fears of 'revenge'. The campaign of the Republican Party's presidential candidate in 2008, John McCain, already tried to capitalize on this fear: A man dubbed "Joe the plumber" by the press, the archetypical representative of the "white middle class" (i.e., classical petty bourgeoisie), was repeatedly invited to speeches of McCain to warn people of Obama's detachment from—or even contempt for—the 'little guy' that wants to start his own business (Rohter 2008). In the following, I will illustrate how Barack Obama as a metaphor actually symbolizes the merging of these two figures, the malicious or ignorant authorities and the undeserving poor. This will then again be put in context with the results of the analysis of another focusing metaphor reoccurring in the TP discussions.

5.1.2 Barack Obama as the Symbol of Dangerous Ambivalences

Interestingly, all of my interviewees in the TP explicitly agree on the election of Barack Obama as the president of the USA being a central reason for the emergence of the TP. Other than the foreclosure crisis, the election of Barack Obama as a moral shock seems to have entered the realm of explicit communication without great distortions. This, however, is only partially true. As already discernible in the first passage quoted in this chapter (p. 100 f.) in lines 24–27, the racial dimension of this shock, though clearly relevant, cannot be expressed by my TP interviewees without keying.[11] For example, here, S expresses "hate" at the fact that she has to admit that she was irritated by the foreignness of Obama's name. In other conversations, activists explicitly stated that Obamas 'race' has nothing to do with their opposition to him.

That Obama figures so prominently in the TP activists' explicit communication about their reasons to protest has to be understood by analyzing what he symbolizes for the TP. As a symbol or metaphor, he is located at the intersection of the two patterns sketched out above. First, S' evocation of the name that "doesn't look like an American name at all" but rather like that of a "terr-(orist)" clearly connects to the conspiratorial motive. The "Middle-Eastern" name signifies Obama's connection to powers outside of the USA. The qualification of this as 'terrorist' is probably partially suppressed because of the racist connotation of equating the two terms. It nevertheless powerfully sums up the idea of him being an 'enemy within'. He is thereby blurring the binary of the inside and outside—or to use the analytical vocabulary of Boltanski for capturing the structure of conspiratorial thinking, his appearance on the top of the institutional ensemble guaranteeing the stability of reality is an event that calls into question the very essence of this reality itself.[12]

Second, even if it is denied on the explicit level, the color of Obama's skin of course plays a role for him attracting this degree of opposition: In the discourse of the groups and interviewees from the TP, 'People of Color' and 'people being poor' is almost used interchangeably. At the face of it, it seems irritating that S also refers to Obama having "no experience" since she expressed strong sympathy for those she perceives as "outsiders" to politics in other parts of the discussion and in other group meetings I visited. But "no experience" has a different meaning here, which has to be understood in connection to the metaphorical potency of 'race' I just mentioned: It is to be read as a stand-in for the fact that *Obama* 'did not stand in line'—he simply *is not supposed to be where he is.*[13] Thus, while Obama's name designates him as the 'enemy within', the color of his skin connects him to the 'undeserving poor'.

It is this double ambivalence (on the vertical axis of the governing and the governed and on the horizontal axis of the inside and the outside) which makes the discourse that developed in the TP around the person of Barack Obama so enormously rich and arcane. One example being the often-raised questions about Obama's supposedly 'missing' birth certificate that was brought up on many TP posters and banners in the first years of the movement. While some of my interviewees still insisted on this question being open for debate, or found some way to rerationalize the argument that he is not a natural born citizen, even though he might be born as an American citizen, most did not bring up the topic in conversations with me. The metaphor of the birth certificate, however, reappeared again and again, as in this short passage from the first group discussion, in which the group explains their constitutionalism with reference to the right-wing manifesto "the 5000 year leap"[14]:

B: But basically the constitution was written based upon human nature. And you see that in that book. And human nature doesn't change. Human nature is in the nature, you know. And and, again, I like to say, the constitution and our declaration of independence, that's our birth certificate. Just like YOU have a birth certificate. It doesn't change, it doesn't change, you're still Nils no matter how old you are. (TPG1)

Another interviewee jokingly remarked that his "birth-certificate is a living, breathing document" when I asked him for his age after the interview. Both incidents do not explicitly refer to the person of Barack Obama, but they both document, in an ironically pointed way, the negative horizon that is defined by the inversion/ambivalence of the very contours of reality itself, in which documents do not really mean what they are supposed to mean and thereby "erode the country". Without explicitly commenting on it, this also indicates how the TP activists interpret the empirical fact of Barack Obama having a birth certificate in the light of the conspiratorial mode of interpretation described above: If this document is real (as they might have to accept as an empirical fact), then, in a sense, they prefer to conclude that *reality itself is not real.*

In other instances, the collaborative search for conspiracies has an almost pleasurable, triumphant tone to it, in which the participants reaffirm each other's deeper insights in what holds the world together.[15] But when the group homes in on conspiracies they connect with the person of Barack Obama, anger and aggression—often already at quite high levels in the group discussions with TP activists as compared to the discussions I conducted with OWS activists—escalate very fast. An example being this passage that concludes the group's discussion on the naivety of most Americans who do not know "what the signs are, along the road" (to impending doom):

M: So we are trillions in debt, nothing's gonna happen.
S: └ don't worry ┘
M: and he's not worried in ten years
about balancing the budget.
T: He doesn't know what a budget means!
L: └ (unintelligible) ┘ he didn't have a
budget. He didn't have a budget.
M: No! Because he wants us to have a big buzzle, ah, a bubble,
ha buzzle // S: @.@ // whatever that is, a bubble, and have us brought to our KNEES.
S: Yes exactly,
well that's why he, that's why he acts the way he does.
D: └ And that's what all those things are all about ┘ it's not about saving the economy.
S: no, it's not
D: It's not about saving the environment. It's all about pulling the country down,
S: └ yeah, exactly ┘
D: our strong country in the world (.) and (unintelligible)
M: └ It is about redistribution of wealth all the way up to the top, ┘ and giving it not to other
countries, but to other leaders. (TPG3, "People Asleep")

Or, in another group discussion in which one participant seeks to explain the heterogeneity of the groups the TP is fighting against:

P: There are those who believe that communism is great, there are those who just are selfish, there are those who have an ideological aspect like Obama who wants America down in size because he's an anti-colonialist who hates what happened to his father's country of Kenya, you're also finding individuals who have a mindset, of, of everyone who has a philosophy towards a deity is somehow wrong and needs to have that changed. Ah, there are those who worship the earth-goddess Gaya and have an environmental motive above others, so there's many different things. Amongst them is also the Islamic desire to recreate the caliphate which was destroyed when the Ottoman Empire fell. (TPG1)

What is striking about this last passage is that among all the groups enumerated, only the Islamists and Barack Obama are attributed an actual plan, and only the latter is understood as driven by purely destructive aims. In this figure, the anger toward the 'undeserving poor' and the experienced powerlessness in the face of economic and social developments both are perceived as one strong and purely destructive aggression directed toward the USA (i.e., toward oneself). This feeling of being subject to aggression permeates a lot of the movement's discourse on state repression: Statements such as the one by L in the opening passage of TPG3 (p. 100 f., ll. 7 f.) that they felt "their right(s) were being taken away" after Obama's election or the fear of a "militarized police" expressed at different occasions are expression of this. It is also one reason why many activists are such strong opponents of any attempts to limit the individual's rights to carry firearms:

S: You lose your gun-rights. (.) You lose your right to the 2nd amendment – you'll lose all the others! When they disarm you, what happens when they disarm you? Look back in history. What happens when the people were disarmed. Ok? You have NOTHING. Can we fight a battle with our army? No. Ok. I don't have nuclear warheads in my living-room, but they would still rather you have nothing. They, because it would be so much less messy. (Susan_TP)

This aggression is perceived by all TP activists I spoke to. As I already indicated above, however, the exact contours and the actual practices of the conspiracy on which this aggression is projected remain, to some degree, open for discussion. When P, seconds after the second-to last passage, explains that he 'personally' believes the Anti-Christ, born into the body of a Muslim, is behind all this, the others in the discussion express disagreement with this proposition. Remarkably for such a strong statement, however, they do not state that what he says is wrong, but only insist that they have other 'opinions'.

But even if the perceived conspiracy is fuzzy in a lot of respects, the content of it is not completely arbitrary, but has certain formal features that are remarkably constant across its variants. These basic structural homologies of the orientations documented in these stories are to be understood through connecting them to the experience of crisis as it was sketched out above, and also shed more light on the habitus that processes these experiences. The most prominent of these homological patterns is documented in focusing metaphors that reappear in all three group discussions. Again, the most concise passage is from TPG3, but the examples in other discussions are numerous[16]:

T: You know, you're gonna, you're gonna, ah, have, you gonna tell people how much they can make? You're gonna tell an executive, oh, you're making too much money, you should make less money? You're gonna tell somebody in scho- in the school, and even in the school system! Oh, we don't wanna judge teachers on how, on how they perform! You know, you just wanna have, you know, ah, ah, an agenda
S: └ happy (unintelligible) ┘
L: └ (unintelligible) ┘
T: Where everybody does whatever. And they're not gonna be rewarded, or, or, or thrown out of school, you have stupidity!
S: └ same thing where everyone, everyone gets a trophy ┘
L: └ right ┘
S: and everyone gets to, everyone gets to pass I can't believe that -
T: └ you know I ┘ have one leg, I can't be runner.
S: well no, I said that, that's what I said, that, what were they talking about, something I said, if you're, if you're blind, you cannot drive a car.
L: Yeah
S: And people can't face anything anymore. It's like, you can't say that. Well you know, you have to have everybody be able to do anything and be successful at everything.
R: └ right, exactly ┘
T: And you have to be polite with your, with your fellow citizens // S: oh// and instead of calling somebody an idiot or a moron, you have to say, you know, maybe you don't have the right (unintelligible) now excuse me!
S: └ the right intelligence you can't use the word FAT ┘ you can't say the word skinny, you can't (unintelligible)
T: └ we're educated idiots ┘ (TPG3, "Tipping Point")

Note the high metaphoric and emotional density of this passage, which clearly indicate a shared habitually relevant structure underlying the exchange. There is no negating or contradicting each other's statements (despite S' claim for 'copy-right' on one metaphor, which is in effect an affirmation). The group is effectively speaking as one person.

What is documented here is a central structural feature of the negative horizon that is connected to the experience of the current socioeconomic and political developments: the erasure of all 'natural' differences that define and legitimate social hierarchy. This also allows for a better understanding of the metaphor of the 'standing in line'. One possible interpretation of this metaphor could be merely the idea of some form of distributional justice being harmed (and it surely has elements of this, even if only on the level of rationalization). The connection to the last metaphor, however, brings a more uncanny latent structure to the surface: The outrage at the collapsing 'line' is that it violates one's understanding of the natural order of things, in which oneself is self-evidently supposed to stand in the front of the line,[17] while the idea of an African-American president or a working-class homeowner is equivalent to the idea of 'blind people driving cars': dangerous nonsense.[18] The conspiracy that is postulated as unifying all these attacks against the ordered world one bases one's claims on material and social recognition is, symbolized in the person of Barack Obama, the alliance of the unworthy elite above with the undeserving poor below.

5.1.3 *Disappointment Without Disillusionment: The Inner Tragedy of the TP's Interpretation of Crisis*

The orienting frame that structures the TP's core constituency's experience of the crisis can be described as being spanned by, on the one hand, a (dominant) negative horizon, which is defined by a loss of orientation and one's sense of place and a blurring of all 'natural' differences undermining one's social status and promised wealth. On the other hand, it is spanned by a very vague positive horizon which can be described as a return to the 'right order of things'. As is already indicated by the asymmetry between these two horizons' resonance with the groups discourse, this frame seems to be invested with a very low or rather no potential for enactment.

At the very core of the habitus generating all these patterns of perceiving and interpreting the way in which one is exposed to the political economic crisis dynamics is what one could call the inner tragedy of the TP—a constant *disappointment without disillusionment.* The anger and aggression caused by the abstinences that are part of their classical petty bourgeois life (the 'standing in line') and the fear caused by the revelation of the very precariousness of all gains achieved, and with it the loss of status and orientation that defines this group's negative horizon, are not directed toward the social relations producing these frustrations or even actors directly involved with them. Instead this very social order is affirmed as something that should, if everything would run correctly, ensure the rewards one was promised as a vague positive horizon that is barely invested with any potential for enactment.

This constellation is stabilized by the high emotional and biographic investment into the social order one is disappointed with: One of the TP activists' biggest fears is to be forced to realize that one has strived for wealth that turns out to be unreachable. Thus, one's fear is channeled into aggression against those that are held responsible for the experienced precariousness of the social and symbolic universe, partially because they are not suffering enough to make oneself feel superior, partially because their strategies for improving their standard of living are perceived as subverting the basis of the legitimacy of one's own claims for social recognition and material rewards.

However, the very precariousness of this symbolic universe constantly reinvades the reality thus constructed. This is articulated by the activists themselves as a kind of panic as soon as elements of this reality are called into question. It is in this light that the slogan of the biggest national TP organization, the Tea Party Patriots, is to be understood: "Pursue your American Dream". If the American Dream can be understood as a very peculiar type of pursuing happiness, then the ideological function of this slogan is to be understood as the expression of the negated consciousness of the very unfeasibility of this endeavor for many: It is the imperative to not give in to the reality principle in acknowledging that the abstinences made so far might have been in vain. This aspect of the habitual structure has very important political consequences: The TP activists' staunch opposition against any kind of higher taxation for the rich, even if they themselves would materially profit from it, is to be understood (at least partially) as the inner resistance against acknowledging that they themselves will never become rich.

This structure bears many similarities to the figure of the (pseudo-)"rebel" developed by Adorno et al. as part of their typology of the "Authoritarian Personality" or that of the "conformist rebellion" of modern anti-Semitism (Adorno 1973a, 328–31; Claussen 1991). Just as these figures, the disappointed but not disillusioned TP activists have a very ambivalent relation to authority and the institutions of government that is defined by the coexistence of submission and rebellion—the rebellion itself manifests the desire for 'real' authority.[19]

This ambivalence is documented in the doubling of institutions or markers of distinction that reoccur throughout the interviews and discussions, one of which is then embraced and the other rejected. This is, for example, documented in the conclusion of the passage "standing in line" in M's contempt for the left's "lawyers" (who are to be read as a stand-in for legalism), while he himself embraces over and over again the constitution and the rule of law as the "framework" of this country. In the same manner, "cronyism" is confronted with "capitalism" or the "liberal elite" with a "citizen government", the latter of which is associated, seemingly arbitrarily, either with the founding fathers or with Ronald Reagan.

Maybe the most persistent variant of this theme in which this orientation is documented is the ambivalent relation to 'education'. My interviewees had, as part of the classical petty bourgeoisie, rather low degrees of incorporated or materialized cultural capital (most activists I spoke to did not have college degrees, very few had higher educational degrees). However, many of them presented themselves as very keen readers, explaining what books they were currently reading and suggesting sometimes quite lengthy reading-lists to me. One of the activists I interviewed introduced himself (and was referred to by others) as a historian and scholar, even though he never finished college and worked in construction. The authority attributed to him was explained by the fact that he was able to trace his genealogy back to the war of independence (he told me that he lived in his current state of residency "since 1776"). In contrast, universities and colleges, sometimes also high schools and even the very word 'education' itself were treated with outright contempt: spaces of indoctrination and moral decay that lead to Americans being "educated idiots".

This peculiar habitual structure and its inner conflict of affirmation and rebellion help to better understand some of the dynamics of the interplay between the developments in different social fields and the TP. First, it should be clearer now why the TP activists were so open to cooperation with the Republican Party, even though on the level of explicit communication they quite often rejected the party as 'part of the establishment' and called themselves 'independent'. The first reaction to crisis for them was the look toward an established authority that might reinforce the 'rules' that they felt were betrayed: While the 'elite' was equated with corruption, the elimination of this corruption was nevertheless hoped to be the act of a 'real authority'. The inner conflicts in the Republican Party between moderates and 'fundamentalists' leant itself toward an adaption through the TP's interpretative structure of splitting the 'real reality' from its appearance[20]: While the party as a whole was perceived corrupted, it still supposedly had a 'true kernel' that could reinstate the true, uncorrupted authority they longed for.

The fear of the vanishing of all natural differences, which was reconstructed as the negative horizon orienting the experiences of the crisis, makes plausible why especially the activists of the TP were so prone to accept the slogan of Obama being a 'Socialist'. Anti-Communism has a long tradition in the USA, at least reaching back to the first red scare in the 1920s. However, the great success of this accusation is somewhat astonishing, given that the Cold War lay more than 20 years in the past. That the openness to this orienting scheme was anchored in a lived experience and not just in inherited figures of interpretation is supported by the fact that in many cases the same resentment was articulated not as anti-Communism but explicitly as "anti-Democracy", an orienting scheme that clearly documented the same negative horizon:

T: Liberty and Freedom, because that's what we are supposed to promote. Not a democracy. Because we know what the word democracy means. That's really change the country, change the laws. So, in this case, in the United States, we have the process of elections, so we can uphold the rule of law. (TPG3, "People Asleep")

A participant in another group stated, even more directly, "democracy is really nothing else than organized mob rule", thereby again connecting it to the negative horizon of a collapse of order that was developed above. What is tragic about the interpretations resulting from this habitus confrontation with the crisis is their systematic inability to address the sources of their discontent in a direct manner. Enormous interpretative efforts are collectively made to preserve one's attachment to USA's political system and capitalism in the face of all the problems one is experiencing. One very persistent structural feature of these interpretative operations was the inversion of what I sometimes perceived as the 'elephant in the room' by blaming "the left" or similar actants for developments that these actants themselves would attribute to capitalism or other structural features of US society:

T: there is the other MYTH
P: └ mhm ┘
T: that they created about this whole economic collapse. You know, that, oh, it's the bad, evil people on Wall Street. (deletion) The best book on it is by two New York Times reporters, who went all the way back into the nineties, and, and really did an honest job in describing exactly how it all happened. Um, the name of it escapes me right now. But it was, a lot of it was, government caused!
M: └ Yeah ┘.
P: └ oh yeah, they, ┘ the what is it, the Glass-Steagall, they repealed that, which they-
T: └ NO! well I actually ┘ I read that there was no real connection between, um, you know, the separation between the, the investment banking and the ah (...)
P: └ It's the, it's the, ┘ I don't think it was any one-one. It was also the fact that they started lending money to people, lending money to people, who like you said, the bad, the bad loans
T: └ sure, sure ┘
P: which was pushed by the federal government-
T: sure, and there were a lot of private mortgage-
P: └ because everybody deserves ┘ t's a right to have a home that you own
T: └ right, right ┘
P: instead of living in an apartment
T: I mean there was a push, there was a push, in the government, on banks, don't be caught redlining,
P: └ yeah ┘
T: or we gonna, don't you, don't draw a red line around this, and they gonna call them racist, because they don't have any loans in this impoverished area. Well, you know, it's not WISE to loan money to impoverished people. So that redlining was outlawed, and, and, so banks would start to lower their standards. (TPG2: "DebtII")

Below the seeming disagreement around the question of the deregulation of the banking sector, an overall interpretative *scheme* is clearly discernible: The federal government is to be held primarily responsible for the resulting crisis. This, however, is carried by an underlying *orienting frame* that becomes clearer in the collaborative movement in the end of the passage: Linked to the negative horizon of the vanishing of all natural differences is the proposition that it is the irresponsible promise of a "house for all" that is ultimately behind the collapse. In the very same manner, the group, in another passage, also explains that the misery of the deindustrialized hyper-ghetto ultimately has to be explained by the "sense of entitlement" that has arisen after the civil rights movement. These interpretations, however, are always reactive; They are preemptive counter-rationalizations employed to preserve the unproblematic status of what is perceived as the "framework" of US society.

The positive horizon orienting the political actions of the TP is therefore necessarily utopian in nature, since it does not address the actual problem of the deteriorating socioeconomic base of the reproduction of the classical petty bourgeoisie in any way. For the same reason, it is—at the same time—hard to even differentiate the positive horizon from the world they are living in, even though this world is otherwise described in the most apocalyptic imaginaries: Since everything that goes wrong with the world around them is ultimately blamed on attempts to change this world, there is very little room for imagining any enactments of the positive horizon beyond an overwhelming rage resulting from the experience of the precarity of the social order.

Thus, the discussants in one group discussion, asked for the best world they could imagine, presented accounts of a world that is pretty much exactly the world they are living in. In an awkward contrast to the apocalyptic scenarios they just gave of the current state of US society, changes seem really peripheral, such as the wish for more "wholesome TV shows", "or that rather than saying, ah, Thanksgiving is the start of the genocide upon the indigenous population of native Americans, (there) would be an understanding that Thanksgiving is an opportunity to thank our creator", and that politicians would 'fight less' and care more about "their constituency"—that is, them.[21]

And finally the conspiracy logic that can be seen as processing the tragic tension between the overwhelming feeling that the world is disintegrating, on the one hand, and the insistence on nothing having to change fundamentally, on the other hand, also helps to explain the escalating nature of the political practice of the TP in two aspects. First, the electoral success especially of 2010 never really could live up to its promise—the staged conflict over the debt ceiling that reinvigorated some TP groups had to end in compromise, which could not be seen other than as "treason" by the TP activists. Second, when the support by donors and parts of the Republican Party dwindled together with the support in the polls and on the demonstrations, the activists I spoke to interpreted this as further proofs of the all-encompassing nature of the conspiracy.

The answer of many parts of the TP was a broadening of the thematic scope of their groups. The early TP's insistence on speaking only on matters of "fiscal responsibility and constitutionality", which my interviewees in 2012 still adhered to, was relaxed the grassroots level: My interviewees openly embraced other topics of the classical right, such as abortion or immigration, as topics for their political practice in the course of 2013 and 2014. The Tea Party Patriots as well started to lobby on topics besides the classical thematic focus and, for example, concentrated very much on questions of immigration policy. However, while this broadening of the thematic scope is plausible both from the sprawling logic of the conspiracy that represents the social conflict as it is perceived by the TP activists and from the free-floating aggression that accompanies the repression of one's own original fear, it—at the grassroots at least—also facilitates emotional detachment. What starts as a perceived opening of the group for issues (and the avoidance of conflict about its further trajectory) turns into a process of dissolution, on the one hand, and in the ever-increasing scope of political arenas to be covered and with it the adversaries to confront, also into the disempowering feeling that 'they' are all the same anyhow. The always latently generationalized conflict of a class whose reproduction is in jeopardy is then, for example, articulated as the suspicion that one and one's values are dying out:

> T: I really don't, I really, I'm not, I feel like America has changed. And that I, here I am, here, I could not convince my own nieces and nephews who really do respect me. I couldn't convince them. (TPG2: "Opening Passage")

This sub-chapter reconstructed the orienting frame structuring both the TP's core constituency's experience of the crisis and their affectability of the protest-practice and the criticism articulated through it. It is spanned between a negative horizon, the fear of a loss of status and orientation through the vanishing of all 'natural' differences, and a vague positive horizon, the restoration of the 'right framework', and invested with very low or no potential for enactment. It also identified the habitual dynamic and the socio-genesis that shape this orienting frame: The deep disappointment with a social order one at the same time bases one's claims to wealth and recognition on.

Throughout the three sections of the sub-chapter, this basic orienting figure was shown to explain different peculiarities of the TP's core constituency's discourse: Sect. 5.1.1 showed the *conspiratorial mode of interpretation* as documenting the fear associated with the perceived disintegration of the socio-symbolic orientation ("the line" in which everybody just "cut in"). Displacing this fear onto sinister and subversive forces rationalizes this fear in a way that does not call into question one's own basic orientations—thus 'repairing' reality and allowing for the disappointment not to result in disillusionment. Section 5.1.2 explained why the habitus of the TP was so affectable to the attribution of their experience of crisis to the figure of Barack Obama. As the *symbol of dangerous ambivalences*, he in a sense functioned as the condensation point of their fear of a vanishing of all natural differences. The final section of this sub-chapter, Sect. 5.1.3, finally showed how the basic habitual dynamic of this orienting figure, namely, *disappointment while refusing to be disillusioned*, is connected to a peculiar oscillation between rebelliousness and the desire for authority figures to legitimize one's fear and aggression, and thereby helps to understand how the TP was so open for collaboration with the right wing of the Republican Party, but also partially explains why it had such great difficulties to develop a protest-practice that did not ultimately reproduce the original feeling of being at the mercy of forces beyond one's reach.

5.2 Occupy Wall Street: Between Exodus and Protest

To delimit the core constituency of OWS' social movement practices is, as I indicated in Sect. 3.2, an endeavor more complex than in the case of the TP. The identification of this social group went hand in hand with the process of the generation and analysis of the data that formed the basis for the habitus analysis. Since what this meant for the course of the inquiry itself will not be transparent from the following presentation of its results, I want to address this issue shortly beforehand.

In the TP it was comparatively easy to recruit discussion groups with (relatively) homogenous patterns of practical and interpretative orientations simply from the respective group meetings. The TP groups' clear social profile and their private or semi-public meeting spaces seem to have limited the participation in the events to the core constituency or those that very closely resonated with them. In the case of OWS, however, the group discussions I conducted at first did not seem to display the typical features documenting a common habitus. The praxis of the occupations and actions, such as Occupy Sandy, which was my main entry route into the mobilization, attracted diverse sets of actors beyond the actual core constituency. Only the additional use of the available survey data and the finer analysis of some individual interviews allowed to delineate the core constituency from the other groups participating in the protests and thus to begin understanding the peculiarities of this group's habitus. An additional difficulty, beyond the relative social heterogeneity of the group, was that the habitus of this group was, via its proneness to constantly emphasizing and negotiating personal difference, additionally veiling itself from a first, rough-grained analysis even in passages where it was, ex post, clearly documented.[22]

After the delineation of the core constituency, the discussion OWSG3 had to be considered unsuited for the kind of analysis done here, since the group brought together participants too demographically different for analysis and some of the participants were not actively involved during the occupation of Zuccotti park but only afterward. OWSG2 and OWSG4 formed the core of the data analyzed for this chapter—together with the individual interviews conducted with participants that belong to the core constituency of OWS. This chapter, mainly for the sake of being comparable, is solely focused on the habitus and the perception of crisis of this specific group. The dynamics of the interplay between the different groups' habitus are going to be taken up in Chap. 7, in which I will also take up the results of the interpretation of OWSG1, which was conducted with Occupiers from a different social class, which I called the urban precariat.

I will first discuss how the basic orienting patterns of OWS' core constituency can be described in comparison to that of the TP and then connect these orienting patterns to this groups' specific experience of crisis. I will then elaborate on the groups' specific relation to and perception of 'society' and institutional politics and give some suggestions on the socio-biographic roots of this interpretation, before I finally sketch out some consequences of the analyzed structures of habitus for OWS' political practice.

5.2.1 *"It Just Resonated with Me": OWS Between Socio-Biographical Detachment and Euphoria*

The discussions with activists of OWS diverged substantially, from the very outset, in thematic focus, but also in their discursive form, from the discussions with TP activists, as can be illustrated with the following opening passage of the discussion with OWSG2:

Interviewer: cool, so, um, why don't you just tell me what brought you to Occupy Wall Street, like, I mean, what, what happened? (2)

P: I'll tell you. Um, I mean it is sort of a number of ah, I can tell you (deletion) from many different angles, but I, I'll try and keep it brief, so I think I'll tell you in a sense like, what ACTUAL um, EVent happened, that attr-, that attracted me. And gave, and ah, gave me notice of, of, of the group. um. Philosophically, I, it just resonated with me. And is something that I eventually would have been drawn to. But it happened that I was, um, down in So-Ho, coming out of REI, the camping store, um, and there was a march going up Broadway. (deletion)

M: ((Clearing her throat)) Um, I was the one, um, who, like in the months leading up to, September 17th, when everything started, I, was kind of becoming really disillusioned with, just the structure of society, and and, I wanted something to change, but didn't think anything would happen? And then I saw the Adbusters advertisement going viral on Facebook. With um, the ballerina on the bull. Kinda like ((takes a deep breath)) yeah, maybe this could be something, it probably won't be, because, it never is // R: @.@ // but I go check it out. // P: mhm// and I went, and there they had the bull barricaded, so we couldn't meet there, we met in front of a museum, um, and heard a few people speak. And (2) you know, it sounded promising, but I had to leave for work, I went ahead and, went. And, um, believe I saw a video of um, like in the couple of days following that, you know because people camped out immediately that night.

P: └ ((coughs)) ┘

M: And the police started going in, just taking people randomly. And, I saw that video, and, went like I'm gonna go back down to see, and, I got to Zuccotti Park, and there were only maybe 20 people there, and oh no, there isn't, there isn't anything. But then you walk in, and immediately hear conversations, and, they're the right conversations, they're the conversations you wish that everybody, you know, had been having for, you know, years! And, that, that first day, um, another arrest happened, and I was there to film it? And, then I realized that there, there is no media there. And you know, there are no newspaper article about it, there is nothing on, you know, the six o'clock news. And, obviously what was happening was important. (deletion)

R: Hey I'm Rob. Um, so I will give you my story, before I (incomprehensible) um, what was your name?

M: Max

R: Max. I have, I guess a similar, like, lead up, um, as Max did. Um I mean my, my political positions haven't really changed like before or after, hopefully I became a little more educated. But, I basically was um, relatively, like, I guess cynical? Um, as toward there could be like a change, like maybe I studied the political economy of capitalism or something like that. But I didn't really think like we could have a mass movement in the US kinda thing. Um, and so I went down on September 17th, um, and I was basically like still pretty cynical? Just like, and as she said like, um, and ah, in the park like, there is, like on the first day, there is like relatively few people? So there's just, and then just like, ah, these silly anarchists, like chanting the same anarchist things

M, P: └ @.@ ┘

(OWSG2, "Opening Passage")

Two things are especially striking about this opening passage: First, all three interviewees proceed very directly to narrations about their first encounters with OWS, which they fully unfold before another speaker presents her or his story (a part of these is deleted above for the sake of brevity). This is a common feature of all group discussions with OWS activists, and of almost all interviews with them, but it barely appears in TP discussions or interviews I conducted. While the latter present (often collaboratively) elaborated argumentations and scenic descriptions that explained the fear and anger with social developments leading to the engagement in the TP, the OWS activists articulate their perception of OWS itself as something that "resonated with" them as the primary, or at least more 'noteworthy', reason for their engagement in the protests.

Second, this resonance is presented in contrast to an emotional atmosphere of detachment and withdrawal that permeates the (often very short and superficial) descriptions or narrations about the months and sometimes years leading up to the encounters with OWS. It is plausible to interpret both these aspects as documents of the same interlinked orienting frame spanned between a negative and a positive horizon orienting their behavior in—and perception of—society. The negative horizon in this figure is associated with "society" or "the structure of society", and is defined by a lack of resonance, while the positive horizon, almost exclusively associated with OWS, is defined precisely by this resonance.[23]

This orientation frame's basic structure is interesting to contrast with that of the TP analyzed above. The TP's negative horizon not only has much clearer contours, its descriptions are also highly emotionally charged; more specifically, it was connected with fear and anger. Furthermore, it bears a clearly discernible temporal index: Independent of its concrete communicative explication, it was linked to the present and the future, while the past (or a de-temporalized 'redeemed' future) was the locus of the positive horizon. In the case of OWS, the negative horizon does not have a clear temporal structure, while the positive horizon is fixated on the duration of the camp as a metaphor for a possible present: In M's account, the day of the occupation of the park is "when everything started" (11), while her discontent is building up for months (10–11) or years (26) and not connected to any specific event. Other than the TP activists, who discussed various candidates for precipitating events or reasons for their engagement, the OWS activists do not mention any of them but a diffuse discontent.

Another peculiarity of many discussions and interviews with OWS activists, which is absent from the discourse of the TP activists, is also documented in this passage: The original mistrust even toward one's own political action (at least before OWS), which is perceived to be useless and over-routinized rather than new and exciting (as was the case in the accounts of the TP). R affirms the statement of M (13–15) with a laughter that seems to indicate him feeling caught red-handed about having had the same 'defeatist' attitude that he then elaborates on in the following. This elaboration culminates in the image of "silly anarchists, (...) chanting the same anarchist things (they always chant)" (41) which in turn again is affirmed in the laughter of M and P.[24]

This affective disinvestment of the negative horizon and its lack of temporal markers make it difficult to search the discourse of the OWS activists that spoke to me for indicators of their interpretation and perception of crisis in the same manner as I did in the case of the TP. In the case of the latter, the form of the 'uncanny truth' behind reality allowed one to reconstruct some elements of both the experienced fear they reacted to and the very vague and mostly implicit positive horizon of a return to the social order of an imagined past. In the case of OWS, this will be inverted, and I will instead take as a starting point the positive horizon as it is documented primarily in the dense descriptions of the movement itself and only then reconstruct the processes and experiences that lead to the high affective attachment to this positive horizon. This mode of presentation also mirrors the actual course of the inquiry. As was explained in Sect. 4.2, the focusing metaphors, that is, the passages of the highest emotional and metaphorical density, are the key to reconstructing the groups' habitus. In the case of the TP, these passages were thematically centered on processes of perceived social decay; in the case of OWS, they were centered on the movement itself, which is why the reconstruction of this group's habitus proceeded from these propositions on one's relation to the movement in the case of OWS.

Just as in the case of the TP, I will mostly bracket the content of the explicit political statements given and concentrate on their form and the latent metaphorical potential of the discourse instead. "(T)he political economy of capitalism" (35) or that they wanted "something" to change (12) are in that sense read not so much as actual political claims or concepts but rather as documents of the detachment of society perceived to process out of one's reach, and the diffuse discontent connected to the feeling of a lack of resonance. This course of interpretation can claim plausibility also through the fact that figures like these are brought up but never taken up again for further elaboration in the groups' discussion.

Especially M's narration of her encounter(s) with the movement is interesting in this regard. It is very poignantly contrasting the original disappointment with the positive surprise by the situation in the park and might therefore serve as a first window into how the positive horizon can illuminate the implicit negative horizon of the orienting frame: What is striking about this part of the passage (22–29) is that the negatively and the positively connoted propositions, albeit presented as directly interrelated, are measured in seemingly disparate terms. What is disappointing for M, on the one hand, is the small number of people in the park, which seems to demonstrate that it "isn't anything" (24). This is, in all its vagueness, an unproblematic statement referring to the fact that one does not feel 'heard' or 'relevant' as a political group. Positively surprising for M, on the other hand, are the "right conversations" (25) that this small number of people is having, which is not relating to the quantitative argument explicit in the first statement but designating a qualitative peculiarity. This euphoria about the dialogical character of the movement is a thread that runs through all accounts given to me by activists in OWS: With surprising constancy, the mode of communication (or even the fact that there was communication at all) was treated as a topic more important than the actual content of this communication.

Taking this as a starting point for interpretation, one can understand that the negatively connoted element of this proposition ('not being politically heard') is not to be read as the primary element of perceived crisis, and thereby as the negative horizon of the orienting frame, but in fact as its secondary rationalization. In other words, the fear of not having enough people on the streets is already embedded in a certain idea of how to "change something" (through protesting), but is not necessarily connected to any specific "something" to be changed. I would argue, however, that the desire for conversations, as it is expressed in the positively connoted element, does document something about the discontent that gives rise to this desire to "change something".

M and R graduated, as typical members of OWS' core constituency, with a degree in the social sciences/humanities/arts, but worked in numerous clerical jobs since then. One understands only a part of the blockage of their biographical trajectory if one points out that they, as 'graduates without a future', face dire prospects for employment, are extremely 'overworked and underpaid' and highly indebted. In other words, the thesis of the rapid devaluation of cultural capital as the primary source of discontent formulated in Chap. 3 has to be further accentuated: During their studies, they not only worked and paid to accumulate incorporated and materialized claims on economic profits and social recognition that proved much less transferrable than they might have anticipated. Furthermore, this process prepared them for specific careers in the educational or cultural sector or as advisors for political or economic actors. It therefore predisposed them to expect a very specific kind of social recognition beyond the missing material reward as it is measured in their levels of debt and experience of unemployment, namely, in one way or another, to be included in conversations on the future of society and culture.

The importance of this specificity of the core constituencies' educational history, which now to me seems obvious already at the level of the demographic composition of the movement, for example, in the study of Milkman et al., and especially at the level of observations of meetings and protest events, for a long time escaped my attention. Comparable to the symptomatic processing of their biographical crisis (as it was triggered by their plummeting real estate values and the contracting market for the services their businesses offered) by the TP activists, accounts by onlookers and participants in the movement to my knowledge do not reflect on this fact, even though it is often evoked indirectly: David Graeber, for example, in one of the earliest reflections on the sources of OWS's 'success', sketches out a general hypothesis on the generational specificity of the problem of finding a job after college. However, he does not substantiate this hypothesis with a story of an unemployed community college graduate (which would be the fitting illustration for this very general explanation since for those the unemployment-and-debt crisis was probably the most severe). Instead, he recounts the anecdote of someone who has an Ivy League school degree in renaissance literature and now has to work as an escort to make a living (Graeber 2013, 67 f.). What gets scandalized thereby is not so much the fact of people in general having to confront poverty and a loss of perspective, but the drastic discrepancy between an anticipated biographical trajectory that promises the social recognition for taking part in the most *sublime* academic debates, and the *vulgar* reality of sex work to make ends meet—which is a very strong metaphor for having to "bring one's own hide to the market" (Marx 1969, 191, translation N.K.).

In that sense the 'positive surprise' of OWS helps to understand at least one aspect of the crisis dynamics as it was experienced by its core constituency and thereby to give a little more contour to the so far undefined negative horizon of the frame orienting their activism. But it also suggests that we have to understand the praxis of OWS not only through the lens of an activism for or against a certain social change. Instead, we have to note that it, at least in part, also has the character of a redirection activity, fulfilling desires connected to the implicit 'original' positive horizon of the orienting frame that oriented their biographical trajectory before the crisis. In this sense, it is not only a movement to make certain voices heard, it is also itself a platform for talking.

This characteristic allows us to better understand why the activists narrate the encounters in and with the movement with such euphoria, describing it in almost religious vocabularies—such as describing it as a "square full of soulmates".[25] Even if those kinds of description are common in activist's accounts on their involvement in social movements in general (cf. Poletta 2006), it is still noteworthy that this feature is almost absent in the discourse of the activists in the TP I interviewed.[26]

Maybe nothing encapsulates this desire to be involved in a dialogue (and how OWS was able to fulfill it) better than the practice of the "peoples' mic" and the activists' fondness of this practice: The people listening to someone speak would collectively repeat every sentence this person said, and thereby amplify it for those standing further away, who would then, if necessary, also repeat what was said. Originally this practice was a response to the NYPD's insistence on preventing the use of any sound-amplifying equipment in the park (Appel 2011a). Over the course of the occupation, however, it would become a signature of the movement, and one which many participants found especially exhilarating:

I: And then we went to the GA, we thought it was awesome the peoples' mic, you know we had
kind of seen it, on livestreams and stuff,
A: mhm
J: but being there? for it? was amazing. Just the idea
that like, people could all, you know, people that had something to say, as long or as short as that
might have been
A: └ @.@ ┘
I: └ @ @ ┘
J: ah, that people would amplify their
L: └ °hopefully shorter° ┘
J: you know, that people would amplify their,
the, you know, share those thoughts, just, it was really pretty amazing. (OWSG4, "Peoples Mic")

The socio-biographical background thus on the one hand helps to better understand the high affective investment of the OWS activists in their respective protest-practice as contrasted with that of the TP. On the other side, it also allows us to reconstruct some reasons for the noteworthy affective disinvestment from 'society' on the side of OWS' activists. As argued above, the TP activists perceive their discontent as "standing in (a) line" that gets manipulated from all sides. Since their claims on social recognition are nevertheless based on the existence of this very "line" (and their, prima facie, promising position in it), this object, which ultimately symbolizes the current class society itself, remains central not only to their discontent but also to their longings, even if in distorted or, better, displaced ways.

The core constituency of OWS on the other side finds itself in a social situation in which this very object of desire—the aspiration that orients and affectively legitimizes the reasonably expected trajectory through the social structure—itself has disappeared. Not only the vanishing point of their biographical trajectory is put in jeopardy, but they find themselves 'hanging in the air' without the institutional recognition or the material base for the social role their habitus is geared toward. The affective detachment from the institutions that failed to guarantee this position should not be taken at face value however, since it shields an even stronger (often implicit) affective attachment to the social role that would have been associated with this position—and the recognition that is connected to this role. The slogan "I awoke in a sweat from the American Dream" (Milkman et al. 2013, 37) that was written on signs and posters at OWS rallies nicely captures this ambivalence. On the one hand, it expresses disorientation and fear in the image of the nightmare one awoke from. On the other hand, it also hints at a certain pride to be smarter and more aware than those still 'dreaming'—preserving the positive distinction via cultural capital that is typical for self-perception of the new petty bourgeoisie.

Another slogan written on many posters on OWS rallies "lost my job, found an occupation" (Milkman et al. 2013, 11) also has to be read in the light of this relation of the practices of the movement to social reality as redirection activities that articulate a lack or desire not explicitly articulated in relation to this social reality itself. On the face of it, it is a mere play on words ironically pointing out the suffering from high youth unemployment. On this level, it is a comic response to the anticipated interjection by the non-sympathizing public to "get a job": One is out here demonstrating because one lost a job, not because one did not look for one. The real irony, however, stems from the fact that the juxtaposition of the 'job' with the 'occupation' is done in a way that suggests that the one *replaces* the other: The seemingly disparate terms reveal, via the metonymy, to be connected. The slogan, however, not only implies an un-anticipated relation (OWS is a kind of job) but also a reversal. The actual employment lost gets reduced to the generic 'job' (something one has to do for a living), while 'occupation' is in its connotation closer to 'vocation' (something one does, in a certain sense, live for)—OWS in this sense represents the realization of desires and ambitions that one found to be non-realizable even if one was lucky enough to have a 'job'.

That this is not a 'mere' joke is documented by the following focusing metaphor from an individual interview with an activist in OWS in which she elaborates on the contrast between OWS and 'society' and explicitly mentions the topic of 'unfulfilling jobs':

Max: Like, people were going about their daily lives, you know, am I making enough money to survive, and, doing the things that, you know, people expect you to do. Find a mate, get children, buy a house, but something is not quite right. And, you know a lot of people say, don't complain about the way things are, unless you have a suggestion on how to fix it. But the problem was, the problems are too big for one person to figure it out and say, oh, here is the solution, we needed to come together and talk. And once you started talking to each other, you started to realize, everything was solvable. But we needed each other @(.)@ to do it.

And another thing that people were experiencing is, that they would come to the park and would be like, I had this job, you know, it used some of my skills, but, I feel I was wasting away, just living to make money. And when I got to the park, I finally, I am using my full potential, I'm using everything that I know how to do. Like, I'm helping in the kitchen, I'm helping the city plan, I'm um, like learning how to build a WiFi-tower, how to make bicycle generators and, like, people who were helping, marching all day long and they would do that and go to sleep feeling completely fulfilled. Like they had done something worth doing. And they were helping to hopefully improve the country by getting people to do something about the corruption @(.)@. That's the main thing about Occupy, that people don't know. (Max_OWS, "people together")

As one would expect from the interpretation above, the passage contrasts a rather diffuse discontent—"something is not quite right"—with the satisfaction of a "fulfilled" life in the park. It is furthermore noteworthy that the enumeration of the different tasks one could help with in the park, even though it in some way represents a variation of the 'classical' theme of bridging the gap between intellectual and manual labor, does not feature an intellectual/creative task such as writing or discussing something (even though Max's role in the park, as I could reconstruct it from her and others' accounts, would make that in fact a more plausible example), but instead brings up the rather 'administrative' activity of "city plan(ning)" (11).

This description presents in metaphorical and textual proximity two elements that were 'fulfilling': First it makes explicit that the lack filled by OWS is in a way connected to the very suspended biographic aim of a career in administration. Second, it also brings up an issue that has so far been bracketed in this discussion: That OWS and the permanent presence in the park also were perceived as an answer to the isolation and loneliness that many activists perceived as part of their work in numerous precarious jobs and short-term living arrangements. Others expressed that they felt 'alienated' in New York, where they came to work after they finished school and where they ended up 'isolated'.

Another part of this passage, however, points beyond the interpretation presented so far. The articulated urge to "improve the country by getting people to do something about the corruption" (14–15) is, on the face of it, in its very modesty and vagueness surely not incompatible with the desires mentioned above. However, it is telling that the phrase that they "had done something worth doing" (14) is not specifying this last proposition, but the one that stated the fulfilled living. This indicates that the relation between the two propositions in this description, the 'fulfilled life' and the 'improvement of the country', is problematic to a certain degree: If the tasks are in themselves rewarding, it seems as if the 'positive effect' is almost too much, something that has to be added for moral reasons even though it implicitly already was pushed aside by activities that were in themselves already "worth doing". The laughter after "corruption" (15) additionally indicates that Max herself experiences the juxtaposition of the two as contradictory or at least problematic: It is as if she 'got lost' in her detailed account of the joy of the fulfilled life in the park and then 'calls herself to order' in stating that, 'obviously', this was not the real reason for her being there.

5.2.2 *The Impossible Exodus: Prefiguration and Protest*

This tension is itself not arbitrary but running through all discussions and interviews with OWS activists. In a sense it points back to the original observation of the asymmetry in the first passage quoted on p. 123 (21–29):

> M: And the police started going in, just taking people randomly. And, I saw that video, and, went like I'm gonna go back down to see, and, I got to Zuccotti Park, and there were only maybe 20 people there, and oh no, there isn't, there isn't anything. But then you walk in, and immediately hear conversations, and, they're the right conversations, they're the conversations you wish that everybody, you know, had been having for, you know, years! And, that, that first day, ahm, another arrest happened, and I was there to film it? And, then I realized that there, there is no media there. And you know, there are no newspaper article about it, there is nothing on, you know, the six o'clock news. And, obviously what was happening was important. (OWSG2, Opening Passage)

While the interpretation so far concentrated on that which is documented in the positively connoted proposition, namely, the surprise by the fact that people were finally having the "right conversations" (5), the two propositions framing it were temporarily left aside—namely, that she first was afraid that "there isn't anything" (4) and later on convinced that "what was happening was important" (9). What these two propositions document is, in some sense, obvious: That OWS was, by its activists and the public perception alike, foremost perceived as a political protest in society and not as a form of subtraction from or even substitution for it, even if it was criticized for its 'stubborn insistence' on practices that point into the direction of the latter.

One could formulate this tension as the contradictory coexistence of two political projects in one mobilization: One of these is aiming at the radical 'rupture' with the existing society and the focusing on what was called the 'prefigurative' politics of OWS. The other is the classical 'protest' that is directed at a transformation of this very society one is at the same time subtracting from. In some form or another, this conflict was brought up in all group discussions and interviews with OWS. Usually, it was discussed in terms of a political conflict in which the first of the two positions was identified as 'radical', while the latter was, depending on the position of the speaker, called 'rightist/reformist' or 'realist'.[27] This has a lot to do with the dynamic of the different social groups forming OWS and the position of OWS vis-à-vis the political field proper as they will be discussed in the Chaps. 6 and 7.

For the understanding of the habitus of OWS' core constituency, however, it is important to recognize that these are not just projects of different social groups, but that this contradiction also relates to a conflict in the group's habitus as it unfolds in the lived experience of the socio-biographical crisis. To some degree, this ambivalence might be documented in every social movement practice: Exercised by living, feeling subjects, they never purely are means to an end but also activities that are rewarding in themselves, and often this aspect will at least over some periods become the dominating force shaping the practice of the movements. In the case of the core constituency of OWS, however, this ambivalence is tilting into conflict, since the investment in the praxis, as result of the socio-biographical crisis, is too high to be handled 'pragmatically'. Yet, no matter how affectively invested the people were in the practice of the occupation and the park, they themselves, to a certain degree at least, always had the feeling that this is 'not it'. This is not only indicated by the classical protest-practices that were maintained throughout the whole time (daily demonstration and the like), but also in the accounts by my interviewees.

This points back to the reasons for which I above, rather in passing, introduced the term redirection activity for the occupation and its connection to the positive horizon of the orientating figure of OWS' core constituency. The problem with this terminology is obviously that it can easily be read in a dismissive manner. This, however, is not how the term 'redirection activity' is used here. It is not chosen to indicate a kind of 'misguidedness' in the eye of the observer: If the activists would simply do one thing instead of another, for example, setting up camps as democratic spaces to live in after originally expected biographical trajectories became unfeasible, this would not be a redirection activity, but simply the development of an alternative lifestyle, no matter how disappointed many social movement researchers and journalists would be with this development. The term as it is used here refers to the very ambiguity that the actors themselves invest their practices with[28]: It was in their eyes neither a mere form of protest—a much circulated slogan was "this is not a protest, this is a process" ("This Is Not a Protest, This Is a Process" 2011; but see also Schneider 2013, 86)—nor an alternative to the world outside of it.

Indeed, and this would be a parallel to compulsive redirection activities and religious rituals as conceptualized by both Pfaller and Freud, the very practice of 'occupying' as a redirection activity over time not only lost its effectiveness, it also assumed more and more characteristics of the object of the desire it originally kept at bay (Freud 1973b; Pfaller 2002, esp. 151–59): Articles written by activist-academics began to mock the "Bureaucracies of Anarchy" (Appel 2011b) and all throughout the discussions and interviews, the movement practices were at points described as slowly transforming into something that people again felt alienated by in a way very similar to what was documented in statements about "society". Sometimes this emerging affinity between the practices intended as 'prefigurative', on the one hand, and 'society', on the other hand, was explicitly stated, as in this passage from the interview with Max[29]:

Max: But once the tents came up, it was kinda like seeing the formation of society @(.)@ from the beginning, like we were all living together in this community, and then buildings came up, and everyone started staying inside of their building and developing a neighborhood, like this is my space, and, you would, you were wandering through the camp, and you would get to a corner where you're like, oh, I don't feel safe here, I want to leave @(.)@. It was just because there were neighborhoods coming up, and there were fights coming up between the neighborhoods, ahm, the tents just weren't good. (Max_OWS, "tents came up")

In a passage in OWSG4, the group also engages in collaborative reasoning on this process, the analysis of which is illuminating not only the process itself but also its interpretation by the activists themselves:

J: But being there, and just getting that sense, and how everybody just like, people would like "oh, I'll jump in and help with whatever"
A: mhm.
J: And I know it wasn't, you know, wasn't always as, as good as it could have @been@ but,
A: It was also like this learning process,
J: └ it was, yeah ┘
A: It was just really new to a lot of people.
L: Yeah, yeah, I think for a lot of people it was their first contact with, you know, radical organizing and anarchism and socialism and things like that // J: mhm// which ((sighs)) I, I think one of the problems was, that because new people were coming so often, it was hard to get passed that first stage. A lot, you know, every day we had to teach the same thing over and over, because there were new people who never learned it before.
A: And it was like something totally new to them, whereas of, like, I don't know, I remember being really, when we started, when we started having tables, and setting like having different areas, I was like, why are we like, we're setting up offices, where we are like recreating, like recreating a microcosm of the macrocosm, where like, to me it felt a little bit like we were (2) re-creating the same structures, just very slightly differently
L: mhm
A: but to other people who hadn't interfaced with that before it was very different.
L: yeah, yeah
A: and it was a very new thing. And so like, I think, like, I often felt like it wasn't that big of a step away? But a lot of people needed that tiny step first.
L: It's a process.
A: It's a process.
J: @.@
A: And I think I (incomprehensible) for a while, after a while I remember saying, be often like, ah, ah, the revolution is a lot of tiny steps in a circle
L: └ tiny steps @.@ ┘
A: tiny steps @.@ (OWSG4, "Tiny Steps")

At first this passage seems to contradict the interpretation according to which the conflict is internalized in the group's habitus: A and L clearly name another group, the newcomers to the park, as responsible for the practices to fall short of their potential (8–9; 10–16). Seen in context, however, this rather seems to be an ex-post rationalization. The first argument for this interpretation is that in the biographic interview, A, just as Max in the passage quoted before, described the problems as elements of a decay, and therefore rather as part of the establishing of the practice than as one of not really adapting to it. The example she chooses in this passage (16–18) points in the same direction: The tables were obviously not set up by newcomers or people new to "radical organizing" (10–11), but by the inhabitants in the park who developed a more and more sophisticated infrastructure. The 'others' in this instance are rather to be understood as a displacement of the ambivalence: In 1–4, J himself displays an excitement that is later attributed to the newcomers. Only when he, as a reaction to A's skeptical "mhm", dampens his praise do the others introduce this figure as a bearer of an enjoyment that oneself feels embarrassed by and that at the same time can be held responsible for the failure of the practices to live up to the hopes one just had projected onto them.

The very urge to state that the protest-practice was 'not perfect' because people were 'not there yet' on the side of the activists is another feature that runs all throughout the discussions and interviews and that also points into the direction of the redirection activity and its inherent tensions—the TP activists I interviewed did not give comparable accounts. They of course discussed strategic 'limits' to their movements, but never seemed to be invested in the idea that the movement would be morally obliged to being 'radically different' from the society around it. In other words, 'not being perfect' was nothing that had to be explained or legitimized. The symbolic conclusion[30] of the passage brings this tragic dilemma into an ironic form: The big step, which is in this passage already rather identified with the transformation of the self than with that of society at large, is not only revealed to rather be a lot of little steps, these steps are ultimately leading back to square one.

Interestingly, this tragic element also appears, in a very similar form—again as a joke—in the discussion with OWSG2. After a highly emotional exchange on the issue of racism within OWS, the group reaches the following symbolic conclusion:

1 R: (incomprehensible)
2 L: └ @.@ ┘
3 P: what's that?
4 R: Occupy needs to be occupied.
5 P: yeah, exac-
6 L: └ @.@ ┘
7 P: yeah, @yeah@, occupy Occupy,
8 man.
9 M,L,P,R: @(2)@ (OWSG2, "Occupy occupy")

Again, the dilemma posed by the practice, that is the impossibility of an exodus from the society surrounding the camp, is symbolically 'solved' by repeating the initial gesture. What better symbol is there of an unresolved social deadlock than answering the recognition of a problem with a repetition of the problem-ridden operation, ad infinitum, in "tiny steps in a circle"? It does not come as a surprise, therefore, that many activists experienced the raid of the park and the end of the occupation not only as traumatic, but in some sense also as a relief.

While the corresponding propositions might also be read as ex-post rationalizations of the acceptance of that which is beyond one's power anyhow, the analysis of another focusing metaphor of the discussion with OWSG4 indicates that this is indeed to be explained through the ambivalence inherent in the practices of the occupation itself. Thematically, the passage deals with collaboratively narrating a very peculiar situation in December 2011: The crime series "Law & Order, Special Victims Unit" had set up a film-set to film an OWS-themed episode at Foley Square, not even a mile from where OWS had been forced out of Zuccotti Park a few weeks before. Outraged by what they perceived as a scandalous act of profiting off their movement, a few hundred activists gathered and quickly decided (and this only further affirms the results of the interpretation thus far) to 'occupy' the film set.

The passage reaches its climax with the arrival of the police that forces the activists from the set, resulting in a short but intensely experienced reversal of the roles. After they forced the occupiers out, the police forces were now standing in the film set camp itself, while the 'occupiers' stood in a circle around the camp—just as the police had done numerous times in the 'original' camp in Zuccotti Park:

J: I remember, at some point, the cops,
L: └ and like the security guards ┘ had no idea what to do @.@
A: @.@
J: Well at some point the cops showed up, right, and kicked everybody out? And I remember a, people gathering,
A: └ @(incomprehensible)@ ┘
J: And the cops were in the camp.
L: yeah
J: And Occupiers were outside. And the Occupiers are yelling "what are your demands! get a job!" @.@
L: └ @(5)@ ┘
A: └@(4)@ ┘ it was super therapeutic!
J: └ it was ┘ like "why are you here!" like "what do you want!" "who are your leaders!"
L: └ @(3)@ ┘
A: └ @(2)@ ┘
J: @And the cops were looking at each other@ and I could see some of the cops were trying not to laugh
L, A: └ @(3)@ ┘ (OWSG4: "OSVU")

The relief about throwing all the objections one had been confronted with over the course of the last months back to the police as a stand-in for social authority is obvious. What is "super therapeutic" (13) about this, however, is not simply 'revenge', but the possibility to articulate, in an ironic way, one's own doubts and fears: Especially these objections from the public (and not those that pointed to OWS' supposedly violent and disorderly character, etc.) stuck because they haunted the activists themselves. In this sense, the laughter one seeks on the face of the police is welcomed as a sign of empathy, a recognition of one's inner conflict by the other.

5.2.3 Dealing with the Tension: Direct Action

The orientation frame of OWS is spanned between a negative horizon of a society that does not seem to hold any promise and a positive horizon of a fulfilled life, in which one has the feeling to be in 'resonance' with one's surroundings. This figure gives rise to conflicting behavioral and interpretative orientations: One of them is pointing toward the horizon of a social exodus, the desire to let go of all contradictions and resistances that are thrown into one's way, and to realize in this exodus the very social existence that (implicitly) oriented the biographical trajectory blocked by the crisis. The other is pointing back to the realization that one remains bound to this very context one is revolting against and cannot enact the implicit aims of the protest-practice without fundamentally changing the social context. This change, however, would in turn call for a strategic involvement with this context, which is perceived as always potentially corrupting.[31]

Understanding this basic structure already contributes substantially to the understanding of the movement's practice. Generally, what struck observers was that the "protest", that is, the practice (implicitly and explicitly) oriented by the horizon to fundamentally change society (if one's action should not be simply be "tiny steps, in a circle"), was not enacted in 'productive' ways (which often implicitly seems to be understood as some form of 'lobbying'). This has to be understood from the tension just described—in the following, I will illustrate and develop on this point by showing how the conflicting habitus as it is documented in the discourse of the core constituency of OWS[32] found a temporary relief in a form of practice that OWS' activists themselves called 'Direct Action', which became a very central figure in the movement's discourse on its protest-practice. The exact meaning of this term seems often to be rather elusive, but in general it connotes practices that supposedly do not 'ask' somebody else to do something but instead themselves try to 'achieve' this something directly.

One visible trace of the habitus' predisposition to this specific form of the protest-practice is the absence of what, in social movement research, typically would be called diagnostic framing or, more specifically, the blame attribution aspect of diagnostic framing (Snow et al. 1986), from the discourse of the groups. In the TP, the panorama of the negative horizon seems to be densely populated by all kinds of culprits and villains from different classes and epochs, while for OWS, this scene is almost empty.

There were protests at the home of Mayor Bloomberg and some actors from the financial industry, such as Lloyd Blankfein, but these protests never had more than a few hundred participants.[33] In the discussions, those who are spoken about as opponents or adversaries were usually of secondary character, such as the police, alleged provocateurs, or specific groups in the park, all of them seen as disrupting the protest, not as the actual addressees or adversaries of the protest. If political opponents are mentioned, it is in a distanced and almost disinterested manner.

Furthermore, corresponding to what will be developed further in Chap. 6, the political field as a whole is perceived as sealed and corrupted beyond repair—to the point that it is not even really criticized but merely ignored in the discourse. It is striking that none of my interviewees from OWS even mentions Barack Obama, especially given the fact that the first wave of interviews began only days after his reelection, which was still very topical, not only in interviews with the TP but also in everyday conversations. Corresponding to the 'lack of resonance' which marks the general perception of society by OWS' core constituency, the field of power is perceived as a closed-off external whole without contradictions or fissures to clasp your fingers into, as is documented in the following passage from OWSG4 that concludes a conversation on the failed attempt to occupy a new park on December 17, 2011:

L: Right, it was never going to happen.
J: └ it was just a ┘ symbolic thing.
L: Which is weird, I, I'm
J: Yeah, there is legitimate criticism.
L: └ Symbolic tactics ┘
J: I know.
L: Especially like, at this point in time? Maybe three years ago. They worked.
J: Yeah, I don't know.
L: Yeah. Symbolic tactics don't work so well anymore. (OWSG4, "Symbolic Tactics")

Two things are striking about this passage. First, the temporal index, according to which "symbolic tactics" still worked "three years ago" (8): 2008 is the year in which Obama got elected.[34] The self-evidence with which this point in time is referred to is a strong indicator that the perception of the political field as being sealed and this perception being connected to the strong disappointment with the (lacking) consequences of the election of Obama is sedimented also on the level of the group's interpretative patterns.[35] Second, the very rejection of "symbolic tactics": What was the occupation of Zuccotti Park if not a strong symbolic gesture? Obviously, what is rejected here cannot be the symbolic dimension of political action, since this would contradict most practices that the discussions just euphorically recalled, but the very 'appellative' character of political actions. The discontent or 'critique' implicitly articulated is yet another variant of the dilemma of protesting under circumstances that one perceives as being immune to protest.

The imagined alternative to these appellative forms of protest, implicit in the passage above, was called "Direct Action" in OWS' discourse. Even though this terminology has a rich history, especially in Anarchist political thought, reaching at least back to the "propaganda of the deed" of the late nineteenth century, I would argue that its widespread popularity in OWS has to be understood from the very contradiction described above, as a kind of acting out of the tension between the urge to do something and the perception that the environment is totally unresponsive. Even in the definition of "Direct Action" by one of its most vocal propagandists in OWS, this dimension of 'short-circuiting' the foreclosure of political agency by denying the tangible social reality of this foreclosure, still simmers through:

> Direct action (…) is a matter of proceeding *as one would if* the existing structure of power did not exist. Direct action is, ultimately, the defiant *insistence on acting as if* one is already free. (Graeber 2013, 233, emphasis added)

As a seasoned activist-academic writing an edited book, Graeber is of course more nuanced in the elaboration of the argument than most of my interviewees were—but nevertheless, in a symptomatic way, all his examples and argumentations given to illustrate this very prominent and much quoted definition are clearly contradicting its basic premises: Mahatma Gandhi's salt march, for example, was all but an acting "as if the existing power-structures did not exist". Presumably, if one would be "already free", one would barely walk hundreds of miles for a handful of salt. The very point of this action is a highly publicized small transgression forcing those in power to publicly surrender or over-react, not to act as if they were not there. In that sense, the salt march (and many other allegedly 'pacifist' forms of protest) are staged spectacles for the 'naïve' observer who is supposed to see exactly the image that Graeber presents as the actual nature of the event. Just as the activists in the discussion, he thereby essentializes a basically strategic question to an 'ethos' of political practices that corresponds neatly with the contradiction at the heart of the core constituency's habitus' processing of fundamental socio-political crisis: It allows for staging (for oneself and the others) a form of strategic involvement with the world that itself supposedly remains pure from any corrupting influences of the latter.

OWS' core constituency's orienting frame as it was reconstructed in this sub-chapter is spanned between a positive horizon—a dialogical, resonating relationship to one's social environment and society in general—and a negative horizon which is defined by the absence of such a relationship. The socio-biographical genesis of this orienting figure was traced to the socialization of the aspirants of the new petty bourgeoisie. The three sections of this sub-chapter showed how this basic orienting figure is documented in and explains a number of peculiarities of OWS discourse and practice.

Section 5.2.1 reconstructed the basic orienting frame and showed that the prominence of the positive horizon in the group's discourse on its own practice is to be understood as documenting OWS' protest-practice's character as a *redirection activity*. This practice resonated so strongly with the participants because it met a socially specific need that had remained unfulfilled because of this class-generational unit's blocked biographical trajectory. Section 5.2.2 argued that the practice of OWS as an *impossible exodus* (and the discourse on this practice) document a reoccurring tension between what the actors themselves call *prefiguring*—and in which they are strongly and affectively invested because of its character as a redirection activity—and the feeling that this is 'not it' which is documented in the logic of *protest*, which is also documented in the practice of OWS. Section 5.2.3, finally, argued that the prominence of *Direct Action* in the practice and discourse of OWS has to be understood as a form of 'acting out' of this tension—it is the attempt of a protesting, strategic involvement with an environment which one perceives as deeply corrupted and corrupting.

5.3 The Habitus in Crisis

Two key findings explaining the peculiarities of the protests can be identified in this table. First, the core constituencies of both protests experience their potential for enacting the positive horizons implicated in their habitus as blocked or redirected. This is the practical or actor-centered expression of the deep objective socio-biographic crises that was identified in Chap. 3. It is this objective deadlock that is also documented in the contradictory and conflicting tendencies in their habitus' processing of the crisis and that (to a relevant degree) explains both OWS' 'stubborn' insistence on protest-practices that the activists themselves often saw as unfit to meet their own explicated goals and the TP constituency's seemingly contradictory insistence to be especially 'critical' and a community of 'believers against all odds'. Thus, both mobilizations can be considered crisis-protests in the fullest sense of the term: They not only articulate critique and dissent in a situation of acute social crisis, but they are also themselves *in* crisis, in that the basis from which they could articulate their demands or discontent is itself problematic. Second, however, this shared situation of the crisis of a suspended future is nevertheless experienced and criticized differently—according to the respective group's habitus. The different class-generational units are invested in a very different socio-biographical 'game' (Table 5.1).

The last part of this chapter further investigates the different ways in which the ambivalences and contradictions of these groups' habitus' processing of the experience of crisis were affectable by the respective mobilization's self-presentation. It does so via the interpretation of non-lingual materials as documents of the respective group's habitus, namely, the pictorial artwork used in two propaganda brochures handed to me during my participant observations. These additional interpretations serve two purposes with regard to answering the research question: First, the triangulation of the analysis of different kinds of documents enhances the validity of the types developed. Second, it turned out that the reconstructive interpretation of the habitus documented in the pictures not only validates the results but approaching the habitus from another angle also provides new insights on aspects that otherwise would have remained underdeveloped. Especially important in that regard was the pictures' potential to reveal the simultaneity of contradicting orientations and affective states in a way that the lingual documents were not able to document in the same clarity. Thus, they allowed for a more nuanced understanding of how the habitus of the core constituencies of the two protest mobilizations, as they found themselves in their respective socio-biographical crisis, resonated with the respective protest-practice.

The first picture to be interpreted is the front matter of a 'pocket constitution' that is distributed by TP groups at their rallies and events, and that was handed to me by the participants in the discussion I conducted with TPG1. The second is the poster-sized artistic form given to the 'Declaration of the Occupation of NYC' by the "arts and labor" working group and was widely distributed in New York and beyond. One version was handed to me by one of my interviewees. Before the actual interpretations (Sects. 5.3.2 and 5.3.3), a short excursus sketches out the method of interpretation.

5.3.1 Methods III. The Interpretation of Pictures as Providing Insights into the 'Gestural' Dimension of the Habitus

In the last years, there has been a growing interest in the role of pictures in social movements, summarized, for example, in a collected volume on *Advances in the Visual Analysis of Social Movements* edited by Doerr et al. (2013). Most of the analyses, however, have focused on what could be called the 'communicative', iconographically interpreted dimension of pictures. They are concerned primarily with the question of what messages are conveyed in pictures or how to translate the pictorial vocabulary for the interested but uninformed onlooker. What is of interest for the "iconic" interpretation of pictures which I will propose in the following, is what we could call, referring to the terminology developed in the last chapter, the 'conjunctive' dimension of pictures: That which is not communicated in the picture but *actualized* in the act of communicating itself (Bohnsack 2009, 300).

Propaganda materials sure have a prominent communicative dimension, as they are by definition trying to get a certain 'point' across. To do so, however, they have to rely on a common structure of meaning in which this point will then be considered meaningful and plausible. The paradox that the prophet in some sense always only preaches to those that are already converted, yet still teaches them something that not only affirms what they knew anyhow (cf. Bourdieu and Passeron 1973, 38), can in this sense be understood via this exact dialectic of the conjunctive and the communicative. This is generally true for what is called 'framing' in social movement studies: Every 'frame' has to rely on already existing orienting frames that allow them to connect to the interpretative predispositions of those they aim to reach. This is all the more important for pictorial artwork used in propaganda materials: As I observed many times, posters and flyers handed out at a protest event are mostly accepted or rejected before the explicable, manifest message is even read.

This makes pictures of this kind an excellent starting point for inquiries into the habitus of the respective movement's constituency: What shared structures of experience and interpretation are encapsulated in these pamphlets' pictures that made them a good and promising way of reaching 'those of like mind' and what affective premium or surplus enjoyment can the picture offer those that resonate with it? The analysis of these materials is furthermore a fruitful addition to the analysis of the protocols of group discussions, since it allows to detach the reconstructed structuring principles of the habitus from its 'verbalized' actualizations and to approach the gestural and affective logic of it—after all, the pre-reflexive, mimetic dimension of the processes of socialization and subjectivation that form the habitus is closely linked to the medium of the image (Bohnsack 2009, 298 f.; Bourdieu 1987, 134ff.; cf. Kastl 2004).

The method chosen for this analysis is the so-called iconic interpretation as it was developed in the theoretical framework of the documentary method following mainly the work of Panofsky and Imdahl (Imdahl 1994; Panofsky 1955). This method was explicitly designed for the reconstruction of habitus documented in pictures and is 'by design' compatible with the documentary method that guided the reconstruction of habitus from the protocols of the group discussions and interviews. As I already argued in Sect. 4.2 "Methods II: Habitus Reconstruction and Documentary Method", to lay out the methodological assumptions and practical steps of the reconstruction would take up too much space here and probably still not do justice to the methodology that is lucidly summarized elsewhere.[36] Therefore, as in Sect. 4.2, the following is merely a short summary of some core features chosen to help the reader estimate the nature and scope of the interpretation results that follow.

One key difference between the logic of the picture and that of the spoken or written word is the sequential character of the latter as compared to the simultaneity of everything present(ed) in the picture. As already mentioned, this allows for expressing or documenting the unity of differing, or even contradicting elements that, in language, would have to be expressed as separated at least by the order of their enumeration.[37] Yet, this also is a methodological challenge for the reconstruction, because this reconstruction cannot rely on following a sequential structure in the course of the interpretation, as it is at the core of the documentary method or objective hermeneutics as two prominent techniques for reconstructing the habitus from protocols of spoken interaction. Instead, the reconstruction has to try to unfold the structure as present in the very constellation of the given pictorial representation.

The analysis of the picture which prepares the ground for its interpretation begins with differentiating a number of different levels structuring the process of interpretation: The *planimetric composition* is the way in which the picture as a two-dimensional plane is structured into different parts and/or one structured whole. The *perspective projection* is determining the way in which that which is presented in the picture is implying a certain perspective of the onlooker that is thereby also himself 'put in perspective'. The *scenic arrangement* is the way the actants in the picture are positioned in relation to each other, thereby also implying a certain (distanced or engaged, sympathetic or repelled) perspective of the onlooker and maybe, even more importantly, a distribution of possible points of identification and the gaze through which one is being seen 'from within' the picture.

This last point is, to my knowledge, not developed in the methodological texts of the documentary method on the interpretation of pictures: As, for example, Lacan argued in his Seminar XI, images are not only passive objects of contemplation for the subject but in a sense also 'look back' at it (Lacan 1996, 73–128, esp. 115). This point was also convincingly argued for and laid out by art historian Wolfgang Kemp in his seminal text "Der Betrachter ist im Bild" (Kemp 1985. The title, which translates to "the viewer is in the picture" plays on the double meaning of "im Bilde sein", which in German also means that one is well informed or 'in the know'). Acknowledging this implies a reflexive move that is of high relevance for the question of the political habitus discussed in this chapter, since it implicates that the onlooker is implicated as being seen in a certain social position vis-à-vis the picture in front of him and thereby her-/himself becomes a part of the scenic constellation in the picture. In looking at the object, the subject itself becomes (unconsciously) aware of being a (socially specific) object visible to the world. In other words, the picture is not just a document of the habitus of the social group that uses and consumes it in the sense of its *expression*, but also in the sense of a more or less fitting *context for resonance*. Successful pamphlets and brochures, such as the ones that the pictures interpreted in the following are taken from, in this sense always work as interpellations in the Althusserian sense of the term. They function as gestures that recognize the subject by instituting it

Table 5.1 Orienting frames of the core constituencies of the protest mobilizations

	The Tea Party	*Occupy Wall Str.*
Negative horizon	Collapse of order, loss of status	*Vague*: Loss of perspective, non-resonant environment
Positive horizon	*Vague*: Restoring of the 'right framework'	Fulfilled life, mutual recognition, shaping society
Potential for enactment	*None*, delegating the agency to others	*None*, displaced into redirection or acting out
Practical unfolding	Disappointment without disillusionment, repairing reality	Impossible exodus, redirection activity

in a socially specific form of being implicated in ideology (Althusser 2008, 44–51): In feeling addressed, the subject accepts as binding the structures in and through which it is addressed.

To avoid that the interpreting reconstruction is unnecessarily pre-structured by knowledge that is externally 'imposed' on the picture, which is instead understood as a self-referential system with 'meaning' in its own right, the reconstruction employs a kind of 'ignorance-as-method'. This means, among other things, that only after all the hitherto mentioned dimensions are analyzed is the title or any other kind of 'frame' of the picture included into the analysis. For the sake of readability, however, this is not employed rigorously in the following, where I, for example, from the very beginning presuppose that everyone knows that the man depicted on the brochure is George Washington.

5.3.2 *The 'Constitution of the United States': Interpretation of a TP Brochure*

The picture, which depicts George Washington, standing beside a desk with the constitution of the USA lying on it, and offering a feather to the onlooker who is apparently asked to sign the constitution, is painted in warm ochre colors. The foreground of the picture is occupied by the hand offering the feather, the constitution spread out on the desktop and the inkstand holding two additional feathers. Washington's body and face are positioned in the middle ground of the picture, while the background is, again, the text of the constitution (Fig. 5.1).

The proportions and main axis of the picture convey a conventional, comforting impression: George Washington's body is dividing the picture

Fig. 5.1 National Center for Constitutional Studies "The Constitution of the United States" (2010), cover, emphasis added. Painting by Robert Schöller, design by Bill Norton and Bryan Crockett

at the horizontal golden section and the feather offered to the onlooker at the vertical golden section. Shoulders, eyes, and the corners of the mouth are arranged strictly horizontal, while the nose, chin, collar, and crotch are arranged on one vertical axis. The *perspective projection* of the picture is centered on a horizon that runs horizontally through the (strong) hand holding the feather and the zenith of the body. The brightest elements of the picture, the face and collar, the hand offering the feather, and the shining silver inkstand holding two additional feathers, are arranged along an elliptical arc that accentuates the light shining on the scenery from above the upper-left corner of the picture: The illumination of the depicted scene parallels the most convenient 'reading direction' of it—from the upper-left to the lower-right corner.

Planimetrically, the horizon divides the picture in two. The upper two-thirds of the picture are defined by orthogonal, orderly, and clear lines of Washington's upper body, while the lower third is defined by skewed and intersecting lines, such as the feathers in the inkstand, the slightly wrinkled pages of the constitution, the table, the folds in the frock coat, and the left leg that is slightly stepping out to the side. The feather, which is lifted above this horizon, 'disturbs' this neat separation and directs the attention away from the upper part of the picture, which is centered on Washington's calm gaze, and unto the 'disorder' of the lower part of the picture.

This constellation introduces an ambivalence that permeates the whole *scenic arrangement* of the picture and the onlooker's implication in it: The look on Washington's face, seen in the context of only the upper part of the picture, suggests calmness. The lifted hand offering the feather, however, introduces an authoritative dimension to it—he practically 'commands' the onlooker to sign the papers on the table. In a way it is as if he holds the onlooker accountable for the 'unfinishedness' and disorder documented in the lower part of the picture, an impression that is intensified by the very socially isolated nature of the encounter between Washington and the onlooker: There are no other people present in the picture, and nothing in the gaze of Washington signals that he is looking at more than one person.

The writing in the background of the picture, which is discernible as the same text of the constitution that is put down on the table, dislocates this encounter. Its skewedness toward the picture's perspective projection makes it impossible to see it as a kind of 'wall' or any other kind of object positioned in the same geometric space that the rest of the scene is placed in. This also gives the warm, comforting colors of the picture an uncanny, dream-like quality. Washington, whose legs and left side of the body seem to emerge from the darkness in the lower right corner of the picture, might just as well be fading back into it at any moment. This dislocation corresponds with an irritation about the temporal structure and locale of the encounter between the onlooker and Washington: Does the lifted feather 'bridge' the more than 200 years since the original signing and invite the onlooker to simply 'take part' in it, or did he and the constitution wait for all these years, incomplete, because the onlooker's signature was missing?

The interpretation of the brochure's title affirms this interpretation: The quote by Washington is to be read as a dedication. This dedication evokes pride because it addresses the onlooker as the one to whom this gift is dedicated, it is activating in that it calls the onlooker to be the constitution's 'keeper', and it elevates in a position of power and domination, since one is the only one capable of being its 'keeper' (as opposed to others that are excluded from this 'people'). On the other hand, it also imposes the law unto this very people and thereby submits the onlooker to it, turning him into the passive recipient of the document.[38] The specification that one is the 'only' keeper of the constitution furthermore at least potentially conveys guilt, since it places the responsibility for everything that goes wrong with one whom Washington projected his hopes on.

The ambivalence of the way the scene is depicted in the picture implies an ambivalence in the habitus of those onlookers that it 'speaks'. This ambivalence can be articulated along three dichotomies. (i) *Pride and guilt*: The onlooker is singled out to take part in the historic event of the 'birth' of the USA, yet he is also held responsible for something that apparently went wrong, that is broken or incomplete about the USA, so that the Founding Fathers cannot 'rest in peace'. (ii) *Domination and submission*: While the gesture of the raised feather invites the onlooker to become one of the 'Founding Fathers' of the USA, the gesture is also a forced one, an act of obedience to the very Founding Fathers' authority, embodied in the person of Washington. (iii) *Activation and passivation:* The calm gaze and posture of Washington presents itself as the object of contemplation and passive admiration. The juxtaposition of the gaze and the offered feather implies an urgency to act, to become involved in the scene thus depicted. This activation, however, is of a very peculiar kind, since the documents for signature are presented in a non-negotiable form to the onlooker, almost as a contract or a list at a recruitment office. The act itself is therefore a passivizing 'binding' of the signer. The back of the brochure, on which the recipient is asked to sign a pledge to read and uphold the constitution while "George Washington" as the witness of the recipient's signature has already signed below, fits this interpretation. The image of the recruitment desk might be a good metaphor for the contradictory unity of the couplets enumerated above: In signing the document, the recipient is in fact asked to symbolically 'sign over' her-/himself to the 'Law'.

The habitus that, empirically, finds itself as being addressed by this picture and the brochure is the same habitus that is documented in the group discussions and interviews: The brochure was distributed and read by the very TP groups I recruited my interviewees from. The interpretation shows that this is not coincidental. The dispositional structures documented in the protocols of the discussions and interviews have a lot of affinities with those documented in this picture. Even more importantly, however, the latter in some regards also helps to better understand the former. While all the contradictory couplets enumerated are in some sense discernible in the interviews and discussions, the spoken accounts and propositions emphasized mostly the first, 'heroic' part of the couplets: One was proud to be a hard-working American, someone who masters difficult situations and triumphs over those that are less driven and dedicated and someone who actively takes a stand. The corresponding, shameful part was usually only hinted at or repressed from the accounts: That one also felt guilty and powerless and that one hoped that others take the initiative in enacting the necessary change for all to return to the state of things one nostalgically longs for. Three aspects of the analysis of the TP habitus' processing of the crisis which became more nuanced through the reconstructive analysis of the picture will shortly be discussed before the analysis of the picture from OWS and the following comparison: The affirmation of the 'standing in line' metaphor and its relation to authority, as well as the importance of 'guilt' as an affective dimension.

The metaphor of 'standing in line' while everybody 'cuts in' has been discussed as documenting the experience of a precarious symbolic universe that regulates what is perceived as 'natural differences' in status and rights and that becomes visible or problematic since it is threatened and therefore has to be insisted on. What the analysis of the picture allows us to understand is that the "countries original framework", the "constitution", and the "republic" or simply "the rules" in the discussions and interviews also have to be read as metaphors for this symbolic universe guaranteeing what the TP activists perceive as 'naturally theirs'. In the picture the all-encompassing character of the imaginary encapsulated in these metaphors is documented as the constitution being the very space in which the scene takes place.

What is further documented in the picture is the importance of authority in legitimizing the order to be defended: the paternal figure of George Washington handing the onlooker the feather gives the law to be signed a normative power it would otherwise be lacking. Propositions documenting similar patterns in the discussions and interviews were, for example, expressing outrage at Obama for not mentioning "God" in his oath, because "God" is the only instance that is guaranteeing the "rights of man", the mentioning of the close and warm relationship to authority figures such as teachers and especially fathers to explain what is different about the TP members, but also, in an inverted manner, the countless instances of expressing anger at Obama illegitimately occupying an authoritative position.

The reliance on an external(ized) authority corresponds with the blocked enactment of the positive horizon which was reconstructed from the interviews and discussions above: Since one cannot imagine a feasible strategy for doing anything about the apparent 'wrongs' in the world, one has to rely on strong allies or authorities for reinstating the "line" as the order guaranteeing one's claims to social wealth and recognition. However, the 'uncanniness' of the way the scene is depicted in the picture also points at a dimension of the blocked enactment that was so far not elaborated on: The mentioned repression of the traumatic discovery of having no control over one's economic and social future not only produces a kind of aggressive powerlessness that tries to hold others responsible. It also, and maybe primarily, is accompanied by nagging insecurity and guilt resulting from the fact that one might, in the end, be oneself responsible for one's potential failure. Precisely because one is not willing to let go of the idea that the existing inequality is in the end 'just', it can never be ruled out that one might rightfully be one of those that fail.

What makes the picture an attractive mobilizing document is that it not only documents all these conflicts but also offers redemption from this conflict to those that subject themselves to its affective interpellation: the fantasy of signing up for a higher authority's cause. The scenic arrangement not coincidentally reminds one of an army-recruitment desk: It is highly untypical that Washington is represented as looking straight ahead, usually he is rather looking slightly to the left or the right. The widely known character that looks straight into the face of the observer and points at him is not the founding father, but the more demanding 'Uncle Sam'.[39] The founding father as recruitment officer offers a kind of affective premium or a 'surplus enjoyment' binding the group addressed and constituted by its interpellation. This premium, which makes identifying with the subject addressed by the picture attractive, is a legitimization of one's aggressions. The identification transforms the subject into an instrument of the authorities' will, and the wish to be in front of the line is thereby turned into the rightful insistence on how things 'ought to be'. The same movement resolves one of one's guilt by transforming the inner tension between the idealized self and its empirical failure into an externalized conflict between those that work hard and upright and those that undermine their strivings.

5.3.3 The Declaration of the Occupation of New York City: Interpretation of an OWS Poster

The picture chosen to be analyzed in comparison to the front-cover illustration of the TP's pocket constitution is a poster based on the text of the declaration of the Occupation of NYC, one of the very few 'GA-consented' documents of OWS. It is a more experimental, non-representative artwork, which is why I dedicate a little more space to the description of its formal composition (Fig. 5.2).

The picture is an arrangement of five rectangular blocks of text (of varying font size) that form a square as an outer frame of the picture. Inside this square, a number of 'bubbles'—irregular, round forms—of different sizes, are arranged (mostly) on concentric circles and filled with text (again of varying font size). The bubbles are connected with each other through a multiplicity of lines that follow no clear pattern. In the center of this arrangement is one circle. The group that discussed the picture with me spontaneously associated the arrangement of 'bubbles' with depictions of an atom, an abyss, a vortex, or the Gordian knot.

The picture has, since it does not represent a discernible object, no clear *perspective projection* structuring it. However, the composition of the different non-figural forms creates a similar effect: The framing text-blocks and the outer circle of 'bubbles' are comparable to a foreground of the picture, the middle ground is taken up by the second and third circle of 'bubbles', while the inner circle forms the background of the picture (which, since the text displayed in this bubble is written in larger letters, in some sense also 'jumps' to the foreground). If this is so, then the 'perspective' implied is a central perspective centered on the intersection of the two diagonal axes of the picture.

Planimetrically, the picture is decisively structured by the concentric circles. The shared center of these circles is further accentuated by the fact

Fig. 5.2 "The Declaration of the Occupation of NYC" (2011), drawn by Rachel Schragis, based on text by the Call to Action Working Group of the Zuccotti Park general assembly, edited in Zuccotti Park through a crowd-sourcing process

that it lies at the intersection of the image's axis and that the rotated text in the bubbles surrounding the inner circle is arranged centrifugally (like 'rays' shining from the center) around it. The bubbles forming the concentric circles are arranged slightly irregularly, which causes the eye of the onlooker to err through the picture in search of a starting point. This starting point is then found in the sentence 'all our grievances are interconnected' on top of the picture which is one of the lines that is printed in comparatively big letters. Furthermore, it follows the conventional horizontal direction of reading and is 'carried' by the cross of the two diagonal axes. From there the eye glides along the axis to the center circle and reads 'let these facts be known' and, against the 'gravity' of the concentric circles, then begins to search its way through the different 'bubbles' texts from the outside in, albeit again and again thrown off by the complexity of links between the different bubbles.

The association of the atom is caused by the closed character of the overall form: the bubbles form a whole with no connections to the outside, but plenty of internal interconnections. The first sentence to be read, "all of our grievances are interconnected", can be read as a proposition documenting exactly the same basic structure—it is all one, self-containing object of contemplation. The association with an abyss/vortex on the other hand points to the fact that the very structure of the picture opens the form toward the onlooker. This impression is created by the bubbles getting not only smaller but being arranged closer and closer to each other, the smaller their distance to the center. They also display smaller and smaller writing that in the middle seems, since it is rotated, to be 'stretched', by some gravitating force. In this sense the onlooker can be understood as being her-/himself addressed by the 'our' in the proposition, so (s)he cannot simply contemplate a completed whole of other peoples' grievances, but, through her/his own grievances, is her-/himself also implicated in the picture.

At the bottom of the abyss is the interpellation, "let these facts be known". The bigger font size gives this center, albeit being at the bottom of the abyss or located at the vanishing point of the central perspective, the appearance of 'jumping' to the fore and activating the onlooker absorbed by the picture.[40] Yet this interpellation's command is undermined by the very text it is referring to—as the association of the Gordian knot captures, the seemingly endless different interconnections of 'bubbles' representing grievances and their relation to each other make it impossible to find out what facts the onlooker is supposed to 'let be known'. The sentence on the bottom part of the 'frame', "Let us not be weight down by the complexity of our situation", cannot but seem tragic in this regard, also because the graphic representation of the sentence itself seems to suggest that it is weighed down by the concentric circles as the object representing the complexity of the situation.

The onlooker is therefore positioned in a contradictory position relative to the picture: (S)he is simultaneously assumed to take a contemplative, distanced position (corresponding to the playful, experimental character of the picture) and to be drawn into it; to identify with the gaze implied in the picture and being subjected to it; commanded to 'spread the word' yet also confronted with the impression that all this is too complex to understand anyhow. Just as the front matter of the pocket constitution documented the ambivalence in the habitus of the TP's core constituency, it is not difficult to recognize the contradictory orientations of the habitus in crisis that was described as being torn between the *impossible exodus* and *protest* in the structures unfolded in this picture.

Furthermore, and this occurred to me only after the first systematic reconstruction, the picture's composition can also be seen as mimicking the very practice of the general assembly in the park: a round gathering of people in a rectangular plaza, centered around a speaker, and loosely structured by the repetition waves of the 'human mic'. Analyzing the folded poster as an artifact further nuances the social situation in which the onlooker is implied in the picture: Other than the front matter of the constitution, which offers itself to the 'quick glance', this picture is a large format poster. It therefore does not lend itself to be quickly glanced at on the street or wherever it is passed out, but rather to be unfolded and contemplated, for example, at home or wherever one finds the calm and space for it. In a sense, the picture is a park to take home with you, including the chaos and the loss of orientation that the latter provided.

Just as the habitus of the TP, the habitus of OWS' core constituency as it is documented in this picture is also marked by contradictions, which constantly seem to ask the respective subject to do two things at the same time. This is maybe best illustrated by the reoccurring call to become active and the difficulties and limitations that are erected against becoming active in a transformative sense: Here it is the injunction to 'let these facts be known' while simultaneously systematically obscuring which 'facts' are actually the important ones to 'let be known'. This basic conflict arises from a habitus that finds its accustomed/anticipated fields of practice, and therefore its potential for enacting what is 'right', blocked, and which therefore is in a sense 'haunted' by the more or less diffuse urge to do something that does not exist as a concrete potentiality.

However, this conflict takes a different shape in the case of OWS, as is also discernible by comparing the two pictures. As discussed above, the image of George Washington offers a powerful affective premium to those that let themselves be addressed as the 'Founding Fathers' sons and soldiers: siding with authority and thereby legitimizing one's aggressions and overcoming one's guilt and fear by delegating the responsibility to others.

At the face of it, the picture of the declaration does not seem to offer such a premium but, in an artistic way, merely to display the contradiction.

At a closer look, there is of course a kind of surplus enjoyment offered in exchange for identifying with the subjectivity interpellated by the picture—otherwise, the picture would not have worked as a mobilizing document. This premium's most obvious trace is the very form of the picture as 'art'. Other than the form of the picture of George Washington, which primarily conveys solidity and clarity (which might even heighten its uncanny potential), the picture's form here is experimental and in its juxtaposition of text and form also occasionally ironic: Those who identify with the basic structure of the picture thereby find themselves confirmed in their position as being culturally educated and 'hip'. The basic insecurity of the habitus in crisis, which is so clearly discernible, is not resolved, but processed as a form of a cultural lead vis-à-vis the rest of society: One does not know a way out, but knowing about this itself is insisted on as something that should be rewarded with social recognition. This interpretation also seems to be affirmed by the very character of the picture as an artifact. The poster is, other than the brochure, a large and very visible object not only of contemplation for the onlooker but also as a signature to display objectivized cultural capital. By putting the poster on the wall, one presents oneself as one of those that not only sympathize with but also 'get' OWS in all its irony and complicatedness.

5.3.4 Summary: The Third-Cut Theory of the Crisis-Protests

In his essay on *Sociology and Psychology*, Adorno (1973b) argues that attempts to conceptualize these two disciplines as one unitary scientific project that will one day merge into one discipline would be doomed to fail. Not so much, other than his contemporary Parsons had argued, because of some contingent lack of scientific knowledge that is not yet able to close the gap between the understanding of the moving forces of the individual and those of society, but because this gap itself is a necessary element of capitalist societies: The logic of capitalism has 'emancipated' itself from the desires of the individual subjects to a degree that makes it impossible to understand its development as the emergent product of interacting individuals and their desires.

He also emphasizes that this must and cannot be understood through the ideological contrasting of "rational" society and the "irrational" psyche. Instead, he points to the fact that the two spheres, albeit following their own, contradicting logics, are complexly mediated and mutually dependent. Not only would it be questionable if the economic rationality of the bourgeois subject's behavior can in fact be called rational given the sacrifices and abstinences it implies. For its functioning, it also depends on psychological mechanisms that would be considered irrational from the standpoint of the economic rationality that is referred to in the ex-post rationalization of this behavior.

In much the same way, the theory-of-practice approach of this book aims to capture the protests as the result of the complex mediations between the logics of the development of social space before and during the Great Recession, which was to an important degree driven by the crisis dynamics of the finance-dominated regime of accumulation, the long-term shifts in the morphology of social space, and the different subjectivities with their socially specific perceptive and behavioral predispositions grounded in their lived experiences that shaped their affectability by these developments. In this complex of mutual dependency and mediation underlying the practices, the habitus is not a residual category, explaining the 'subjective', 'irrational' aspect of the protests as measured against the 'rational' behavior the 'objective' circumstances would have required instead. Rather, it points to the immanent logic and rationality of the specific discontent and interests as they are enacted in protests as a social practice of specific class-generational units.

The reconstruction of the habitus in this sense is the central element for the understanding of OWS and the TP as crisis protests. Deciphering the structures of the subjects' experiencing of the crisis and their articulation of discontent as protest showed that these protests are not only to be understood as responding to crisis dynamics of society at large but also as symptoms of the subjective processing of the crisis, which is, however, itself socio-genetically rooted in the subject's trajectory through social space. The explosive growth of the protests from this perspective is not only to be understood via socio-political polarization and the contradicting 'class interests' that accompanied the escalation of the economic crisis in the USA. They are also to be understood via the resonance of the protest-practice with the way in which the habitus as the pre-reflexive 'class ethos' of the core constituencies predisposed them to react to the crisis.

The TP's strong criticism of the Obama administration (often with conspiratorial undertones) which was accompanied by demonstrative affirmations of the political and economic system of the USA, resonated with the *disappointment without disillusionment* with which the older classical petty bourgeoisie tended to react to the crisis. The critique brought forward by the TP allowed for the rationalization (and also the acting out) of the fear and aggression that was evoked by the eclipsing of their economic horizon while at the same time reaffirming this group's claims to social status and wealth. The desire to reaffirm the precarious socio-symbolic universe—the "eroding country" or the "line" in which everyone "cuts in"—an endeavor which I called *repairing reality*, also helps to explain the willingness of this group, despite all its rebellious rhetoric, to align with authority figures, be it symbolic ones like the "founding fathers" or "God" or be it the apparatus of the Republican Party. This in turn helps to explain why the TP was far less hesitant to directly connect to conflicts within and to get directly involved with official electoral politics than OWS. When the higher authorities however failed to deliver on the hopes that were projected onto them, this euphoria quickly tilted back first into aggression and then into resignation.

OWS' political practices were so attractive to the young new petty bourgeoisie because they allowed them to act out the social libido associated with their hitherto anticipated social role that was foreclosed by the economic crisis and the long-term development of social space. The dialogical and caring practices of OWS provided a form of social resonance that they missed in their everyday surroundings. The accounts of those active in OWS however also document that this *redirection activity*, even though it was perceived as rewarding and exciting, was nevertheless clearly experienced as '*not-quite-it*'. As a result, the practice of OWS was shaped by two contradicting orientations of its core constituency's habitus: on the one hand, the wish to live the social role one aspired and, on the other hand, to voice one's discontent with the difficulties perceived as being thrown in one's way. Referring to the vocabulary used by the protesters themselves, I called these orientations *prefigurative politics* and *protest*.

The resulting tension left its mark on the tactics and practices chosen by OWS' participants and played an important role in "*Direct Action*" becoming such a central metaphor in the protesters' discourse on their practices. From this perspective, the often 'ironic' and 'original' style of the protest's slogans and aesthetics should also be read as affirming the protesters' cultural capital as their most important marker of social status. While the TP activists sometimes even seemed to be proud to be believers even if that means to explicitly disregard empirical facts, the Occupiers present themselves as disillusioned and enlightened—they seem to take pride in the fact that they "awoke in a sweat from the American Dream".

The understanding of the socio-genesis of the prominence of 'prefigurative practices' as rooted in the ethos of the aspiring new petty bourgeoisie and the reconstruction of the tension between prefiguration and protest as springing from the habitual patterning of an experienced situation of crisis allows one to better socially and historically contextualize the peculiarity of the prefigurative practices of OWS that some academic observers have highlighted. Ingolfur Blühdorn, from a system theory-informed perspective, categorizes OWS as the latest blossom of a development that already permeated the older 'new social movements' (Blair Taylor, albeit arguing from a critical theory rather than from a system theory perspective, comes to a very similar conclusion). As practices of 'simulative democracy', they allow to practically satisfy the need of the late modern subjects for radically democratic practices in the context of a society whose degree of functional differentiation and structural complexity makes actual democratic politics impossible (Blühdorn 2006, 2013, 2014; Taylor 2013).

This concept of simulative democracy nicely captures the character of these 'prefigurative' practices as redirection activities that the reconstruction of OWS' core constituency's habitually patterned relation to the protest-practice also pointed. The results of my habitus reconstruction can add two points to this understanding. First, the socio-spatial locality from which this "problem-solving instance"[41] emerges: It is the new petty bourgeoisie, whose expansion as a class has accompanied the long arc of the development of the new social movements since the 1960s, whose class ethos reverberates with these forms of practices.[42]

Second, the reconstruction supports a more dialectical understanding of the development thus described. Both Blühdorn and Taylor emphasize that Occupy's heavy fixation on direct-democratic forms marks a new high point of the development toward an ever-higher importance of these practices for social movements. My reading of OWS' core constituency's high affective investment in this form of practices suggests that the increasing importance of this form of practices of protest points to the crisis of the very class position in which the form itself is habitually rooted: It becomes so important exactly because it increasingly becomes unfeasible as a form of other everyday practices. The discontent that results from this impossibility in tendency pushes the practice beyond prefiguring and toward the articulation of a more systemic critique as protest.

Indeed, as other observers have highlighted, questions of the political economy and material redistribution, which had lost prominence in the discourse of the new social movements, regained importance in OWS

(Langman 2013). The reconstruction of the conflict between 'prefiguration and protest' indicates that one should interpret both—the high importance of direct-democratic forms of practice within the protests itself and the new prominence of questions of political economy—as being rooted in the socio-biographical crisis which OWS' core constituency is experiencing. In that light one would understand OWS' position in the development of the new social movements as more ambivalent than the reasoning of the mentioned authors would lead one to expect: It can be seen as the most consequential realization of the ethos implicit in many of the new social movements, but this also points to social dynamics that could define it as a turning point in this development.

However, the protest-practice is still not sufficiently explained by referring to the habitus as a class specific ethos on the one hand (as it was reconstructed in these last two chapters) and the development of the respective national economy and the classes' being-exposed-to these developments on the other hand (as it was described in the second and third chapters). What is still missing is the interplay between these predispositions and experiences with the socially patterned environments in which the practices unfolded. This is why the following chapter will turn toward the social fields as the socially patterned 'playing fields' in which the social meaning of the strategies and investments of the protests developed.

Notes

1. This follows the trend in the practice of the Documentary Method to shift away from single-case descriptions and toward comparative typologies in order to better emphasize the nature of its research object (the habitus) as being objectively differentiable from its realization in a concrete practice (Bohnsack 2010, 141).
2. This grammar of "reality" and "the world" is systematically developed in Boltanski (2010).
3. For the concept of contingent necessity, see Jessop (1982, 212–19).
4. For the more thorough interpretation of this conclusion in the context of the whole focusing metaphor, see "Appendix 3: Exemplary Interpretation of a Focusing Metaphor: TPG2 "Standing in Line"".
5. This sequence is followed by a break, after which another participant turns to the interviewer and asks for another question, while the rest of the group chuckles, signaling that they perceived the rising emotional density of this passage as having gotten a little 'out of control', and that the sequence also marks the thematic exhaustion of the passage, to which there is nothing more to add.

6. Both forms of rationalization can be read as variations of the avoidance of a repressed experience, namely, that of either powerlessness or moral insecurity that would otherwise be evoked by the fact that one did not act for a long time, even though the problems had de facto already surfaced: The 'opening of the eye' proposition negates that one could have even wanted to act earlier (because one was still 'asleep'), the 'enough is enough' proposition transforms the passive endurance of what is perceived as injustice into a claim to moral superiority, since one had stood by because one was, until the breaking point, above the petty deviances of the others. That both propositions are offered by the same speakers is reminiscent of the famous "Kettle-Logic" that Freud presents as typical of the logic of dreams and jokes. The apparent contradiction in simultaneously arguing that one did not borrow a kettle, that the kettle was already broken when borrowed, and that one did return it in fine shape points to the suppressed true experience: That one has broken the kettle (Freud 1970, 191). In the same fashion, insisting on the 'opening of the eye' and simultaneously declaring that 'enough is enough' points to the fact that the emergence of the TP was a more than welcome opportunity to act out aggression that was repressed before. The affective coupling of guilt and aggression that is reconstructed in the analysis of the cover of the TP brochure (Sect. 5.3.2) points to the same tension in the affective processing of the experiences of the TP's core constituency.
7. This condensation of the basic affective structure of the experience is of course a causal hypothesis on the affective genesis of their conflict that would most likely be disagreed with by the TPers themselves, since they, as was discussed with regard to the conspiratorial mode of interpretation, deem themselves especially critical and 'aware', and thereby without illusions. However, as was also already touched upon, at the same time, they often also present themselves as a community of 'believers against all odds'. In fact, the two self-perceptions sometimes seem to merge or oscillate, as in the case of Obama's citizenship, which is 'critically' questioned, but at the same time 'believed' to not be real if the evidence seems to render the questioning unreasonable.
8. The concept of the scenic as it is implied in this interpretation was developed by the critical psychoanalyst Alfred Lorenzer: In his meta-theory of psychoanalysis, he develops the idea that the patient in his discourse unfolds certain scenic drafts and interaction forms, which, via their affective and interpretational structures, reveal his phantasies and experienced social relations as well as their relation to the traumatic scene that gave rise to them. In a similar vein, the metaphors chosen by the discussants and interviewees display an affective and interpretative logic that is revealing their experience of the 'scene' of the foreclosure crisis, while this experience

itself is absent from the level of explicit communication (Lorenzer (1972, esp. 104–160); for an English introduction into the theory of Lorenzer and the depth-hemeneutic method, see Bereswill et al. 2010; Olesen and Weber 2012).

9. On the socio-psychological consequences of the 'foreclosure' of this object of desire, especially the ensuing rage, see Andrews (2014). However, it is worth noting once more that the TP activists I interviewed did *not* lose their homes, in contrast to the people whose experiences Andrews is describing, but only the economic value attached to it.
10. For the French case, Bourdieu and his team have argued that the suppressed feeling of being duped is widespread among petty bourgeois homeowners, even in the absence of an escalating foreclosure crisis, and might partially explain the resentment and anger toward those they deem 'irresponsible' (1998). Michael J. Thompson (2012) has even suggested that the lived environment of the US-American suburb might explain the psychogenesis of a mindset that he holds (partially) responsible for the rise of the TP. Even though the last argument is not implausible, it is hard to see how it can be checked empirically, especially since many of the OWS activists I interviewed were raised in a suburban environment as well, and many TP activists only moved to suburban environments when they were grown up.
11. "Keying" is a term borrowed from Goffman's frame analysis, and designates the process through which something with an apparently clear meaning, via reframing, is turned into something that the participants treat as something completely different. An example being 'fights' that are assumed to be 'fun' when they are keyed as part of a 'game' (Goffman 1974, 40–82). As Bourdieu pointed out in his analysis of Martin Heidegger's rhetoric, one should bear in mind that keyings often function as negations in a psychoanalytical sense: They allow one to simultaneously say and not say something, and thereby, for example, give in to one's aggressions, yet not in a way that can be socially sanctioned without disputable interpretations—'this is not what I said' being the reply that a critique will often get, even though it is perfectly clear that this is what the speaker 'meant' (Bourdieu 1988; Freud 1975. For a very similar form of negation of racist projections, see: Adorno 1973a, 127 f.).
12. Boltanski himself points to the uncanny similarity between the figure of the "Arab" in contemporary islamophobic discourse to that of the "Jew" in early twentieth century conspiracy theories and literature (Boltanski 2013, 263).
13. During my visits to the TP groups that form the basis for this analysis, anecdotes of more or less open racism that aimed at degrading Obama were, however, rather frequent—for example, one of the leaders of a Tea

Party group called Obama "Chris Christie's boy" in a public meeting in which I participated.

14. This book was written by the anti-communist agitator Cleon Skousen in 1981. It advertised the right-wing extremist John Birch Society and proclaimed that the US constitution was based on natural law, as well as that the founding fathers never had the intention of separating church and state. The popularity of this book, which was recommended to me by some TP'ers, had increased enormously after Glenn Beck had advertised it on his show (Skousen 2009; Zernike 2010).
15. At these instances, the conspiratorial interpretations seem to function analogously to what Boltanski describes as the logic of the circulation of 'fables' (as opposed to narrations), where pleasure is drawn from enriching the story with more and more paradoxes and ornaments, that nevertheless are symbolically coherent (Boltanski 2013, 397 f.).
16. Not only are they numerous, but also thematically diverse with regard to their explicit content. While the topic of school and school sports is the most common metaphoric, the activists discuss the problem of 'access to college' by the less talented and the access to housing by the less wealthy in pretty much the same form: The 'elites' erase differences and ignite a 'false sense of entitlement' in the poor to ultimately undermine the very institutions that guarantee the solidity of reality.
17. In an interesting switch of perspective, Jeffrey Prager suggests that a powerful social dynamic in US-American Racism is its capacity to *legitimize* social inequality, thereby affectively stabilizing one's affective relation to conditions that would be perceived as revolting if this protective veil was lifted, which effectively means that people cling to their racism because it renders social inequality more bearable (Prager 2014).
18. Two other common elements of most elaborations on the 'agenda' supposedly behind the current social developments, the supposed erosion of national sovereignty and the use of environmental policies to further plans for a 'totalitarian' society, were also mentioned frequently, but never gained the status of focusing metaphors in the discourse. The most plausible interpretation of this is that these elements emerged from the ex-post rationalization of the perceived conspiracy. This is supported by the fact that these themes are cornerstones of the conspiracy theory according to which the UN's "Agenda 21" is a secret plot to bring down the USA. This theory is propagated by the John Birch Society (JBS), among others. The journal and the leaflets of the JBS were often to be found in the meeting spaces of the TP groups I visited.
19. A feature of the TP's discourse that points in that very same direction is their frequent references to the 'Founding Fathers' as a legitimizing authority: One of my discussion partners, for example, wore a T-shirt with

the Thomas Jefferson quote "a little rebellion now and then is a good thing" printed on it (TP_28.11.2012), which seemed to be popular with other TP activists as well. In the light of the interpretation above, one could read this as the 'father's' permission to rebel.

20. Occasionally, this figure was also deployed vis-a-vis the Democratic Party: The rare members of this party active in the TP (I spoke to none, but they were frequently mentioned), or one's own parents (of whom nobody ever spoke but in the highest praise) if they had been Democrats, were always portrayed as being "true Democrats" as opposed to the "Democrats of today".
21. The 'utopian question' at the end of the interviews, which was a tool that I 'inherited' from a research project of the Institute for Democracy Research in Göttingen, was mostly dropped when my methodological framework became more and more geared toward systematic habitus reconstruction. Its analytical value should not be overstated, since it confronts the interviewees with contra-factual scenarios not all of them might be equally routinized in addressing. It is, however, noteworthy that the OWS participants that were confronted with this question, other than the TP activists, gave answers that explicitly acknowledged their own utopian character.
22. The specific discourse-oriented habitus of OWS' core constituency with its insistence on constantly negotiating difference made it difficult for me to understand that, in fact, a common orienting figure is lying behind this very display of disagreement. Most probably understanding this was made even more difficult by the relative closeness of the generational and class background between the core constituency of OWS and me and the participants in the group that helped me to interpret the results, who were all PhD-candidates from the social sciences and cultural studies.
23. One might object that this may well be due to the fact that the interviewees from OWS sensed a greater class-generational closeness to the interviewer and therefore left their 'grievances' more implicit since they did not find it necessary to explicate them. However, the very formulaic structure of the propositions that do explicate their discontent, such as the "political economy of capitalism" above, indicate that the interpretation of the affective detachment is valid, even if it is not the only factor explaining this discursive peculiarity.
24. The self-critical dimension of this image is enforced by the fact that R in other passages signals that he is considering himself a part of exactly the milieu he is ridiculing here.
25. Amy_OWS: "Square full of soulmates", p. 188.
26. With one exception: Patricia told a very similar story about her meeting the TP in TPG2 and in the biographical follow-up interview I conducted with her. In an article reflecting the very first analyses of my empirical

material, which had started exactly with this discussion, I considered it a trait common to both movements (cf. Kumkar 2014). However, this was proven wrong by the analysis of other TP discussions and interviews that never showed something comparable. Closer analysis of the discussion of TPG2 and especially of the autobiographical follow-up interview revealed that Patricia is an exception to the general TP demographics: she comes from a family rooted in a very different socio-political milieu she now felt increasingly alienated from as a result of her social upward mobility from a working-class background to an administrative petty bourgeois life—an alienation that mirrors what was felt by many OWS activists with regard to "society" in general.

27. It is worth noting that the 'radical' position is called the same independent of the speaker, and is treated as the 'gold standard' of OWS even by its opponents, which means that deviations from this standard have to be legitimized, for example, by referencing a public that might not be 'there yet'. This observation further supports the thesis that the core constituency of OWS in fact has a leading role with regard to the form and content of the protest-practice, which caters to their specific habitual orientations and dilemmas.
28. As the philosopher Robert Pfaller pointed out, the trouble with avoiding terms with pejorative connotations for the noble aim of sparing those the insult who are already harmed by stigma or ridicule in society—he himself is mainly concerned with the terms "perversion" and "superstition"—is the difficulty to systematically deal with the ambiguous stance these very subjects have toward the practices connoted by these terms. What he suggests, therefore, is a shift away from any 'material' or 'substantive' definition of these terms, which is based on accepting social stigma as grounded in the assumed nature of the designated object (i.e., homosexual desire is perverted, since it is not the 'natural' sexual desire; believing in horoscopes is superstitious because it is neither 'proper' scientific nor religious). Instead, he suggests a 'topical' or 'relational' definition that is based upon the actors' own relation to the praxis or phenomenon thus designated (homosexual desire might be perceived and lived as perverted and subjects might derive pleasure and pain from this, which is of course not in any sense 'external' to the desire itself; someone wants to, or even 'must' read her or his horoscope, even though she or he might 'know it's stupid') (cf. Robert Pfaller 2002, esp. 164–170).
29. Max was chosen as an example again to underline that these propositions were made by the very same people that also were the ones so euphoric about the practice of the occupation, and thus documents an actual ambivalence toward the practice, not just two diverging points of view. Very similar statements regarding the increasing professionalization of tasks,

departmentalization of space etc. were also made by the others belonging to the core constituency.

30. In her theory of conversation analysis as Documentary Method, Przyborski differentiates between two kinds of conclusions, "real" and "ritualistic". The former thematically conclude a passage (such as M's description what a TP' activist is "in a nutshell" in TPG2, "Standing in Line"), while the latter conclude a conflict between different and opposing orienting frames, for example by changing the topic or suggesting a kind of 'meta-framing' (Przyborski 2004, esp. 74–77). The conclusion cited above, however, points to another possibility, that is, a dilemma or blockade inherent to the habitus itself rather than between two habitus: It's not A's and L's orienting frames that are in conflict with each other, but both their orienting frames are structured by the same conflict. I labelled the conclusion that corresponds with this kind of tension 'symbolic'. Much like the myth in Levi-Strauss´ theory, the function of these conclusions is not to suppress/postpone the conflict (which would be the meta-function of ritualistic conclusions) but to render it 'speakable' (cf. Lévi-Strauss 1977, 226–54).
31. One incident that can serve as a pointed example of this refusal is the rejection of monetary support from "Ben and Jerry's" by OWS activists in 2012, as described in an article in the Rolling Stone—not because the rejection of the support is politically irrational, but because its rationalization clearly documents the moral-affective repulsion by the activists, and their fear of being 'corrupted' (Binelli 2012).
32. It is interesting to note that the two widely quoted but atypical sub-groups of OWS that engage in classical lobbying-practices, namely, "Occupy the SEC" and "Alternative Banking", are comprised largely of activists that are from a different socio-biographical background. Many of them work in academia, or are organizers or advisers of unions. Ann_OWS, another activist of OWS I spoke to that was highly critical about their abstinence from institutionalized politics, also works in academia and is the board member of an important leftist discussion platform in New York City.
33. Some have wondered if OWS' concentration on "Wall Street" as the symbolic target without a broader, more nuanced critique of capitalism does not leave broad openings to structurally Anti-Semitic imaginaries of parasites plaguing an otherwise healthy social body. However, while especially at the beginning, groups from the extreme right tried to use this motive to connect to the movement, these attempts were ultimately futile (cf. Sunshine 2014; Ogman 2013; Taylor 2013; Arnold 2012). I would argue that this is due to the fact (among other things) that the "Bank-Blaming" was in fact not a frame that connected to the habitus of the people involved in the movement, but mostly a more or less contingent secondary rationalization of the fact that one did not know whom to blame. This might also

explain why the only protest events I witnessed that targeted an individual banker as a 'culprit' ended up rather small and barely attracted any activists I reencountered at other protest events.

34. The alternative interpretation according to which she would refer to three years before the interview was conducted can be ruled out since this would be the year 2011 itself, for which she just articulates her criticism of symbolic tactics.
35. In fact, the very subtleness of the link is what makes it especially strong—disappointment with Obama almost became a Cliché in explanations of OWS. The way in which it is only implicitly brought up, however, indicates that it indeed corresponds with conjunctive experiences shared by OWS' core constituency, much as it is with the implicit omnipresence of the housing crisis in the case of the TP. The using of the time reference of the original action rather than that of the 'now' of the interview indicates that, albeit the proposition has the form of an argument, it still is closely connected to the conjunctive experience of the collective praxis of OWS.
36. The following summary is based on Bohnsack (2009, 2010), Przyborski and Slunecko (2012).
37. In "The Order of Things" Foucault highlights that this difference arises as an epistemological problem at a certain historical point in time and sums it up in referring to a quote by de Condillac "to my gaze 'the brightness is within the rose'; in my discourse, I cannot avoid it coming either before or after it." Interestingly, Foucault opens this book with the analysis of an image that, in many respects, resembles the method suggested by Bohnsack (Foucault 1994, 82; Bohnsack 2009, 305).
38. Other, more classical depictions of the signing of the constitution are showing the signers and framers of the constitution as a group. A scenery like this could, in contrast to that presented in this image, be read as an invite to take part in the 'making' of the constitution, and not just submitting to it.
39. I owe this insight to my friend Holger Kuhn.
40. This gives the image of the abyss a certain affinity with that of an eye—which curiously did not come up as an association in the analysis group—and which brings to the mind one of Friedrich Nietzsche's aphorisms: "And when you stare for a long time into an abyss, the abyss stares back into you." (Nietzsche 2002, 69)
41. For the concept of "life-forms" as systems of inert and habitualized practices functioning as "instances of problem-solving", see Jaeggi (2014, esp. 200–260).
42. This perspective on the new social movements in some sense can be read as an empirical-reconstructive validation and class-generational nuancing of the "New Class" hypothesis in social movement research (Rose 1997; Kriesi 1989).

Bibliography

Adorno, Theodor W. 1973a. *Studien zum autoritären Charakter*. Frankfurt am Main: Suhrkamp.

———. 1973b. Zum Verhältnis von Soziologie und Psychologie. In *Aufsätze zur Gesellschaftstheorie und Methodologie*, 7–54. Frankfurt am Main: Suhrkamp.

Althusser, Louis. 2008. Ideology and Ideological State Apparatuses (Notes Towards an Investigation). In *On Ideology*, 1–60. London/New York: Verso.

Andrews, John. 2014. Foreclosure from Freud to Fannie Mae. In *The Unhappy Divorce of Sociology and Psychoanalysis: Diverse Perspectives on the Psychosocial*, ed. Lynn Chancer and John Andrews, 269–283. Basingstoke/New York: Palgrave Macmillan.

Appel, Hannah Chadeayne. 2011a. The People's Microphone. *Social Text*. https://socialtextjournal.org/dispatches_from_an_occupation_the_peoples_microphone/. Accessed 30 Oct 2017.

———. 2011b. The Ritual of General Assembly and the Bureaucracies of Anarchy. https://socialtextjournal.org/the_rituals_of_general_assembly_and_the_bureaucracies_of_anarchy/. Accessed 30 Oct 2017.

Arnold, Sina. 2012. 'Bad for the Jews'? Antisemitismus und die 'Occupy'-Bewegung in den USA. In *Jahrbuch für Antisemitismusforschung 21*, ed. Stefanie Schüler-Springorum, 370–391. Berlin: Metropol.

Bereswill, Mechthild, Christine Morgenroth, and Peter Redman. 2010. Alfred Lorenzer and the Depth-Hermeneutic Method. *Psychoanalysis, Culture & Society* 15 (3): 221–250.

Binelli, Mark. 2012. The Battle for the Soul of Occupy Wall Street. *Rolling Stone*, June 21. http://www.rollingstone.com/politics/news/the-battle-for-the-soul-of-occupy-wall-street-20120621. Accessed 30 Oct 2017.

Blühdorn, Ingolfur. 2006. Self-Experience in the Theme Park of Radical Action? Social Movements and Political Articulation in the Late-Modern Condition. *European Journal of Social Theory* 9 (1): 23–42.

———. 2013. *Simulative Demokratie: Neue Politik nach der postdemokratischen Wende*. Berlin: Suhrkamp.

———. 2014. A Massive Escalation of Truly Disruptive Action...? Bürger Protest und Nachhaltigkeit in der postdemokratischen Konstellation. *Forschungsjournal Neue Soziale Bewegungen* 2014 (1): 27–37.

Bohnsack, Ralf. 2009. The Interpretation of Pictures and the Documentary Method. *Historical Social Research/Historische Sozialforschung* 34 (2): 296–321.

———. 2010. *Rekonstruktive Sozialforschung*. Opladen/Farmington Hills: Barbara Budrich.

Boltanski, Luc. 2010. *Soziologie und Sozialkritik: Frankfurter Adorno-Vorlesungen 2008*. Berlin: Suhrkamp.

———. 2013. *Rätsel und Komplotte: Kriminalliteratur, Paranoia, moderne Gesellschaft*. Berlin: Suhrkamp.

Bourdieu, Pierre. 1987. *Sozialer Sinn: Kritik der theoretischen Vernunft*. Frankfurt am Main: Suhrkamp.

———. 1988. *Die politische Ontologie Martin Heideggers*. Frankfurt am Main: Suhrkamp.

———. 1998. *Der Einzige und sein Eigenheim*. Hamburg: VSA.

Bourdieu, Pierre, and Jean-Claude Passeron. 1973. *Grundlagen einer Theorie der symbolischen Gewalt*. Frankfurt am Main: Suhrkamp.

Claussen, Detlev. 1991. Angst vor dem Anderen. Über den Zusammenhang und Unterschied von Antisemitismus und Fremdenhaß. Evangelische Akademie Arnoldshain. http://www.comlink.de/cl-hh/m.blumentritt/agr60s.htm. Accessed 30 Oct 2017.

Doerr, Nicole, Alice Mattoni, and Simon Teune, eds. 2013. *Advances in the Visual Analysis of Social Movements*. Bradford: Emerald.

Foucault, Michel. 1994. *The Order of Things: An Archaeology of Human Sciences*. New York: Vintage.

Freud, Sigmund. 1970. Der Witz und seine Beziehung zum Unbewussten. In *Psychologische Schriften*, 9–219. Frankfurt am Main: S. Fischer.

———. 1973a. Psychoanalytische Bemerkungen über einen autobiographisch beschriebenen Fall von Paranoia (Dementia Paranoides). In *Zwang, Paranoia und Perversion*, 135–203. Frankfurt am Main: S. Fischer.

———. 1973b. Zwangshandlung und Religionsausübung. In *Zwang, Paranoia und Perversion*, 11–21. Frankfurt am Main: S. Fischer.

———. 1975. Die Verneinung. In *Psychologie des Unbewußten*, 371–377. Frankfurt am Main: S. Fischer.

Goffman, Erving. 1974. *Frame Analysis: An Essay on the Organization of Experience*. Boston: Harvard University Press.

Graeber, David. 2013. *The Democracy Project: A History, a Crisis, a Movement*. New York: Spiegel and Grau.

Hofstadter, Richard. 2008. *The Paranoid Style in American Politics*. New York: Vintage.

Imdahl, Max. 1994. Ikonik: Bilder und ihre Anschauung. In *Was ist ein Bild?* ed. Gottfried Boehm, 300–324. München: Wilhelm Fink Verlag.

Jaeggi, Rahel. 2014. *Kritik von Lebensformen*. Berlin: Suhrkamp.

Jessop, Bob. 1982. *The Capitalist State. Marxist Theories and Methods*. Oxford: Martin Robertson.

Kastl, Jörg Michael. 2004. Habitus als non-deklaratives Gedächtnis: Zur Relevanz der neuropsychologischen Amnesieforschung für die Soziologie. *Sozialer Sinn. Zeitschrift für hermeneutische Sozialforschung* 2004 (2): 195–226.

Kemp, Wolfgang. 1985. *Der Betrachter ist im Bild: Kunstwissenschaft und Rezeptionsästhetik*. Köln: DuMont.

Kriesi, Hanspeter. 1989. New Social Movements and the New Class in the Netherlands. *American Journal of Sociology* 94 (5): 1078–1116.

Kumkar, Nils C. 2014. Events of Emancipation and Spectacles of Discontent. How the Tea Party and Occupy Wall Street 'happened'. In *Protests as Events. Politics, Activism and Leisure*, ed. R. Ian Lamond and Karl Spracklen, 211–231. London/New York: Rowman & Littlefield.

Lacan, Jaques. 1996. *Die vier Grundbegriffe der Psychoanalyse.* Weinheim: Quadriga.

Langman, Lauren. 2013. Occupy: A New New Social Movement. *Current Sociology* 61 (4): 510–524.

Lévi-Strauss, Claude. 1977. *Strukturale Anthropologie I.* Frankfurt am Main: Suhrkamp.

Lorenzer, Alfred. 1972. *Sprachzerstörung und Rekonstruktion: Vorarbeiten zu einer Metatheorie der Psychoanalyse.* Frankfurt am Main: Suhrkamp.

Marx, Karl. 1969. *Das Kapital 1. MEW 23.* Berlin: Dietz.

Milkman, Ruth, Stephanie Luce, and Penny Lewis. 2013. *Changing the Subject: A Bottom-Up Account of Occupy Wall Street in New York City.* New York: Joseph S. Murphy Institute for Worker Education and Labor Studies. https://www.documentcloud.org/documents/562862-changing-the-subject-2.html. Accessed 30 Oct 2017.

Nietzsche, Friedrich. 2002. *Beyond Good and Evil: Prelude to a Philosophy of the Future.* Cambridge: Cambridge University Press.

Ogman, Robert. 2013. After the Evictions: The U.S. Occupy Movement Struggling at the Front Lines of the Crisis. *Socialistproject.ca*, November 6. http://www.socialistproject.ca/bullet/895.php. Accessed 30 Oct 2017.

Olesen, Henning Salling, and Kirsten Weber. 2012. Socialization, Language, and Scenic Understanding. Alfred Lorenzer's Contribution to a Psycho-Societal Methodology. *Forum Qualitative Sozialforschung/Forum: Qualitative Social Research* 13 (3). http://www.qualitative-research.net/index.php/fqs/article/view/1906

Panofsky, Erwin. 1955. *Meaning in the Visual Arts: Papers in and on Art History.* New York: Doubleday Anchor Books.

Pfaller, Robert. 2002. *Die Illusionen der anderen: Über das Lustprinzip in der Kultur.* Frankfurt am Main: Suhrkamp.

Poletta, Francesca. 2006. *It Was Like a Fever. Storytelling in Protest and Politics.* Chicago/London: The University of Chicago Press.

Prager, Jeffrey. 2014. Melancholia and the Racial Order: A Psychosocial Analysis of America's Enduring Racism. In *The Unhappy Divorce of Sociology and Psychoanalysis: Diverse Perspectives on the Psychosocial*, ed. Lynn Chancer and John Andrews, 284–316. Basingstoke/New York: Palgrave Macmillan.

Przyborski, Aglaja. 2004. *Gesprächsanalyse und dokumentarische Methode: Qualitative Auswertung von Gesprächen, Gruppendiskussionen und anderen Diskursen.* Wiesbaden: Springer.

Przyborski, Aglaja, and Thomas Slunecko. 2012. Linie und Erkennen: Die Linie als Instrument sozialwissenschaftlicher Bildinterpretation. *Journal Für Psychologie* 20 (3). http://www.journal-fuer-psychologie.de/index.php/jfp/article/view/239. Accessed 30 Oct 2017.

Rohter, Larry. 2008. Plumber from Ohio Is Thrust into Spotlight. *The New York Times*, October 16. http://www.nytimes.com/2008/10/16/us/politics/16plumber.html. Accessed 30 Oct 2017.

Rose, Fred. 1997. Toward a Class-Cultural Theory of Social Movements: Reinterpreting New Social Movements. *Sociological Forum* 12 (3): 461–494.

Schneider, Nathan. 2013. *Thank You, Anarchy: Notes from the Occupy Apocalypse*. Berkeley: University of California Press.

Schütz, Alfred. 1981. *Der sinnhafte Aufbau der sozialen Welt: Eine Einleitung in die verstehende Soziologie*. Frankfurt am Main: Suhrkamp.

Schütz, Alfred, and Thomas Luckmann. 1984. *Strukturen Der Lebenswelt*. Frankfurt am Main: Suhrkamp.

Skousen, W. Cleon. 2009. *The Five Thousand Year Leap: 28 Great Ideas That Changed the World*. Franklin: American Documents.

Snow, David A., E. Burke Rochford Jr., Steven K. Worden, and Robert D. Benford. 1986. Frame Alignment Processes, Micromobilization, and Movement Participation. *American Sociological Review* 51 (4): 464–481.

Sunshine, Spencer. 2014. The Right Hand of Occupy Wall Street: From Libertarians to Nazis, the Fact and Fiction of Right-Wing Involvement, February 23. http://www.politicalresearch.org/2014/02/23/the-right-hand-of-occupy-wall-street-from-libertarians-to-nazis-the-fact-and-fiction-of-right-wing-involvement/#. Accessed 30 Oct 2017.

Taylor, Blair. 2013. From Alterglobalization to Occupy Wall Street: Neoanarchism and the New Spirit of the Left. *City: Analysis of Urban Trends, Culture, Theory, Policy, Action* 17 (6): 729–747.

"This Is Not a Protest, This Is a Process." 2011. Printed Ephemera Collection, PE.029, Box 25, Pat de Angelis Donation. Tamiment Archive, New York City.

Thompson, Michael J. 2012. Suburban Origins of the Tea Party: Spatial Dimensions of the New Conservative Personality. *Critical Sociology* 38 (4): 511–528.

Zernike, Kate. 2010. Movement of the Moment Looks to Long-Ago Texts. *The New York Times*, October 1. http://www.nytimes.com/2010/10/02/us/politics/02teaparty.html. Accessed 30 Oct 2017.

CHAPTER 6

Fields and Conjunctures: The Thick Opportunity Structure of the Mobilizations

The socially structured exposition to social strain—even if combined with a socially specific interpretative predisposition to experience this strain—only explains the disposition of certain social groups to more or less virtually 'agree' with a given protest mobilization. Even if one casts aside the mentioned contingency of the individual case, it is still feasible and plausible for social groups to react to the experienced crisis in other ways than by protesting: They might campaign for a presidential candidate, support a lobbying network or a union, take antidepressants, or join a millennial sect to seek comfort and pray for or against change instead of embarking on the endeavor of semi-illegally camping in a public park to protest against economic injustices in general or to disrupt town hall meetings to prevent the USA from stepping on the slippery slope to Socialism. And indeed, all these are in fact strategies pursued by the different constituencies before their respective mobilizations took off.[1] Their actual behavior is, at this level of abstraction, still strongly underdetermined or, as Smelser would put it, "ambiguous" (1967, 53 f.).

As Smelser already highlighted in his theory of collective behavior, to understand how a precipitating event and social strain(s) are connected to the factually occurring collective behavior, one has to include the "general situation" as constituted by "social conduciveness (…) and generalized belief" into the equation. The habitus of a given group, even if it as a socialized interpretative disposition can be considered the condition

N. C. Kumkar, *The Tea Party, Occupy Wall Street, and the Great Recession*, Critical Political Theory and Radical Practice,
https://doi.org/10.1007/978-3-319-73688-4_6

of the possibility of "general belief" in and across certain social classes, does obviously not fill this gap completely: As a "generative grammar", it can be the basis of innumerable and quite diverse practices (cf. Bourdieu 1974, 143).

What narrows down the choice of objectively and subjectively meaningful and possible responses to a given situation is that the practice unfolds in a specifically structured social environment. In the praxeological formula for deciphering and explaining an observable social practice—(Habitus) (Field) + Capital = Praxis (Bourdieu 1994, 175)—the term that designates this specifically structured environment is that of the social *field*. This last analytical chapter will, after briefly introducing the concept of the field and discussing some of the difficulties that arise when this concept is used for understanding protest-practices, explore the social environment of the protest-practices of the three protest mobilizations as it is structured by the development in different social fields.

6.1 The Concept of the Field and Protests: Synchronizing Unruly Practices

That a social practice unfolds in a specific field means that it is articulated in a peculiar, to some degree institutionalized, setting of objective relations in which certain implicit and explicit rules of conduct apply. These rules are naturalized regularities assuming normative power over the course of the specialization of a social practice and the corresponding increase of autonomy of the social sphere being spanned by this practice. Even though these rules are the constant object of renegotiation, as *faits sociaux* (Durkheim), they are experienced as more or less independent of individual will and action and therefore become the basis of strategizing as much as its object.

These rules regulate conduct not only in the sense that they prohibit certain practices but in the sense that they constantly hierarchize styles of practices and even the goals one is allowed to pursue via these practices: As I argued in Sect. 4.1, a scientist that seems to try too openly to become famous and/or economically successful as a primary goal of her research will most probably become the object of critique for behaving immorally or, which is pretty much the same in this peculiar field, 'unscientific', even if there is nothing in her practices themselves that is explicitly forbidden (Bourdieu 1993; Bourdieu and Wacquant 1996, 124–47).

As Bourdieu notes about the field of religion (2010), even disagreement in a given field on what is correct, or what one should and should not do, often masks the deeper agreement (for which he coined the concepts of *doxa*, the unquestioned body of common sense assumptions [1979, 325], and *illusio*, the personal and moral 'investment' of the subject in the social order it is acting in [1987, 123; Bourdieu and Wacquant 1996, 148]) on the specific rules and regularities of the field and its institutions structuring these disagreements, at least on what can be meaningfully be spoken about in this field and about what one must be silent. It is in the constant dialectic between internalized and objectivized social structures, or between habitus and field, in which these two shape and reshape each other, that the basis for a non-conscious synchronization of different actor strategies is established.

To transpose this concept into the inquiry of the praxis of protest mobilizations brings some difficulties with it. Bourdieu himself has, in his writing on the protests of May 1968 in France, focused on the developments of different social fields, the crisis of which created the objective chances for the events to unfold, but he did not conceptualize them as unfolding in a defined field themselves—there is, at the explicit conceptual level, no "protest-field" in *Homo Academicus* (cf. 1988).

Social movement scholars have problematized this gap and suggested that a praxeological perspective on protests would have to develop a concept of a social movement field (Crossley 2003; Mayrl 2013). However, as this chapter will show, the degree to which one can actually speak of the logic of an own, delineated and relatively autonomous field stabilizing the protest-practices as meaningful actor strategies with a common logic has to be treated as an open question, especially in the case of crisis protests such as the Tea Party (TP) and Occupy Wall Street (OWS). It turns out that the social environments in which they unfolded are actually better understood as examples of a dynamic quite similar to that described in *Homo Academicus*: as emergent effects of developments in different social fields, occurring outside of them, but remaining dependent of the dynamics of their developments.

In the case of the TP, my research shows that actors in the political, the economic, and the journalistic field followed strategies that remained focused on bettering their position in their respective field, but in doing so sought to gain legitimacy through a *mobilized audience*, which contributed heavily to the explosive growth of the TP. Albeit allowing for the synchronization of actor strategies, the social environment created and shaped by these strategies never really became the harbor of a logic of practices autonomous from these external fields, and the mobilization ceded with the dissolution of this conjuncture. I therefore labelled the social space in which the TP unfolded a *quasi-field*. OWS, which also emerged from the conjuncture of developments in different social fields, did develop a greater autonomy from this conjuncture itself, but more importantly also displayed early signs of the development of an own field logic. Since, however, this tendency did not fully unfold and proved to be instable, I decided to call this corresponding social space a *proto-field*.

6.2 The Tea Party: Emerging with a Quasi-Field

In the case of the TP, there are some very visible indicators that a social movement field in the sense of a semi-autonomous realm of (quasi-)institutionalized behaviors and groups in which the peculiar constituency of the TP could articulate their discontent in a way they themselves experienced as meaningful and appropriate cannot plausibly be presupposed. First, there is an interesting time lag between the alleged 'spark that ignited the flame' and the actual mass mobilization: The mentioned "rant" of Santelli, although broadly broadcasted by news platforms and advertised by right-wing lobbying groups, did not result in spontaneous mass demonstrations, but first in rather small TP events—only on April 15, 2009, that is, almost two months later, did the mobilization really gain momentum.[2] Furthermore, even the activists who were involved in the organization of these events expressed a feeling of inner distance or caution about this kind of social movement practices, or as one of my interviewees expressed this foreignness to political protesting, "I never protested a day in my life. Most conservatives don't, it's not in our DNA".

This does not necessarily mean that something like a social movement field did not exist on the right of the political spectrum of the USA. The activism of the Christian right against reproductive rights, or against the so-called gay marriage and so on, clearly suggests otherwise. However, my observations do indicate that TP activists were, before and even during their protesting, not really moving in this particular field, as none of the groups I observed built alliances with grassroots groups from this spectrum, and only very few members of the groups had been active in it beforehand.[3] In my observations and interviews, classical civil society institutions were almost never mentioned—neither churches nor any sorts of clubs or neighborhood associations seemed really integrated or involved in the TP groups' activism.

The founders of a TP group in Southern Connecticut, which was later on quite active and successful, recalled how they were finding themselves somewhat clueless on their rally on Tax-Day about what to actually *do* on such an occasion—so they ended up "singing all the patriotic songs" and collected all email addresses of those present to an email list, which almost collapsed on the first day because everyone sent emails to everyone else. All this indicates a lack of basic organizational and general practical knowledge. When reflecting on this lack of knowledge, however, this was romanticized as an indicator of one's own authenticity as a 'reluctant hero':

> B: Right. Right. And that's how it all started, really. Very, yeah, nothing elaborate, nothing fancy, just -
>
> A: Just a grandmother who went out and struggled to save the country. (TPG1: "Opening Passage")

This is not to say, however, that the TP activists just 'fell out' of their accustomed fields and then acted in a social vacuum. There was *something* like a field catering to (rather than decisively shaping) their respective habitus, which attracted them and gave their practices a perceived consistency. This 'something', however, is better understood as the emergent effect of the interactions of different social fields, themselves largely exterior to the logic of the protest-practices itself. The emerging practices furthermore remained tied to this specific conjuncture and did not really gain autonomy vis-à-vis these other fields—which would constitute it as a field in its own right.

This emergence of a quasi-field can be modeled analogously to Bourdieu's concept of the "critical event" (Gilcher-Holtey 2001; Kumkar 2014; Bourdieu 1988). The developments in a number of other social fields made it a promising strategy for certain actors in these fields to pursue their strategy by 'going in from an angle'. Finding themselves blocked or hindered to better their position within their own field, they had to rely on strategies that included (or just had the effect of) the mobilization of an "audience" outside their proper field into a legitimizing constituency for their position within this field. As Bourdieu pointed out in his sociology of the political and the religious field, in these fields, the system of objective relations for its inner functioning depends on (and implicates) a legitimizing, yet at the same time excluded "laity" or "audience". These are, on the one hand, deprived of all resources to actively participate in the "game" of the field, but they are also ultimately the only ones that can grant authority to those involved in the game (as the "believers" or "the people") (cf. Bourdieu 2010, 2013).

It is because of this peculiarity of the political and the journalistic field that a conjuncture of developments especially in the political field, the economic field, and the journalistic field together resulted in the temporary opening of a social space that the TP could articulate itself in. In the political field (in the strict sense of the term, the field of organized electoral politics of the two-party system of the USA), the part structured as the Republican Party was in deep crisis after the election of Barack Obama as the president of the USA. "Whither the Republicans?" asked a New York Times article in early 2009, and the Senate Republican Leader of that time is quoted in the same article as being worried "that the Republican Party seems to be slipping into a position of being more of a regional party than a national one"—which did not seem overly pessimistic at a time when a CBS poll found the lowest approval rating for Republicans since it included the question for party approval in their nationwide phone surveys in 1992 (Blow 2009; NYT/CBS 2009).

The election campaign in 2008 had held the party together in the desperate attempt to prevent the inevitable, symbolized in the odd couple of soon-to-be organic intellectual of the TP Sarah Palin[4] and the more 'moderate' John McCain. Now, however, conflict about the interpretation of the lost election and the future course of the party burst into the open. Especially more marginal figures in the party used the opportunity to attack the established center of the party for 'selling out' the core values of America and not resisting Obama's 'socialist agenda'. The emergence of the TP allowed these figures to present themselves to the activist base of the Republican Party which was radicalized considerably to the right during the last three decades (Abramowitz 2011), and which was one of the central recruitment pools for the TP mobilization (New York Times 2010) as the 'true republicans' opposed to the so-called RINO's (a mocking acronym for those that supposedly are 'Republican in name only'[5]), and thereby improve their position in the inner-party struggles for influence. This specific inner-party constellation is a reoccurring pattern of conflicts in the Republican Party, latest since the campaign that made Barry Goldwater the presidential candidate of the Party in 1964, which some identify as the origin of the "new American right" (McGirr 2002). This constellation, which seems implicated in the very structure of the contemporary Republican Party, may be one of the reasons why 'TP candidate' as a brand clearly outlived the actual mass mobilization of the TP, even when organizational structures like the—for a time quite active—TP caucus in Congress had de facto been dissolved too.

As argued in Sect. 2.3, in the economic field especially, the extractive and chemical industry and the inflation-sensitive owners of large financial wealth were fearful that Obama's vision of a Green New Deal might actually materialize and initiate a new cycle of accumulation via a restructuring of the economic field that would devaluate their invested capital. It is therefore hardly coincidental that the groups most heavily involved in the "test marketing" of the TP had strong connections to these industries as, for example, through the right-wing libertarian lobbying group *Freedom Works*, which received generous donations from the Koch family at this time and supported different TP organizations from the beginning (cf. Burghart 2012; Williamson et al. 2011): They publicized Santelli's "rant" on many media channels, sponsored the first TP events, and funded emergent local TP groups to get them involved in campaigning against important policy measures of the Obama campaign and especially in the midterm elections of 2010 (Lo 2012, 100 f.; Trost and Rosenthal 2012).[6] This field's relation to the protests differs slightly from that of the political field (which in its very own constitutive logics is bound to being legitimized by an audience it at the same time excludes from participating in the field), the economic field actors' strategy involved a double mediation: The mobilized audience built pressure on certain actors in the political field to influence policies which in then turn impacted the economic field's structure.

Finally, of key importance for the emergence of the protest that became the TP was the highly differentiated and polarized journalistic field in the USA. Especially Fox News, which is traditionally closely aligned with the Republican Party, was from the beginning very critical of the Obama administration. Many show hosts, especially Glenn Beck, whom many of the TP activists I interviewed admire, seemed to be caught in a self-enforcing spiral of escalating condemnation of the administration in order to keep their audience interested (Stelter and Carter 2009). The often alarmist imaginaries produced in this process very probably contributed to the fixation of the TP's core constituency's fears and discontents on the newly elected president. In early April 2009, for example, Glenn Beck publicly declared that the administration was "flirting with fascism" ("Flirting With Fascism" 2009).

But Fox News not only catered to the fears of the petty bourgeoisie from the ranks of which the majority of the TP was recruited, it also helped to publicize the mobilization while it had not yet developed its own momentum. It, for example, ran over 100 promotion clips for their news coverage of the rallies on April 15 in the weeks leading up to them (Carr 2009).[7] This might have been decisive because it gave the 'demonstration shy' conservative base of the TP the comforting impression that there is already a mass movement that they merely would have to join.

Even though I never asked about this specifically, interviewees from all TP groups I visited told me that they first heard of the TP via Fox News' coverage of it. This is very likely a general phenomenon, given that the NYT/CBS News nationwide phone survey in April 2010 found two-thirds of all TP supporters to rely mainly on Fox News for information about current political events (compared to 23% of the non-TP supporters). All this supports the claim made by Williamson et al. (2011, 30) that Fox News in fact acted "as a national social movement organization" in the creation of the TP.[8] Indeed, even those interviewees that took pride in being the 'founders' of their respective TP group were recruited through Fox News—like the just mentioned "grandmother who went out and struggled to save the country":

> I was watching the news one day and Fox News had on, I believe it was Amy Kremer, and she said how this April, they were gonna have a Tea Party, and if you were interested, you go on her website. (…) So I went on her site, I actually spoke to her, she said, leave a donation, I'm welcoming you at the Tea Party. So I went to (…) her website, so, that was it! (TPG1_Opening Passage)

The importance of this conjuncture between the development in all three fields (journalistic, economic, and political) not only for the establishing but also the sustaining of the TP as a political mass mobilization can be illustrated by pointing out how closely the dissolving of this conjuncture correlates with the decline of TP activism in general, which began in the summer of 2010 and accelerated after the summer of 2011.

After the midterm election of 2010, the funding of TP groups via Freedom Works and other lobby groups diminished—none of the TP groups I spoke to received funding after 2010, while at least two had in the lead-up to the midterm elections—maybe at least in part because the so-called Citizens United ruling of the US supreme court[9] made it easier for these groups to more or less directly inject undisclosed donations into electoral campaigns.[10] Furthermore, when the TP, partially in reaction to the ever smaller numbers at rallies and declining motivation of the activist base, turned to new, socially 'hot topics' like fiercely opposing any immigration reform, they found themselves on collusion course to the politics of, for example, the chamber of commerce (cf. Post 2014).

In the Republican Party, at the latest after the escalation of the debt-ceiling conflict that brought the USA dangerously close to bankruptcy in 2011 and when a record low of approval for both the (then majority Republican) Congress and the TP in the US population could be noted (Cooper and Thee-Brenan 2011), the moderate center had, for the moment, regained the offensive, culminating in the nomination of Mitt Romney (the candidate with the least TP credentials in the whole race) as the presidential candidate in 2012. In June 2011, Glenn Beck left Fox News and catered to a smaller but dedicated group of followers via an internet TV show. There is ample speculation on the reasons for this step, but in any case, Beck had come under severe criticism even from the conservative right, and around 300 companies refused to place ads to boycott Beck after he called Obama a "racist" that "hates white people" (Downie 2011; *Reuters* 2011).

In that sense, the event might be interpreted as part of the broader attempt on the political right to regain the support of the political center by curtailing the influence of the Tea Party 'insurgents', which also meant the demobilization of their legitimizing audience. The TP activists I interviewed sometimes expressed a feeling that fits this diagnosis, namely, that from a certain point onward, their main practical opponents actually were those in the "Republican establishment". Especially the nomination of Mitt Romney was perceived as a humiliation by some:

> And we even (…) had a press conference and endorsed Herman Caine. Well, what did they do? (…) Herman Caine, oh my god, Herman Caine is winning in the polls, this is the Republicans. Ch, we got to do something. (…) People say the left did it? The left didn't do it. Maybe they did a little bit, but I think the Republicans did it. 'Cause it was Mitt Romneys turn. Then, Sarah Palin pshh, ok? Whoever. Michele Bachman. They just went down the line. We, we had an order of who we liked and they just went down like that ((imitates shots fired)) and they got rid of them until who was left? Mitt Romney. Ahm, (2) well, we went to the Republicans and said listen. This was one of these times when I said, we're gonna have a roadside rally for, ah,

> Mitt Romney. We hate it, we're gagging, but, if you guys, you should be involved in this. You're the ones that shoved him down our throats, so come to our, they didn't show up. (Susan_TP)

When I revisited the TP groups in early 2014, most of them had scaled back their electoral activism and withdrawn from the nationwide networks, which they experienced as complicit with the Republican "establishment". However, they never had been able to set up mobilizing structures or shared agendas that were not originating or at least heavily supported by these outside actors, such as lobbyists, the Republican Party, or the mass media. Their earlier attempts to organize locally, for example, via alliances with other TP groups in the respective state, had not developed the momentum they were hoping for, leaving the groups shrinking and the remaining activists resigned.

The explosive growth and the decline of the TP mobilization thus are closely tied to the existence of a specific thick opportunity structure that was defined by a conjuncture of developments in other social fields. Actors in the political, the economic, and the journalistic field all aimed at a bettering of their own field position through the mobilization of a legitimizing audience: the TP. After this conjuncture dissolved, the TP was not able to maintain its momentum autonomously. The thick opportunity structure therefore can be understood as a quasi-field: While it did synchronize actor strategies into a coherent protest-practice, it did not evolve into an autonomous realm of social practice but remained bound to the specific conjuncture of developments in different social fields.

6.3 Occupy Wall Street: The Strategy of Heresy and the Establishing of a Proto-Field

Other than the TP activists I spoke to, interviewees from OWS often had had at least some experience with what they considered 'activism' beforehand.[11] Interviewees from the TP often made statements indicating a kind of inner distance to social movement praxis, or rather to political activism in general, as is documented in statements such as "all I did before the 2008 election, was vote. I always voted. And that was my, the limit to my political involvement" or that all they did was "yelling at the TV" (Skocpol and Williamson 2012, 40). The accounts by the OWS activists, in contrast, document that they saw this kind of practice as a meaningful activity, indicating that they had a kind of 'feeling for the game' as it is associated with the correspondence between a field and its habitus, or at least with the fact that the habitus is containing the virtual possibility of resonating with the structuring of acceptable practices in this field. In other words, they had already practiced protest-activism and incorporated the corresponding strategies and preferences into their habitus, or their hitherto biographical trajectory in other social fields had equipped them with strategies and preferences similar enough to those required for protest-activism that they, other than the TP activists, did not feel alienated by it.

However, there are a number of indicators suggesting that the field in which the more experienced activists gathered these experiences, and which could provisionally be labelled the 'social movement field' in NYC,[12] was not an unproblematic environment in which the protests were articulated, but was itself in a crisis: Numerous attempts were made in the weeks leading up to OWS to mobilize for anti-austerity or pro-democracy protests, sometimes in a manner that seems surprisingly similar to that which finally materialized in OWS, but none of them seemed to quite gain traction with a broader audience.[13] This is one symptom of the field's apparent problem to integrate interested onlookers into protest-activities.

Another document of this difficulty is that those of the core constituency that joined the mobilization on or after September 17, 2011, had little or no experience with activism in NYC itself. They reported a high level of political interest prior to joining OWS (they, for example, passionately followed the 'Arab Spring' via the internet, like Max did), but were not able to connect to groups to become active themselves. When Occupy finally did offer the chance to get in touch with these groups the individual new participants did not join together with friends or as a group, but went down to Zuccotti Park alone. For NYC this indicates that the existing groups of the social movement field had no or very little connection to the social realms of the living environment of the Occupiers.[14]

The reasons for this crisis of the social movement field are without doubt multiple. Very important, however, was the dynamic of the political field at this point and its interaction with the social movement (sub-)field. Other than the TP, which met a strategic opening in the Republican Party, the situation for the clientele of OWS in 2011 can be defined as one of an almost total lack of conduciveness of the political field, which resulted in a crisis of legitimacy of the political field in the eyes of its audience.

Barack Obama had originally euphorized especially the birth cohort of the core constituency of OWS, and his presidential campaign capitalized on the social movement networks and structures that had been worn out by eight years of mobilizing against the policies of the Bush administration. The years following his election as president saw a growing disenchantment, when, not least because of fierce resistance on the right of the political spectrum, even the modest remnants of his redistributive and modernizing campaign promises seemed to fall apart. The slow economic growth barely had effects on employment for the aspiring new petty bourgeoisie, while others from the social classes that had supported Obama's campaign were even negatively impacted (2011 saw dramatic cuts in government employment but also in manufacturing) (The Economist 2011a, b). At least in part this disappointing recovery was due to the stimulus packages and other economic interventions being (in a preemptive bow to the TP-fueled opposition) too restrained to have lasting effects (Krugman 2009). Also because of this, Obama's electoral victory and the ensuing disappointment had a disarming effect on a social movement field that had become increasingly synonymous with the 'all but Bush' alliances that had mobilized for Obama (cf. Taylor 2013).

While Americans across all groups had a historically low opinion of their legislature in the summer of 2011,[15] the disappointment must have been especially high among those that had projected their hopes on Obama—according to the survey by Milkman et al. (2013), almost half of the respondents who were under 30 years old were active in Obama's campaign in some way. After OWS emerged as a noticeable phenomenon, the reaction by politicians from the Democratic Party was mixed, but in general rather reluctant. To the best of my knowledge, none of the nationally known members of the party publicly spoke out against the eviction of the camps in late 2011. It seems like in trying to juggle the already polarized public, barely anybody considered it a promising endeavor to side with OWS to improve one's position in the political field, in a way that would have been analogous to what had happened within the Republican Party in relation to the TP. All this might contribute to explanations of why OWS was, other than the TP, in general not only reluctant, but outright dismissive of any kind of involvement in electoral politics.

This lack of conduciveness did increase the willingness of some actors at the dominated poles of the economic and the political field, such as unions, which had hitherto mostly limited their strategy to (unsuccessful) congressional lobbying in the years after Obama's election (cf. Tilly 2011; Baccaro et al. 2010, 372–76), to support street protests and even occupations as means of building political pressure, as became obvious at the latest with the occupation of the Capitol of Madison in early 2011 to protest the anti-union legislature proposed by Wisconsin's governor Scott Walker—an event which some consider a predecessor of OWS.[16] In NYC itself, however, these kinds of protests had become increasingly difficult to organize in the last decades: 27 years of law-and-order policies under the mayors Giuliani and Bloomberg had resulted in a very repressive atmosphere against civil disobedience and even just minor deviant behavior (cf. Vitale 2005, 2014; Smith 1996). At the same time, the exploding rent levels all over NYC made spaces for political activism beyond the well-funded NGO groups increasingly scarce. All these tendencies increased the relative power of groups from the non-profit sector and some remaining sectarian fringe-parties such as the "Revolutionary Communist Party" over a field whose available resources and mobilizing potential were shrinking at the same time.[17]

The conflict over the nature of the general assembly in August that led to the formation of the planning team for OWS, the NYCGA, as well as OWS' refusal to form structures that would allow for any kind of formalized alliances with political groups and the like, can in this light be interpreted as the attempt to leave the apparently blocked terrain of this field behind. Initially at least, this 'being different', the "rupture"(Sitrin and Azzellini 2012, 29–36), as it was labelled in the protesters' own language, proved to be one main attracting and euphorizing factor for many resigned activists on the radical left. Very similar to the strategy of "heresy" described by Bourdieu in his theory of the genesis of the literary field (2008, esp. 379ff.), a group of actors declared to break with the rules of conduct of a field that they felt to be corrupted and that did not seem to offer any room for a relative improvement of their position. The common complaint by early activists about the "verticalism" of the established social movement organizations and their "institutionalized" character (cf. Holmes 2012, 151ff.; Graeber 2013) in this sense document the perceived deadlocks one tries to break with by propagating a new 'style' of politics, which foremost is defined by its refusal of any kind of formal structure.

Propagating a new form of interaction rather than a political program (the "small-a anarchis(m)" which is "willing to work in broad coalitions as long as they work on horizontal principles" (Graeber 2013, 89)), combined with the expansive aspirations and the rhetoric of the radical break with the 'old' way of protesting, can in this light be read as typical indicators for the (very rudimentary) beginnings of the formation of a new social field. Other than in the case of the TP, the emergence of social space in which the movement unfolded was therefore not so much the effect of strategies pursued by actors in other, independent social fields, but was propelled by a group of actors that tried to break with the logics of the political field and the social movement sub-field that in its logic seemed to be completely subsumed under it. As the historian Jeremy Varon rightfully remarked early on: "(t)his is the Obama generation declaring their independence from his administration".[18] The activists themselves expressed this longing for 'breaking free', for example, in the stylistic affinity of their "Declaration of the Occupation of NYC" with the US "Declaration of Independence".

The format of the occupation and the 'pure' assembly-democracy, which was chosen as a sign of the departure from the social movement field and its "institutionalized" actors, proved to be especially attractive to those that had felt excluded from the social movement field before.[19] After OWS had gained a certain amount of traction, it in turn exerted a considerable attraction to not only those individuals but also to many other actors from the very social movement field just left behind. This in turn became a bone of contention in OWS, since many now feared that OWS and its corresponding small proto-field might be 'co-opted' by 'verticals'. A fear that might even have been amplified by OWS' non-representativist structures that practically ruled out any kind of official alliance building with existing political groups, thereby in effect forcing these groups to unofficially try to influence what happened in the park. In the words of the "Statement of Autonomy", one of very few "GA-consented" documents:

> We wish to clarify that Occupy Wall Street is not and never has been affiliated with any established political party, candidate or organization. Our only affiliation is with the people. (…) Any organization is welcome to support us with the knowledge that doing so will mean questioning your own institutional frameworks of work and hierarchy and integrating our principles into your modes of action. SPEAK WITH US, NOT FOR US. (NYCGA 2011, emphasis in original)[20]

In other words, everyone is welcome, as long as they break with the very logic of the social field they are coming from and unconditionally subsume under the rules of the field in-becoming. All this meant that the difficulties to set up some kind of protest infrastructure were definitely higher in the case of OWS—even if it at times seems as if the participants in OWS put additional spokes in their wheel, as in the case of coordination with established political groups, but also with regard to accepting donations from actors in the economic field that tried, albeit apparently on a much smaller scale than in the case of the TP (Milkman et al. 2013, 16), to in some form align with OWS.[21]

On the other side, the mentioned repressive behavior of the NYPD itself might have at least helped to overcome the original difficulties to gain attention in the journalistic field: Although some have suggested that MSNBC de facto functions as a kind of left-wing advocacy news network counterpart to Fox News (Steinberg 2007), in the case of OWS, they did not play a comparable role in publicizing the movement in its infant state. Yet, while the NYT and other major newspapers in the beginning reported rather reluctantly,[22] this changed with the broadly publicized pepper spray incident and the mass arrest of protestors on the Brooklyn Bridge. After this, the media attention certainly helped to establish OWS as a socially legitimate form of practice in the eyes of those still hesitant to join. However, the attention quickly ceased again after the eviction of the parks made 'spectacles' like the mentioned acts of police violence less likely.[23] As will be discussed in Chap. 7, it is the combination of all these factors and the habitus of the involved actors that made the occupation of the park such a central feature for OWS, which in turn also explains why the mobilization, with regard to numbers mobilized, together with the proto-field it had created, imploded so fast after May 2012.

After the collapse of the decision-making structures of OWS, the remaining working-groups continued to splinter along lines of affinity (and along with these often class) and followed trajectories that were increasingly independent from each other. An interesting still of this development is a survey conducted in early 2012 by participants in the movement itself (Owen 2013), which shows the 'pluralism' of the movement, but also how this diversity is constituted by diverse sub-groups that were in themselves relatively homogenous.[24] In this process, especially those that had established little social connections to other activists and that had more economic difficulties, like the mentioned houseless people and the marginalized youth from the outer Boroughs, splintered off first, until an (albeit enlarged) core of activists remained. It is most probably not by coincidence that two of the most visible remaining campaigns that emerged from OWS in late 2013 and early 2014 were 'Strike Debt', which evolved out of the education and empowerment working group, and 'Occupy the Pipeline'. The former addresses an issue central to the young new petty bourgeoisie's experience of the crisis, namely, possible venues of resistance against personal debts, whereas the latter addresses a classical topic of 'middle class radicalism', namely, environmental issues. Both initiatives are mostly carried out by groups with socio-demographic compositions very closely resembling those of the group which originally started OWS, now reintegrated into the social movement field it originally departed from. While OWS also can be understood as emerging in a conjuncture of developments in different social fields, this conjuncture evolved differently. By declaring their secession from the social movement field in crisis, OWS' activists did aim at the establishment of an autonomous realm of practices with clear boundaries toward other social fields of practice. However, while this attempt showed early success, this proto-field could not be stabilized for a longer period of time.

6.4 Summary: The Fourth-Cut Theory of Crisis-Protests

The fifth chapter reconstructed the habitus of the core constituencies of the respective protests as it structured the socially specific experiences of the social developments that culminated in the Great Recession. This helped to understand why certain social groups were predisposed to resonate with certain protest-practices—one could say it reconstructed the subjectivized mediations of the subjection to the crisis dynamics into a meaningful experience of this very crisis as part of the complex behavioral and interpretative predispositions to resonate with certain protest-practices. To understand the protest-practices as a social symptom of the crisis, however, requires also a reconstruction of the objectivized mediations of the discontent into protest-practice via understanding the socially structured environment in which the practices unfold—this last analytical chapter of the study sought to close this gap by applying (and adapting) Bourdieu's concept of the field to all four protest mobilizations (Table 6.1).

Both mobilizations found themselves without a field that offered itself as a promising terrain for the protests—the thick opportunity structure in

Table 6.1 Social fields of articulation

	The Tea Party	*Occupy Wall Str.*
Social field of articulation	*Quasi-field*, spanned by conflict in other fields	*Proto-field*, secession from social movement field in crisis

which they unfolded was rather spanned by a conjuncture of developments in other fields which I conceptualized as spanning a *quasi-field* in the one case and a *proto-field* in the other. In the case of the TP, an alliance of actors of the economic, the political, and the journalistic fields together established a social space that could supplement a proper field in its function of coordinating and synchronizing different actors' strategies for a while. This functioning *as if* is what the concept of the quasi field seeks to capture. This space however did not gain relative autonomy from the functioning of these fields. Therefore, after this conjuncture dissolved, the TP also lost its momentum and attempts to organize beyond the established lobbying and party structures largely failed.

In the case of OWS, I chose the term *proto-field* to highlight that the dynamics here pointed in another direction. While it can be understood as the result of strategies pursued by actors in other fields, the different 'state of energy' of these fields changed the relation of the newly spanned social space toward the other fields in that the actors did not seem to pursue strategic interests in these fields anymore. They demonstratively chose to 'secede', especially from the social movement field as it defined the extra-parliamentary landscape of NYC before. In doing so, they were able to mobilize many that had not found a way into leftist activism before. After the eviction of the parks, however, OWS could not be stabilized, but its single initiatives faded out or mostly reintegrated into the social movement field of NYC.

Notes

1. Occupy Wall Street's (OWS) participants to a large degree were active in Obama's presidential campaign and some supported anti-austerity alliances before OWS. According to different studies, there has been a remarkable increase in the use of antidepressants in the USA between 1999 and 2010 (Ramin and Olfson 2014). Furthermore, there seems to be a stark increase in the use of antidepressants especially among the relatively well-off during the Great Recession (McInerney et al. 2013), and TP members were relatively often also members in evangelical churches (Hood et al. 2015; Solty 2014).
2. The understanding of the "rant" as a 'spark' is widespread within the movement itself—all of the groups and many of my interviewees from the TP brought the speech up as an important event. However, none of them actually considered the speech as important for their *own* mobilization, but only for that of others. Seen in this light, the commonsensical notion of the

'spark' is rather to be considered as a part of the mythology that the movement created about itself than as an actual element explaining its emergence.

3. This is supported by the findings of a master thesis by Benjamin Rohr, who, via an email survey conducted with TP groups in New Jersey, found that these groups were not cooperating with civil-society institutions, such as churches, and that the members also did not have systematically clustered relations to certain institutions (Rohr 2015).
4. The already mentioned NYT/CBS poll in 2010 found TP supporters to be almost double as likely to think that Sarah Palin would be a good president than non-TP supporters among members of the Republican Party (New York Times 2010).
5. The image of the 'Rino' plays with the iconography of the US party system that pictures the Democrats as donkeys and the Republicans as elephants: The rhinoceros, albeit looking like an elephant, is in fact a member of the zoological class of the odd-toed ungulates, like the donkey.
6. And they did so with great success: As Solty shows, the TP mobilizations that from the very beginning attacked important cornerstones of the Green New Deal contributed heavily to the failure (or underachievement) of the American Recovery and Reinvestment Act of 2009 (Solty 2013).
7. Interestingly, in the week of the events itself, CNN reported on the TP more extensively than Fox News (Williamson et al. 2011).
8. And beyond Fox News, the universe of conservative talk radio displayed a similar dynamic in early 2009.
9. As one consequence of the "Citizens United v. FEC" ruling, public advocacy groups were allowed to make expenditures in political races and to not have to disclose the names of their donors to the Federal Election Commission.
10. The amount of "Dark money" spent on election campaigns, that is, money from organizations that do not report all or only some of their donors, increased notably from $160.8 million in 2010 to more than $219 million in the midterm election 2014 (Post 2014).
11. The study by Milkman et al. likewise found that most early activists in OWS had already had long-term experiences in social movement activism of some sort (2013, 16).
12. While some of these observations are generalizable beyond NYC, the situation in Oakland, for example, seems to have been very different. Here, the mobilization was mostly carried out by pre-existing radical groups who together decided to do 'something like Occupy' when they convened to talk about actions planned against Columbus Day.
13. For an overview, cf. Schneider (2013, 3–11).

14. Participants in OWS from Greece and Germany also recognized this phenomenon as strange. A German participant furthermore brought my attention to the fact that one of the most frequently used media of expression was the sign, handmade from a pizza carton, rather than collectively painted banners or pre-printed posters, as they are common on demonstrations, for example in Germany.
15. In August 2011, a record number of 82% reported that they disapprove of the way that congress is doing its job in a CBS/NYT poll, higher than at any time since this question was included into the poll in 1977.
16. This occupation was an attempt to prevent the signing of a bill that made public-sector union organizing next to impossible, which some consider an early foreshadowing of OWS (e.g., Waisbren 2012; Milkman et al. 2013, 5).
17. A much-read title in left-wing circles in New York during my stays was a pamphlet calling radical activists to leave behind their ties to NGO's and the non-profit sector, which is supposedly concerned mainly with self-reproduction rather than the transformation of the given situation. Cf. INCITE! (2009).
18. Jeremy Varon, cited in Gitlin (2011).
19. See Sect. 7.3.
20. The same document asks paid organizers to "disclose your affiliation at the outset", thereby illustrating that there was a fear of 'hidden co-optation' as a partial side effect of the outright rejection of any alliance building on the formal level.
21. An exemplary anecdote illustrating these difficulties is the failed attempt of "Ben & Jerry's" to support OWS with $ 2,000,000, which is described in an article in the Rolling Stone magazine (Binelli 2012).
22. "Wall Street Occupiers, Protesting Till Whenever" was the title of the first article in the NYT on September 30 (Kleinfield and Buckley 2011).
23. My research on Nexis shows 17 English-language newspaper articles worldwide for the week from September 17 to September 23 featuring "Occupy Wall Street", most of them smaller side notes, 78 from September 24 to 30, 607 from October 1 to 7, and 426 for October 14 to 20, including front-page coverage and extensive commentary. For comparison, "Tea Party" features already in 815 English-language newspaper articles in the week of the big tax-day rallies from April 13 to 19, 2009 (data retrieved on 15.04.2015).
24. When I went to two highly publicized events organized by groups that understood themselves as coming from the OWS lineage, and which both were advertised at the official NYCGA website, only one additional person went to both events.

Bibliography

Abramowitz, Alan. 2011. *Partisan Polarization and the Rise of the Tea Party Movement*. Presented at the Annual Meeting of the American Political Science Association, Seattle, Washington. http://faculty.washington.edu/jwilker/353/AbramowitzTea.pdf. Accessed 31 Oct 2017.

Baccaro, Lucio, Robert Boyer, Colin Crouch, Marino Regini, Paul Marginson, Richard Hyman, Rebecca Gumbrell-McCormick, and Ruth Milkman. 2010. Labour and the Global Financial Crisis. *Socio-Economic Review* 8 (2): 341–376.

Binelli, Mark. 2012. The Battle for the Soul of Occupy Wall Street. *Rolling Stone*, June 21. http://www.rollingstone.com/politics/news/the-battle-for-the-soul-of-occupy-wall-street-20120621. Accessed 31 Oct 2017.

Blow, Charles. 2009. Whither the Republicans? *New York Times*, January 31. http://blow.blogs.nytimes.com/2009/01/31/whither-the-republicans/. Accessed 31 Oct 2017.

Bourdieu, Pierre. 1974. Der Habitus als Vermittlung zwischen Struktur und Praxis. In *Zur Soziologie der symbolischen Formen*, 125–158. Frankfurt am Main: Suhrkamp.

———. 1979. *Entwurf einer Theorie der Praxis auf der ethnologischen Grundlage der kabylischen Gesellschaft*. Frankfurt am Main: Suhrkamp.

———. 1987. *Sozialer Sinn: Kritik der theoretischen Vernunft*. Frankfurt am Main: Suhrkamp.

———. 1988. *Homo Academicus*. Stanford: Stanford University Press.

———. 1993. Über einige Eigenschaften von Feldern. In *Soziologische Fragen*, 107–114. Frankfurt am Main: Suhrkamp.

———. 1994. *Die feinen Unterschiede: Kritik der gesellschaftlichen Urteilskraft*. Frankfurt am Main: Suhrkamp.

———. 2008. *Die Regeln der Kunst: Genese und Struktur des literarischen Feldes*. Frankfurt am Main: Suhrkamp.

———. 2010. Sociologists of Belief and Beliefs of Sociologists. *Nordic Journal of Religion and Society* 23: 1–7.

———. 2013. Die politische Repräsentation. Elemente einer Theorie des politischen Feldes. In *Politik*, 43–96. Berlin: Suhrkamp.

Bourdieu, Pierre, and Loïc J.D. Wacquant. 1996. Die Ziele der reflexiven Soziologie: Chicago-Seminar, Winter 1987. In *Reflexive Anthropologie*, 95–249. Frankfurt am Main: Suhrkamp.

Burghart, Devin. 2012. View from the Top: Report on Six National Tea Party Organizations. In *Steep. The Precipitous Rise of the Tea Party*, ed. Lawrence Rosenthal and Christine Trost, 67–97. Berkeley: University of California Press.

Carr, David. 2009. Cable Wars Are Killing Objectivity. *The New York Times*, April 20. http://www.nytimes.com/2009/04/20/business/media/20carr.html. Accessed 31 Oct 2017.

Cooper, Michael, and Megan Thee-Brenan. 2011. Public Views Congress as Top Culprit in Debt Debate, Poll Finds. *The New York Times*, August 4. http://www.nytimes.com/2011/08/05/us/politics/05poll.html. Accessed 31 Oct 2017.

Crossley, Nick. 2003. From Reproduction to Transformation. Social Movement Fields and the Radical Habitus. *Theory, Culture & Society* 20 (6): 43–68.

Downie, James. 2011. The Decline of Glenn Beck. *The New Republic*, March 3. http://www.newrepublic.com/article/politics/84662/the-decline-glenn-beck. Accessed 31 Oct 2017.

"Flirting With Fascism". 2009. FoxNews.com. April 2. http://www.foxnews.com/story/2009/04/02/flirting-with-fascism. Accessed 31 Oct 2017.

Gilcher-Holtey, Ingrid. 2001. 'Kritische Ereignisse' und 'Kritischer Moment'. Pierre Bourdieus Modell der Vermittlung von Ereignis und Struktur. In *Struktur Und Ereignis*, ed. Andreas Suter and Manfred Hettling, 120–137. Göttingen: Vandenhoeck & Ruprecht.

Gitlin, Todd. 2011. The Left Declares Its Independence. *The New York Times*, October 8. http://www.nytimes.com/2011/10/09/opinion/sunday/occupy-wall-street-and-the-tea-party.html. Accessed 31 Oct 2017.

Graeber, David. 2013. *The Democracy Project: A History, a Crisis, a Movement*. New York: Spiegel and Grau.

Holmes, Marisa. 2012. The Center Cannot Hold. In *We Are Many: Reflections on Movement Strategy from Occupation to Liberation*, ed. Kate Kathib, Margaret killjoy, and Mike McGuire. Oakland/Edinburgh: AK Press.

Hood, M.V., Quentin Kidd, and Irwin L. Morris. 2015. Tea Leaves and Southern Politics: Explaining Tea Party Support in the Region. *Social Science Quarterly* 96 (4): 923–940

INCITE!, ed. 2009. *The Revolution Will Not Be Funded: Beyond the Non-profit Industrial Complex*. Cambridge, MA: South End Press.

Kleinfield, N. R., and Cara Buckley. 2011. Wall Street Occupiers, Protesting Till Whenever. *The New York Times*, September 30. http://www.nytimes.com/2011/10/01/nyregion/wall-street-occupiers-protesting-till-whenever.html. Accessed 31 Oct 2017.

Krugman, Paul. 2009. The Obama Gap. *The New York Times*, January 9. http://www.nytimes.com/2009/01/09/opinion/09krugman.html. Accessed 31 Oct 2017.

Kumkar, Nils C. 2014. Events of Emancipation and Spectacles of Discontent. How the Tea Party and Occupy Wall Street 'Happened.'. In *Protests as Events. Politics, Activism and Leisure*, ed. Lamond R. Ian and Karl Spracklen, 211–231. London/New York: Rowman & Littlefield.

Lo, Clarence Y.H. 2012. Astroturf versus Grass Roots: Scenes from Early Tea Party Mobilization. In *Steep. The Precipitous Rise of the Tea Party*, 98–129. Berkeley: University of California Press.

Mayrl, Damon. 2013. Fields, Logics, and Social Movements: Prison Abolition and the Social Justice Field. *Sociological Inquiry* 83 (2): 286–309.

McGirr, Lisa. 2002. *Suburban Warriors: The Origins of the New American Right.* Princeton/Oxford: Princeton University Press.

McInerney, Melissa, Jennifer M. Mellor, and Lauren Hersch Nicholas. 2013. Recession Depression: Mental Health Effects of the 2008 Stock Market Crash. *Journal of Health Economics* 32 (6): 1090–1104.

Milkman, Ruth, Stephanie Luce, and Penny Lewis. 2013. *Changing the Subject: A Bottom-Up Account of Occupy Wall Street in New York City.* New York: Joseph S. Murphy Institute for Worker Education and Labor Studies. https://www.documentcloud.org/documents/562862-changing-the-subject-2.html. Accessed 30 Oct 2017.

New York Times. 2010. Polling the Tea Party. http://www.nytimes.com/interactive/2010/04/14/us/politics/20100414-tea-party-poll-graphic.html. Accessed 31 Oct 2017.

NYCGA. 2011. Statement of Autonomy Passed by the General Assembly at Occupy Wall Street. November 10, 2011 and Passed Revision by the General Assembly at Occupy Wall Street, March 3, 2012. http://www.occupywallstreet.net/policy/statement-autonomy. Accessed 31 Oct 2017.

NYT/CBS. 2009. *The New York Times/CBS News Poll*, January 11–15. http://graphics8.nytimes.com/packages/pdf/politics/poll_results.pdf. Accessed 31 Oct 2017.

Owen, James. 2013. Occupy's Precarious Pluralism: A Study of the Purposes, Identities and Politics Enabled by the NYC Occupy Movement. New York. http://occupywallstreet.net/sites/default/files/ows_-_occupys_precarious_pluralism_report_final.pdf. Accessed 31 Oct 2017.

Post, Charlie. 2014. The Future of the Republican Party. *Jacobin*. https://www.jacobinmag.com/2014/12/republican-party-tea-party/. Accessed 31 Oct 2017.

Ramin, Mojtabai, and Mark Olfson. 2014. National Trends in Long-Term Use of Antidepressant Medications: Results from the US National Health and Nutrition Examination Survey. *The Journal of Clinical Psychiatry* 75 (2): 169–177.

Reuters. 2011. Glenn Beck and Fox News End Daily TV Show, April 6. http://www.reuters.com/article/2011/04/06/us-glennbeck-idUSTRE73560N20110406. Accessed 31 Oct 2017.

Rohr, Benjamin. 2015. Nestling into Pieces of Social Structure: Organization and Mobilization in the Case of the Tea Party. Master Thesis, Mannheim: Universität Mannheim.

Schneider, Nathan. 2013. *Thank You, Anarchy: Notes From the Occupy Apocalypse.* Berkeley: University of California Press.

Sitrin, Marina, and Dario Azzellini. 2012. *Occupying Language: The Secret Rendezvous with History and the Present.* New York: Zuccotti Park Press.

Skocpol, Theda, and Vanessa Williamson. 2012. *The Tea Party and the Remaking of Republican Conservatism*. Oxford: Oxford University Press.

Smelser, Neil J. 1967. *Theory of Collective Behavior*. New York: Free Press.

Smith, Neil. 1996. *The New Urban Frontier: Gentrification and the Revanchist City*. London: Routledge.

Solty, Ingar. 2013. The Crisis Interregnum: Considerations on the Political Articulation of the Global Crisis. From the New Right-Wing Populism to the Occupy Movement. *Studies in Political Economy* 91: 85–112.

———. 2014. Die Tea Party Als Klassenprojekt. Neoliberale Religiösität in Den USA. *Luxemburg* 2014 (2): 52–59.

Steinberg, Jacques. 2007. Cable Channel Nods to Ratings and Leans Left. *The New York Times*, November 6. http://www.nytimes.com/2007/11/06/business/media/06msnb.html. Accessed 31 Oct 2017.

Stelter, Brian, and Bill Carter. 2009. Fox News's Mad, Apocalyptic, Tearful Rising Star. *The New York Times*, March 30. http://www.nytimes.com/2009/03/30/business/media/30beck.html. Accessed 31 Oct 2017.

Taylor, Blair. 2013. Long Shadows of the New Left: From Students for a Democratic Society to Occupy Wall Street. In *Revisiting the Sixties: Interdisciplinary Perspectives on America's Longest Decade*, ed. Laura Bieger and Christian Lammert, 77–93. Frankfurt am Main: Campus.

The Economist. 2011a. Not Again. *The Economist*, June 13. http://www.economist.com/blogs/freeexchange/2011/06/americas-jobless-recovery. Accessed 31 Oct 2017.

———. 2011b. The Jobless Young: Left behind, September. http://www.economist.com/node/21528614. Accessed 31 Oct 2017.

Tilly, Chris. 2011. An Opportunity Not Taken... Yet: U.S. Labor and the Current Economic Crisis. *WorkingUSA* 14 (1): 73–85.

Trost, Christine, and Lawrence Rosenthal. 2012. Introduction: The Rise of the Tea Party. In *Steep. The Precipitous Rise of the Tea Party*, 1–22. Berkeley: University of California Press.

Vitale, Alex S. 2005. From Negotiated Management to Command and Control: How the New York Police Department Polices Protests. *Policing and Society* 15 (3): 283–304.

Vitale, Alex. 2014. The Rise of Command and Control Protest Policing in New York. In *The New York City Police Department: The Impact of Its Policies and Practices*, ed. John A. Eterno and Eli Silverman. New York: CRC Press.

Waisbren, Harry. 2012. From Wisconsin to Wall Street: A Cheesehead Does Not Stand Alone. In *From Cairo to Wall Street: Voices From the Global Spring*, ed. Anya Schiffrin and Eamon Kircher-Allan, 180–188. New York: New York Press.

Williamson, Vanessa, Theda Skocpol, and John Coggin. 2011. The Tea Party and the Remaking of Republican Conservatism. *Perspectives on Politics* 9 (1): 25–43.

CHAPTER 7

The Acid Test: Reconstructing the *Occupation* of Urban Public Space as a Socially Determined Practice

The findings of the preceding chapters illuminate the social logic of the protest mobilizations—identifying their social 'condition of possibility' on different levels of abstraction, from the political economic dynamics of the crisis up to the thick social contexts in which the protestors articulated their experienced discontent as protest. Before the conclusion ties all these determinants together, this chapter puts them through an 'acid test': Bringing together the findings on the social determinants of Occupy Wall Street's (OWS) protest-practice, it reconstructs the social logics of one concrete feature of this practice, namely, the occupation of 'Liberty Plaza'.

The 'acid test' serves two main purposes. First, with regard to the validity of my findings, it shows that the outcomes on the different levels of abstraction can indeed be articulated as a complex whole of interlinked propositions and not merely as an accumulation of isolated findings, which, at worst, are "not even wrong" because the findings lack a systematic relation between the levels of abstraction (Bourdieu 1991, 64). Second, I chose the practice of occupying as the *hic rhodus, hic salta*, because the occupation of urban public space as a means of protest or for so-called "prefigurative" politics has been very prominent in many attempts to systematize and define the wave of protests and uprisings since 2011 (Madden and Vradis 2012;

Some arguments in this chapter have been originally developed in Kumkar 2016.

N. C. Kumkar, *The Tea Party, Occupy Wall Street, and the Great Recession*, Critical Political Theory and Radical Practice,
https://doi.org/10.1007/978-3-319-73688-4_7

Pickerill and Krinsky 2012; Della Porta and Mattoni 2014).[1] However, these studies offered relatively little explanation why so many actually felt drawn to 'camping' as a protest-practice. Building on my findings on the social rootedness, social meaning, and the context of articulation of the protest-practice of OWS, this chapter will show how the explosive growth of the protests is not sufficiently explained by the inspiration of activists through the occupations of urban public space in protests around the Mediterranean—rather, it was possible only because social groups well beyond the 'usual suspects' *felt* 'occupying' to be a plausible form of practice in the socioeconomic situation they experienced.

The first part of this chapter will show that 'occupying' was, at the outset, rather something considered a symbolic gesture and nothing that most organizers and participants considered a very promising protest-practice in itself. The second part of the chapter will therefore outline how the habitus of the core constituency of the protest resonated with the practice of the occupation—which led, along with media representation of the protest, to 'occupy' becoming both the central element of the 'brand' of OWS and an aim in itself of its protest-practice. The centrality of the park can thus be understood as a characteristic of an explosive but undirected social dynamic wherein OWS emerged from the complex interaction of different social groups and crises. This unfolding also includes a resonance of the practice of the occupation with other social classes, as is sketched out in the third part of the chapter, especially in regard to the habitus of the urban precariat. Relating those findings to the dynamics of the social fields around the protest can further explain why it was so difficult for OWS to transform its practice—even if the risks and deadlocks of occupying were discussed very early on in and around the mobilization itself.

7.1 How "Occupy" Became the Name of the Protest Mobilization: "It's Catchy, But It's Kind of Dumb"

Not only sociological observers perceive occupying as a—or the—defining element of OWS: The very name "Occupy Wall Street" suggests that the mobilization identified itself with this practice. However, documents from the early stage of the protests and accounts from those that participated in the planning and first phase of the mobilization reveal that this *pars-pro-toto* relationship in which 'occupying' assumed more and more characteristics of the aim in itself of the protests, rather emerged over time.

"Adbusters" suggested occupying Wall Street in July 2011. However, the call barely discussed the practice itself. Instead, it focused on the question of the "one demand" that the participants should agree on and then set out to achieve. The heading #OCCUPYWALLSTREET (Adbusters 2011a) was most probably read as a call to action rather than as a name for the action itself. Even on September 17, 2011, the first day of the occupation, it was "still just a hashtag" (Schneider 2013, 12). In much the same vein, the group that prepared the action did not call itself OWS but "New York City General Assembly" (NYCGA).

The call by "Adbusters" and accounts of the debates and the composition of the early NYCGA (Kroll 2011; Graeber 2013; Schneider 2013) all indicate that the idea of an occupation was rather that of a symbolic quote of the protests in Egypt, Greece, and Spain, thought to position one's discontent in the frame of a broader, global 'moment' and not something that would be in itself strategically or even tactically promising. Apparently, even as such, this was not uncontroversial in the NYCGA. Nathan Schneider, for example, reports that Georgia Sagri, a Greek performance artist involved from the beginning of OWS, claimed to not be "interested" in the "metaphorics of the occupation" (Schneider 2013, 27). Another participant in the demonstration on September 17 told me that he saw the idea of occupying as "a shallow imitation of the tactics of Puerta de la Sol and Tahrir Square," which he found irritating and strategically wrongheaded since "you can't just do the exact same thing that someone else is doing in another country (...) because, we have different contexts (...)".

The discussions and preparation meetings leading up to the occupation in the NYCGA document that even those who did not share this very general skepticism did not really believe that the occupation could develop its own momentum. As one of the participants in these meetings recalled in an interview, there was only one person that considered it to be relevant to talk about food supply for the occupation—all others deemed it irrelevant because they believed that they would be forced out of the park by the police before anyone would get hungry.

However, the police did not force everyone out and the participants found themselves surprised that they succeeded in occupying something—even if not Wall Street itself. Turning the arising necessity to improvise into virtue, my interviewees tended to romanticize especially these first moments as the spontaneity of a new beginning, when everything could still be "negotiated on the fly"—in contrast to the "bureaucracies of anarchy" (Appel 2011) that gradually filled this void over the course of the occupation.

After the successful establishment of the occupation, the question for the "one demand" was pushed more and more into the background until the subject became almost taboo.[2] The occupation itself, on the other hand, gained more and more prominence, as is documented in the way the movement talked about itself: Transcripts show that on September 19, 2011, one participant in the NYCGA refers to "Occupy Wall Street" as an actor with an agenda, and on September 23, different participants at the NYCGA already mention the "Occupy Wall Street movement" in their contributions (NYCGA 2011a, b).[3]

Apparently, the actors and processes that met in the Park at this time began to be identified as a more or less coherent body labeled "OWS", not only from the inside but also from the outside:

> I also remember when the media started calling us Occupy (…). And I remember having conversations with people that were like, oh, I hope that name doesn't stick, I mean it's catchy, but it's kind of dumb. And then it stuck, and then, like, that brand happened, and then we became like really attached to it. And then I got kind of sick of it (laughs). (Amy_OWS)

Three things about this short narration appear noteworthy: First, Amy, who took part in the occupation from its very beginning, once more confirms that she, in the beginning, did not consider "Occupy (Wall Street)" to be the label of the protest participated in. Second, the passive mode, in which the establishment of the 'brand' is described—it is nothing experienced as a decision, but the name merely 'happens' to 'stick'. This is especially interesting because there seems to be manifest criticism toward this name. Third, however, there is an affective ambivalence regarding the brand—signaled both by her laughter, but also in the juxtaposition of "catchy, but (…) kind of dumb"—something about the name was apparently appealing to her, despite her criticism.

As the next section will show, this appeal rests on the resonance of the habitus of OWS' core constituency with the practice of the occupation—reaching beyond the participants' own rationalization of their protest-practice.

7.2 The Core Constituency's Experience: "…It Liberated Us from Fear"

Some observers of OWS have highlighted political fault lines as important factors in explaining the development of the protest (e.g., Gould-Wartofsky 2015). In contrast to this explanation, the praxeological-materialist perspective focuses on the socio-spatial positions in which these conflicts were grounded. This is a plausible perspective because the resonance with the practice of the occupation in the beginning seems to have transcended the political fault lines.

In the following, the reconstruction of the habitus' resonance with the practice of the occupation will, therefore, concentrate on the core constituency identified in Sect. 3.2: The young adults who expected to become members of the new petty bourgeoisie but found themselves socio-biographically 'blocked' from this entry as a result of the devaluation of their cultural capital and the contraction of the labor market in the Great Recession and thereby effectively 'proletarianized', resulting in a form of socio-biographical displacement. These actors, whose ethics and incorporated interpretative patterns developed in institutional settings that were implicitly preparing them for very specific (semi-)professional careers, were confronted by a rapidly changing structure of objective chances to employ these ethics and interpretative patterns in a manner perceived as meaningful. My habitus reconstruction therefore aims at delineating how the group's practical "class ethos" (Bourdieu 1994, 655), and this element of the lived experience of this group, resonated with the practice of the occupation.

As mentioned in Sect. 5.2, the dense narrations and focusing metaphors in the interviews and discussions with this group often displayed an emotional density that culminated in a kind of 'rush', centering on the 'first encounters' with OWS—or, more concretely, the events depicted usually 'took place' in the park:

> "Um, it was like nothing that I ever experienced. It was just like, I remember describing it as like, um a square full of soulmates. Like, it was like everybody I met was like, instant, like, connection (…). (Amy_OWS: "Square full of Soulmates")

This euphoria about feeling immersed in a community is connected to a negative horizon of experience—the same interviewees reported feelings of loneliness and alienation that marked their experience of the months and even years leading up to OWS. Furthermore, their elaborations on their feeling of community document a more detailed positive horizon orienting their actions as not only a feeling of community, but rather a peculiar kind of community. What drew them to this particular community was the way in which it resonated with their dialogical predisposition:

> Or I mean, everybody had different ideas, but similar perspectives on a lot of things. And most people were like really interesting (…). um, and, it was just, there was just, there was just, constant like incredible conversations going on, and, um, it was such feeling of like generative, like creative energy in the park. um, and it just felt like something really big (…). (Amy_OWS: "Square full of Soulmates")

The description of the community as one of "different ideas" but of "similar perspectives" and that of the other participants as not only "soul mates" but also as "really interesting" people documents that differences in opinions between occupiers were nothing to be eventually overcome. Instead, it was in and of itself experienced as something to be cherished.

As was argued in Sect. 5.2, in this sense, the protest-practices of OWS functioned also as a redirection activity in which the dialogical, discursive predisposition of the biographically blocked new petty bourgeoisie could unfold—an unfolding for which the occupied park offered an ideal setting. The reason for this can be understood through contrasting it with other, conventional protest-practices such as rallies, which are different from the occupation in at least two important regards: They often have asymmetrically directed communicative relationships—as well as between 'organizers' and 'participants' and between activists and their 'audience'. The question if potential participants want to join these protest-practices therefore becomes a decision that is contingent upon them agreeing or not agreeing with the protest's 'message' beforehand.

The fact that the concrete, precipitating conflict that led to the founding of the NYCGA was a conflict about the use of loudspeakers at a rally (Schneider 2013, 12ff.) might serve as a good illustrative example for the core constituencies' unwillingness to submit themselves to this kind of directed communication.[4] The conflicts between 'horizontalists' and 'verticalists' during the occupation itself, which were discussed in Sect. 6.3, can be understood at least partially as the reoccurrence of this pattern of dispositional incongruence between those accustomed to classical protest-practices and the habitus of the core constituency.

Besides this, another important difference between the occupation and other, more conventional protest-practices is the temporal endurance of the former: Hectic schedules, insecurity about a protest's message—the potential reasons to miss a demonstration are plenty. The occupation, in contrast, allowed people to leave and come back at a time of their choosing to 'feel things out'. The permanent presence in the park also helped to overcome fears such as that of confrontation with the police: A 'legal team', jail-support, and Direct Action trainings might also exist at and around other protest events, but for those unfamiliar with them, the occupied park offered the ideal setting for getting in contact and learning to trust these structures. The opportunity to build and maintain relationships of trust more generally was an important feature of the occupation.

> Since then, I think I realized, having people that were regularly in the park, also um, helped you to trust the people that you were marching with? Because afterwards, once there was no park, and it was always new people. When I would go, like, to the Mayday march, I was, I wasn't sure that I wanted to be there, I weren't sure what they wanted to do, or if they knew, I mean, I didn't know why they were there.
>
> (deletion) (I)t was the biggest thing that Occupy did, that made it work this time, is that it liberated people from fear? (Max_OWS: "Being Together all this Time")

As is already indicated in the last part of this passage, the importance of trust also documents, as its negative horizon, an underlying fear that potentially prevented people from joining forms of collective action:

> 'Cause they were all afraid of something. They were like, oh, if I go out there, um, you know, to live there, and I quit my job, I'll lose my house! And there is always something that you are afraid of.
>
> (...) But if, for a few people, they were able to come out. Because if I come out, there would be other people to support me, we always had food enough for everybody. Um, towards the end we had healthcare (laughs) free healthcare. (Max_OWS: "Being together all this Time)

A plausible interpretation of the social roots of this fear[5] is twofold: First, and already indicated in this passage, is the perceived economic and social precarity of the biographical trajectory, in which a wrong step could set in motion a chain reaction ultimately jeopardizing one's social status. Second, this fear is further amplified by the deeply incorporated meritocratic orientations of the new petty bourgeoisie. Even temporarily suspending ones individualized career ambitions and instead deciding to protest the rules of the game one is losing (or at least not winning) seems to be perceived as 'giving up'. By symbolically reappropriating basic reproductive tasks, and through institutions such as the "Peoples Library" or a medical tent, the activists created a protective community that cushioned these fears.

7.3 Class Alliances and Internal Conflict: "Let Me Facilitate Something"

The reconstructed resonance of the core constituency's habitus and the protest-practice helps to explain why the occupation became such a central plank of this practice. It, however, does not sufficiently explain why OWS encountered such difficulties in developing alternative practices once the limitations of the occupation as a protest-practice made themselves felt. It seems unlikely that this can only be explained by a "fetishization of space" (Marcuse 2011) (or the occupation) on the side of OWS, especially since the core constituency had a rather ambivalent relation to the practice and many had acknowledged early on that it might have an expiration date.

Two more layers will help us better understand this 'inertia' of practice: first, the relation between the core constituency's resonance with the practice of the occupation and that of other social classes also involved in the protests and, second, the thick opportunity structures or social fields in which this practice was able to unfold but which also hindered its transformation.

As discussed in Sect. 3.2, besides the core constituency, at least three more demographic groups played a role in OWS: subaltern, marginalized parts of the population of New York, veterans from previous leftist social movements, and parts of the unionized working class. In the following, I would like to concentrate on the first group and its habitus' resonance with the practice of the occupation. This group, consisting of homeless people and the young 'precariat'[6] of the outer boroughs—the "lower 99%," as they were sometimes called by members of the other groups (Gould-Wartofsky 2015, 162)—was invited early on to participate in the occupation (NYCGA 2011a). Although this group is no doubt internally variegated, it seemed to me (at least in my interpretation of their accounts on the events that I was able to collect) as if they often found themselves in similar positions in relation to the practice of the occupation and in conflicts in and around the occupied parks.

This group's participation in the protests was topical mostly in reports about heated conflict that arose around it—and which was often mockingly cited as proof of the failure of the protestors' utopian ambitions.[7]

However, it is important to understand these conflicts also through the lens of this group's own dispositional affinity to the protests. Their everyday experience of state institutions as absent or repressive and their disillusionment with political representation fit neatly with OWS' anti-institutional rhetoric. The mentioned practices of mutual care fulfilled material needs but also delivered a sense of social recognition. In interviews and group discussions with activists from this group, this lived experience of 'being at home' in the park was documented in almost religious vocabulary employed for describing it:

> A: It's a there is no words for the description of some of the things that happened here, there's no words to describe it, like ah, sleeping on the floor and the floor being warm and it wasn't just your body heat, it was something else, it was like the floor knew -
> C: └It was the most comfortable floor that I ever slept on.┘
> A: The floor knew that you were sleeping on it that night and it was warm before you hit it. You know it wasn't, it was, something special. And I think after the park closed there was a change of mindset of, within the Occupy movement, within our own, you know, wellness and being, because we lost something. It was tragic. (OWSG1: "it was magical")

As is already indicated at the end of this passage, this lived experience and the fear of losing this connection made them staunch defenders of the practice of the occupation and of an uncompromising 'prefigurative' and 'presentistic' practice in conflicts over the development of OWS. For example, they experienced the attempted establishment of a Spokes Council (SC) as a means of unburdening the GA of organizational tasks, as a breach. Its introduction partially failed due to vocal discontent questioning its legitimacy—which was often voiced by members of this sociodemographic group (e.g., Gould-Wartofsky 2015, 164ff.).

In what follows, I will demonstrate the habitus conflict underlying this turn of events, as it is documented especially in two passages from an extraordinary meeting of the Spokes Council (SC) on December 7, 2011.[8] Three weeks after the eviction of the park, ten days before the last bigger attempt at occupying a new space, and one day after the first occupation of a house through 'Occupy our homes', this specific meeting of the SC took place in one of the most heated phases of the mobilization. Conflicts in and around the SC had already escalated. According to a widespread (or at least very vocal) suspicion, the SC purportedly constituted a form of power grab by some who were trying to bypass the GA at the expense of the more marginalized communities in OWS. The facilitation working group accused of being at the heart of this coup d'état reacted to the accusations emerging around this rumor and demonstratively stepped down. The result was a three-hour meeting without a clear agenda that was regulated only by a list of speakers (a 'stack' in the vocabulary of OWS) that was enforced to differing degrees during the meeting.

During this meeting, most of the contributions formed a meta-discussion on the nature of the mobilization, the competencies of its different organizational bodies, and the perception of the power relations behind the current conflicts. The discussion was punctuated only occasionally by attempts to have a 'normal' conversation on the reproductive and infrastructural tasks of the occupation. These contributions document not only vastly different orienting frames structuring the interpretation of the events by different social groups, but also how little these groups were able to integrate the respective contributions of others into their own interpretation of the events. As a result, an alienating distance between what one 'thinks is the case' in the given social situation and the actual development of the situation emerges, which then turns into frustration.

Already the opening of the meeting by a member of the facilitation team documents the high level of tension between those present in the room—and documents basic patterns that help demonstrate the non-understanding between this group's perception of the development of OWS after the park was raided and that of the more marginalized parts of the constituency.

Am: Um, once again, facilitation won't be facilitating

Bm: Hey, I'm Nathan with facilitation, and I'm speaking to you not as, as facilitator for the evening, but as a member of the facilitation working group. As a spokesperson for the facilitation working group. And um, we ah, we have, ah, (incomprehensible) to take us out of the spokes council this evening, we have the sense that there is a lot of really important conversations that need to take place, and we have, tried to participate in a some of these conversations throughout, on a few occasions, and we acknowledge that it has been perceived that we were, setting the agenda, or trying to lead the conversation or dictate the dialogue. Um, that being, that being said, we would like to take place just as an equal spoke in this conversation that happens today. And, we don't take that position lightly? (incomprehensible) we really believe that there are a lot of (incomprehensible) does have a lot of resources, and we want, we hope that, that us stepping out of the center of the room, it will leave the space for that conversation to happen more organically, and we hope give a little more, so, let the conversation happening more organically. Thank you. (5) (SC_07122011, Opening Statement)

This passage is telling in many regards. Most striking is the contradiction between its form and its explicit content. Even though Bm explicitly declares that he does not speak as a facilitator (2), he is nevertheless the first one exercising the right to take turns. In explaining the facilitation group's understanding of the situation and their decision to actively "step out of the center of the room" (12), and finally in closing his statement with "thank you" (14), he acts in contradiction to his own announcements and also sets the parameters for the discussion to follow. This contradiction in the form of the passage corresponds with the contradictory character of the actual proposition elaborated in it. While on the one hand he acknowledges that the facilitation working group has in fact at times overstepped its boundaries, he instantly downplays this as something that occurred only "on a few occasions" (7) and also only acknowledges it as something that "has been perceived" as a problem and not as something that might point to an actual conflict (7–8).

It would, however, be too easy to dismiss this as mere hypocrisy. Rather, these contradictory propositions indicate a difficulty springing from the understanding of the nature of the very problem. From Bm's point of view, the conflict around the SC is the result of an unfortunate chain of events and misunderstandings, and by stepping (temporarily) aside, he therefore feels this conflict can be resolved quickly and naturally (or "organically" 12–14). This is because he perceives the institution of the SC as unproblematic (after all, as other speakers highlight in the course of the discussion, it was authorized by the GA) and as a logical consequence of OWS' development. The conversations that should happen in the SC are "really important" for what he perceives as the necessary development of the mobilization, especially for dealing with "a lot of resources" (11).

This, however, misses the actual conflict at the heart of other participants' fear and anger toward both the facilitation team and the institution of the SC itself. This is most clearly discernible not in the numerous vocal disruptions of the process or in the attacks on any attempt to introduce some sort of moderation to the discussion (some of which obviously have little other interest than the disruption for the sake of causing mayhem), but in the 'constructive' contributions to the discussion made by the members of the marginalized parts of OWS' constituency. It is in these passages that a fundamental conflict between the ways in which the orienting frames of the different socio-demographic groups structure their perceptions of OWS' development is documented. The following passage is one of the most elaborate contributions by this group, brought forward by a speaker for the recently founded "houseless working group":

Stack: Houseless! Houseless working group!
22m: Ok. We have understanding, that people, everybody here tonight, that if we go, the great job that facilitation did do, tonight we just wanna do without facilitators. You do facilitation every night. But one night we don't want no facilitation around. This is corner is keep "facilitation, fa" can we please. If you, now. If you wanna facilitate something, let me facilitate something.
Off: └ @.@ ┘
22m: now, we got all these working groups, we got some new ones that I'm hearing about, and some that been around. I know we are supposed to be the 99%. But we know there's one percenters in here. So we're in here, we just wanna be 100%. Now,
Off: @.@
22m: What? we got working groups out there. We got kitchen, that do have people out there that haven't ate breakfast today. And they are Occupiers. Let's facilitate some breakfast to them. Let's facilitate some food to them. Let's facilitate-
Off: └ @------------4------------@ ┘
22m: I guess you wanna keep feel to facilitate. You got, everybody in this place right here are value to our, our kids future. Now when we first started, started new as Occupiers, prior to this blossom, so we got different working group and stuff like that. I'm like in the Occupier stage right now, when we started with tents and stuff like that. The same, very body of people wanted to X-out the homeless (incomprehensible) wanted to do that, (incomprehensible) we still here, it's funny. We need to all work together, now, we occupying Wall Street, it seems like there is a stock exchange in this very room that we're in.
Off: mhm
22m: (incomprehensible) cut that out. We need to be on the same page, have a understanding of, everybody have a good idea, cause facilitation (2) we could facilitate good things, and not oppression. That's what we, that's what our facilitate, who cares if that's a GA or a spokes council, ideas pop up at any given time, everybody need to speak, this is a spokes council. Let's speak and do the council later. Alright?
Off: └ @--5--@ ┘
22m: I will not stay there and let, I will not stay there and let a bunch of facilitators, that can facilitate or not, stay here and make me look like a crazy man. You know what I'm saying? But let's all do the right thing, it's not that hard. Everybody (incomprehensible) we know that, so we are all 100% here, let's think about now.
Off: thank you
Off: thank you ((Applause)) (SC_07122011, "fucking facilitate")

The non-understanding of this discourse with OWS' core constituency's discourse is discernible in the way in which 22 m seems to ironically twist around core concepts and slogans of OWS: be it the "99%" that in fact should be "100%" (10–11), the suggestion that the facilitators should "facilitate some breakfast" to the hungry (14–15), or the statement that one could "speak and do the council later" (30–31).

This irony, which is acknowledged by applause and laughter in the audience, should not primarily be understood as a sign of a sovereign and playful mastery of the discourse. Rather it documents the attempt to *demonstrate* mastery in a foreign discourse that is endowed with higher social prestige than one's own. This is, for example, documented in the somewhat gruff reaction of 22 m to the laughter that responds to his 100% statement (11–13), which indicates that he does not perceive the laughter as support but, at least partially, also as mockery.

It is also indicated in the tension between the grammatically unsound structure of the opening sentences and the somewhat awkwardly 'formalist' manner of speech ("we have (the) understanding", 2) that is employed in these sentences and that abruptly switches to colloquial, almost slang-like tropes ("we don't want no facilitation around", 4–5).[9] The insecurity that accompanies this act of 'speaking uphill' is clearly discernible in the anger expressed in the pronounced insistence that one will not "let a bunch of facilitators" "make me look like a crazy man" (33–34).

Undergirding the social tension that permeates the unfolding of this discourse within the very speaking situation is a fundamentally different orienting frame that can be reconstructed from the propositional content of this passage. This frame's basic coordinates are in conflict with that documented in the last passage. On the one hand, it is spanned by a negative horizon, which is connected to the metaphors of "facilitation", which is apparently "facilitating oppression" (28), the "stock exchange in the room" (24), and in general the "council" (28–31). On the other hand, it is spanned by a positive horizon that is defined by the unity of the "100%" and doing "the right thing", which is, for example, feeding the hungry. What is feared and resisted is the very process of institutionalization, which is implicitly equated with exclusion and the exercise of power. 22 m even declares that he does not care "if this is a GA or a spokes council" (29), thereby expressing his view that the *form* of this institutionalization is not of high importance. What is contrasted with this negative perspective is the practice of radical inclusion—"everybody needs to speak" (30)—and of doing good deeds.

It is not difficult to understand the habitus articulated in this basic orienting frame as the outcome of a social life that experienced most institutions as exclusionary or absent/irrelevant. Neither is it implausible that this habitus resonated very well with the early practice of OWS, which emphasized the ethos of radical inclusivity and mutual aid as its core principles.

What this habitus, however, does not resonate with is the implicit character of OWS, not only as *prefiguration* but also as *protest*. For large parts of the core constituency and especially for the involved veteran activists who played an important role in the establishment of the SC, the establishment of new structures to improve the efficiency of OWS as a political movement seemed to be a natural consequence of what they had done so far. These attempts, however, seemed absurd (at best) to many that came from the ranks of the homeless and the urban precariat. Politics, in their view, is a divisive and ultimately futile endeavor, something that those 'on top' seem to have the inexplicable urge to practice (5–6), but which ultimately threatens the very community of mutual help and recognition that they had originally perceived and enjoyed OWS as.[10]

While coexistence with the homeless was far from unproblematic for the core constituency during the occupation,[11] it became close to impossible as soon as the protesters were evicted from the park. Attempts at organizational integration, such as the establishing of a homeless caucus in December 2011 (NYCGA 2011c), were only short lived, and the cooperation with them took on a philanthropic bent that many Occupiers felt uneasy with. When I arrived at OWS in late 2012, only rather peripheral 'little occupations' in front of Trinity Church and Goldman-Sachs remained interfaces of contact with this part of the movement. It is no wonder then that they, and everybody working closely with them, had insisted very strongly on maintaining the occupation.

However, this is only part of the answer for why the movement did not really evolve into a new form but rather disintegrated in the years that followed. Most of my interviewees from the core constituency and the movement veterans recalled the feeling that the park evolved from an asset to a burden for the movement, and even Adbusters suggested in their 'tactical briefing' in November that abandoning the park might be a necessary next step for the movement (Adbusters 2011b).[12]

This transformation was not only hindered by internal conflicts but further complicated by the specific thick opportunity structures, especially the 'social movement field' in NYC, as it was discussed in Sect. 6.2. The lack of pre-existing social networks for the core constituency, which research has shown to be crucial for social movements to unfold ("indigenous organizations" (McAdam 1999)), in this sense, had a double-edged effect. It most certainly contributed to both the explosive growth and dynamic of OWS through a kind of pressure cooker effect, but it also added to the difficulties to maintain the momentum of the movement once the dynamic of this first explosion was interrupted. The occupation of the park as OWS' visible center and main expression is also tied to this.

It provided the catalyst for the discontent to crystallize, but it was itself unable to generate the kinds of infrastructures and alliances that would have allowed for the transformation of the practice. In this sense, the potentially transformative moment of the occupation fell on sterile ground.

7.4 Summary: "That's Not a Solution"

The rise and decline of OWS as an internationally recognized protest mobilization is closely linked to the 'signature practice' of the occupation of Liberty Plaza. As this chapter demonstrated, the multi-level theory-of-practice approach can meaningfully reconstruct the conjuncture of different social determinants that shaped the mass resonance with this practice. It also contributes to understanding the difficulties in moving beyond the occupation even when its limitations as a protest-practice made themselves felt.

In a manner not consciously intended by those planning it, the occupation of Zuccotti Park turned out to temporarily overcome the obstacles that had prevented the social groups that built and shaped the mobilization from collectively voicing their discontent. It allowed the members of the proletarianized new petty bourgeoisie to overcome their fears by providing a setting that catered to the needs and expectations for dialogical and discursive practices and by serving as a reliable and durable environment to process and overcome one's fears and insecurities. The practice of the occupation, especially its welcoming and demonstratively non-hierarchical character and its institutions of mutual care, also resonated with the habitus of other social classes, such as the urban precariat, and therefore allowed for practical alliances that turned out to be very difficult to sustain in other settings-

Interestingly, in contrast to what classical theories of movement-repertoire-diffusion would lead us to expect (McAdam and Rucht 1993), this process did not even really require the involved actors to attribute similarity between the situations in Spain, Egypt, and their own. Instead, what began as a kind of symbolic 'quote', which was not even invested with very high hopes, resonated with the socio-structural conflicts in the USA and especially NYC in such a way that it turned into an actual protest-practice with a dynamic of its own.[13]

This very constellation allowing for the occupation's surprising success, however, also hindered the development of new forms of protest for replacing the occupation, and after the park was evicted, the old obstacles against collective mobilization regained their demobilizing force. The interests of important social groups like the homeless began to diverge sharply from those of the core constituency as soon as the shared practice of occupying as the conjunctive object of reference had vanished, and the original fear and mistrust of the participants was reinforced through lack of collective spaces of experience and encounter.

Thus, while OWS revealed the widespread discontent in large parts of the population of the United States, it was not able to give it a durable and concise form. This is not to join the chorus of those that hurried to explain how deluded OWS was as soon as it disappointed the hopes projected onto it (e.g., Frank 2012). What those criticisms frequently ignore is that these 'mistakes' were also solutions that made the mobilization possible in the first place—a paradox that was nicely formulated by the participants in one of the group discussions in regard to the occupation and 'horizontalist' protest-practices in general:

L: You know, and that's why we're not still sitting in a Park somewhere. Or, whatever. That's why,
J: └ yeah ┘
L: that's why like
J: └ (incomprehensible) ┘ things that were like flaws, with how Occupy did things, but always, it really frustrates me, when people are like, the whole organizational thing, and // L: mhm// you know, horizontalism is bad, it's like, nonono. It would, you're trying to solve the problems that there were, by doing something that would have prevented it from ever existing in the first place.
L: right.
J: That's not a solution. That's a, it wouldn't have
L: └ right ┘
J: happened at all. (OWSG4)

Some have argued that addressing the challenge of transcending the original "anarchist moment" (Dean 2012) of the 'movement of the squares' and the obstacles it encountered is a pressing issue for critical theory and the political left in general (e.g., Rehmann 2013; Taylor 2013; Candeias and Völpel 2014; Dean 2016). By identifying the condition of the possibility of the protest practice of 'occupying' developing such a strong momentum while also pointing out what contradictions and blockades to further transformations were already implicated at this very conjuncture, this chapter—and this book—seeks to contribute to this debate. The reconstructive, theory-of-practice-inspired approach allows for leaving behind some of the false dichotomies ("prefiguration" vs. "protest", "horizontalism" vs. "verticalism") and voluntarisms that have plagued the political and philosophical debate between those that emphatically greeted the assembly as the model of the leaderless protest of tomorrow (Hardt and Negri 2017) and those that have challenged this position (Dean 2016). Better yet, it allows for understanding how these categories are rooted in the very social logic of the conjuncture from which the protests themselves emerged. In doing so, it can contribute to a heightened reflexivity in regard to some of the desires and fears that drove and shaped the protests and thereby often non-consciously predetermined the limits of their development.

Notes

1. For the centrality of "occupations" in analyses of the movements of 2011ff, see also, e.g., (Butler 2011; Aalbers 2012; Mörtenböck and Mooshammer 2012; Schrader and Wachsmuth 2012; Hammond 2013).
2. On the level of the lived experience, this is documented, for example, in the group discussion passage discussed in Sect. 5.2.2 in which the question "what do you want?" is cited as an annoying and reoccurring question that the activists saw themselves confronted repeatedly.
3. It is probably no coincidence that this is also the day the first article in *The New York Times* referring to the group in Zuccotti Park as "Occupy Wall Street" was published (Bellafante 2011).
4. For the "people's mic" as the alternative to loudspeakers, a choice that resonated very well with the predisposition of OWS' core constituency, see Sect. 5.2.1.
5. At first, this passage seems to be a rationalization for why others were hesitant to join the protest. However, the switch from the third- to the first-person perspective and the short laughter indicate that what Max presents as other peoples' reasoning is in fact closely connected to her own lived experience.
6. The term 'precariat' is used here not in the sense of a unified new, global class recruiting itself from all over the old class structure (Standing 2011), or some kind of "affective class" (Berlant 2011, 195), but in a much narrower sense as referring to the disintegrating lower ranks of the proletariat's youth—the "urban outcasts", as Wacquant conceptualized them (2008).
7. This discursive strategy was shared from the right to the center-left. Not surprisingly, the conservative *New York Post* mocked that the kitchen team was frustrated by "freeloaders"; however, a liberal television program, "The Daily Show", also ran a clip titled "Occupy Wall Street Divided" (Algar 2011; The Daily Show 2011).
8. An audio recording of this meeting is available online. The reconstruction is based on a transcription of the whole meeting, which was subjected to an interpretative procedure similar to that described in Sect. 4.2: First, it was

fully transcribed, then the whole transcript was subjected to a formulating interpretation, and finally, core passages were subjected to a reflecting interpretation.

9. Bourdieu describes an equally split 'doubled discourse' in his analysis of the language deployed by members of the working class that are trying to make a 'political point' in letters written to newspapers—an endeavor that also constantly oscillates between the desire to demonstrate one's mastery in the legitimate discourse, on the one hand, and to demonstrate that one 'sees through their (the politicians) game', on the other (1994, esp. 678ff.).
10. This is documented also in other contributions to this SC meeting. Another speaker, albeit without discernible irony, employs the same strategy of twisting OWS's vocabulary around, explaining that he is speaking for "Occupy" and not just for "Occupy Wall Street". He presents the latter as the divisive, politicizing faction among the greater community of the former.
11. A document of this was the persistent feature in many interviews that the NYPD had brought drug-abusing individuals and people with mental problems into the park to undermine solidarity. Independent of the factual correctness of this claim, its persistence in the narrated accounts points at the centrality of the associated conflicts for the experience of the life in the park.
12. One should not overestimate the role of Adbusters in any decision-making processes in and around the park. They are referenced here rather as an indication that the idea of the occupation being a tactic with an expiration date was widespread at that moment.
13. A very similar observation was made by Ingrid Gilcher-Holtey apropos the barricades of Paris in May 1968, which also began as a historic quote and assumed their practical-political meaning only through the evolving conflict with the police and other social actors' reactions toward this conflict (Gilcher-Holtey 1998, 20).

Bibliography

Aalbers, Manuel B. 2012. Socializing Space and Politicizing Financial Innovation/Destruction: Some Observations on Occupy Wall Street. *Belgeo. Revue Belge de Géographie*, 1–2. http://belgeo.revues.org/6155. Accessed 17 Nov 2017.

Adbusters. 2011a. #OCCUPYWALLSTREET A Shift in Revolutionary Tactics. https://www.adbusters.org/blogs/adbusters-blog/occupywallstreet.html. Accessed 15 May 2013.

———. 2011b. Tactical Briefing #18 – Occupy the High Ground, November 14. https://www.adbusters.org/blogs/adbusters-blog/adbusters-tactical-briefing-18.html. Accessed 15 Oct 2013.

Algar, Selim. 2011. Occupy Wall Street Kitchen Staff Protesting Fixing Food for Freeloaders. *New York Post*, November 27.

Appel, Hannah Chadeayne. 2011. The Ritual of General Assembly and the Bureaucracies of Anarchy. https://socialtextjournal.org/the_rituals_of_general_assembly_and_the_bureaucracies_of_anarchy/. Accessed 17 Nov 2017.

Bellafante, Ginia. 2011. Protesters Are Gunning for Wall Street, With Faulty Aim. *The New York Times*, September 23. http://www.nytimes.com/2011/09/25/nyregion/protesters-are-gunning-for-wall-street-with-faulty-aim.html. Accessed 17 Nov 2017.

Berlant, Lauren. 2011. *Cruel Optimism*. Durham: Duke University Press Books.

Bourdieu, Pierre. 1991. *The Craft of Sociology: Epistemological Preliminaries*. Berlin: Walter de Gruyter.

———. 1994. *Die feinen Unterschiede: Kritik der gesellschaftlichen Urteilskraft*. Suhrkamp: Frankfurt am Main.

Butler, Judith. 2011. *Bodies in Alliance and the Politics of the Street*. Presented at the The State of Things, Venice, July 9. http://eipcp.net/transversal/1011/butler/en. Accessed 17 Nov 2017.

Candeias, Mario, and Eva Völpel. 2014. *Plätze Sichern! ReOrganisierung der Linken in der Krise. Zur Lernfähigkeit des Mosaiks in den USA, Spanien und Griechenland*. Hamburg: VSA.

Dean, Jodi. 2012. Occupy Wall Street: After the Anarchist Moment. *Socialist Register* 49 (49): 52–62.

———. 2016. *Crowds and Party*. New York: Verso.

Della Porta, Donatella, and Alice Mattoni. 2014. Patterns of Diffusion and the Transnational Dimension of Protest in the Movements of the Crisis: An Introduction. In *Spreading Protest. Social Movements in Times of Crisis*, 1–18. Colchester: ECPR Press.

Frank, Thomas. 2012. To the Precinct Station – How Theory Met Practice…and Drove It Absolutely Crazy. *The Baffler*, 21. http://www.thebaffler.com/past/to_the_precinct_station. Accessed 17 Nov 2017.

Gilcher Holtey, Ingrid. 1998. Mai 68 in Frankreich. In *1968: Vom Ereignis zum Gegenstand der Geschichtswissenschaft*, 11–34. Göttingen: Vandenhoeck & Ruprecht.

Gould-Wartofsky, Michael A. 2015. *The Occupiers: The Making of the 99 Percent Movement*. Oxford/New York: Oxford University Press.

Graeber, David. 2013. *The Democracy Project: A History, a Crisis, a Movement*. New York: Spiegel and Grau.

Hammond, John L. 2013. The Significance of Space in Occupy Wall Street. *Interface: A Journal for and about Social Movements* 5 (2): 499–524.

Hardt, Michael, and Antonio Negri. 2017. *Assembly*. New York: Oxford University Press.

Kroll, Andy. 2011. How Occupy Wall Street Really Got Started. *Mother Jones*, October 17. http://www.motherjones.com/politics/2011/10/occupy-wall-street-international-origins?page=1. Accessed 1 Nov 2017.

Kumkar, Nils C. 2016. The Meaning of the Park – How the New York City General Assembly Became 'Occupy Wall Street' and Never Recovered from Its Success. *City: Analysis of Urban Trends, Culture, Theory, Policy, Action*. 20 (5): 700–718.

Madden, David J., and Antonis Vradis. 2012. From Athens to Occupy and Back: Introduction to Cities in Upheaval. *City: Analysis of Urban Trends, Culture, Theory, Policy, Action*. 16 (1–2): 235–236.

Marcuse, Peter. 2011. #5. The Purpose of the Occupation Movement and the Danger Of Fetishizing Space. *Peter Marcuse's Blog*, November 15. https://pmarcuse.wordpress.com/2011/11/15/the-purpose-of-the-occupation-movement-and-the-danger-of-fetishizing-space/. Accessed 1 Nov 2017.

McAdam, Doug. 1999. *Political Process and the Development of Black Insurgency, 1930–1970*. Chicago: University of Chicago Press.

McAdam, Doug, and Dieter Rucht. 1993. The Cross-National Diffusion of Movement Ideas. *The Annals of the American Academy of Political and Social Science* 528 (1): 56–74.

Milkman, Ruth, Stephanie Luce, and Penny Lewis. 2013. *Changing the Subject: A Bottom-Up Account of Occupy Wall Street in New York City*. New York: Joseph S. Murphy Institute for Worker Education and Labor Studies. https://www.documentcloud.org/documents/562862-changing-the-subject-2.html. Accessed 1 Nov 2017.

Mörtenböck, Peter, and Helge Mooshammer. 2012. *Occupy: Räume des Protests*. Bielefeld: transcript.

NYCGA. 2011a. General Assembly Minutes 9/17/11. http://www.nycga.net/2011/09/general-assembly-minutes-91711/. Accessed 4 June 2016.

———. 2011b. General Assembly Minutes 9/23/11. http://www.nycga.net/2011/09/general-assembly-minutes-7pm-92311/. Accessed 4 June 2016.

———. 2011c. Proposal for Saturday 12/10 General Assembly: Formation of Houseless Working Group & Caucus. http://www.nycga.net/2011/12/proposal-for-saturday-1210-general-assembly-formation-of-houseless-working-group-caucus/. Accessed 15 Mar 2013.

Pickerill, Jenny, and John Krinsky. 2012. Why Does Occupy Matter? *Social Movement Studies* 11 (3/4): 279–287.

Rehmann, Jan. 2013. Occupy Wall Street and the Question of Hegemony: A Gramscian Analysis. *Socialism and Democracy* 27 (1): 1–18.

Schneider, Nathan. 2013. *Thank You, Anarchy: Notes From the Occupy Apocalypse*. Berkeley: University of California Press.

Schrader, Stuart, and David Wachsmuth. 2012. Reflections on Occupy Wall Street, the State and Space. *City: Analysis of Urban Trends, Culture, Theory, Policy, Action* 16 (1–2): 243–248.

Standing, Guy. 2011. *The Precariat: The New Dangerous Class*. London: Bloomsbury Academic.

Taylor, Blair. 2013. From Alterglobalization to Occupy Wall Street: Neoanarchism and the New Spirit of the Left. *City: Analysis of Urban Trends, Culture, Theory, Policy, Action* 17 (6): 729–747.

The Daily Show. 2011. *Occupy Wall Street Divided*. New York: Comedy Central. http://thedailyshow.cc.com/videos/5510me/occupy-wall-street-divided. Accessed 15 Mar 2013.

Wacquant, Loïc J.D. 2008. *Urban Outcasts: A Comparative Sociology of Advanced Marginality*. Cambridge: Polity Press.

CHAPTER 8

Conclusion and Outlook

In April 2014, I participated in and observed an Occupy Wall Street (OWS) event in New York—the so-called people's gong. A ritual of protest held in front of the New York Stock Exchange (NYSE), which initially developed during the "Occupy Spring" of 2012, during the months of reassembling and regrouping that followed the eviction of Liberty Plaza, repeatedly attracted hundreds of people in that period. The performance, a kind of demonstrative people's mic, consisted of people standing in circles, facing outward, and repeating the words of a leading speaker, proclaiming that the bell of the NYSE was a symbol of everything they considered to be wrong with the world and the "people's gong" was the call to join the common struggle, before counting down and then collectively imitating the sound of an actual gong.[1]

Despite the event having been advertised quite persistently on social media and mailing lists, the group that assembled there was rather small (around 50 people), and it seemed as if more people were watching than actually participating. Tourists took pictures, a few policemen and women looked grimly on the scene, and people wearing suits with shiny shoes and briefcases walked a little faster when they passed the group, shaking their heads in disapproval. When it started drizzling, everyone dispersed rather quickly. In hindsight, what struck me the most about this small event was the air of nostalgia that hung over it. People I spoke to on the sidelines told me that they "always loved the people's gong", even though it was

N. C. Kumkar, *The Tea Party, Occupy Wall Street, and the Great Recession*, Critical Political Theory and Radical Practice,
https://doi.org/10.1007/978-3-319-73688-4_8

happening right in front of them and even those actively participating in it afterward told me that it felt good to do it “once again”. It seemed that for almost everyone involved, there was no doubt that—two and a half years after the occupation of Liberty Plaza, and six months after the last personal story had been uploaded on the “wearethe99percent” tumblr-blog—OWS was history. It had morphed into something which one could cite and reenact, but not really continue.

During the same month, I revisited a Tea Party (TP) group which I had stayed in contact with in the two years before. When I wrote an email beforehand to announce my intention to attend the group’s public meeting, I was told that they were not meeting in their office anymore, but rather in a nearby roadside diner, since it did not make much sense to pay the rent for the office anymore. And indeed, the group that still gathered could comfortably sit around a larger diner table, and the conversations happening, despite still being driven by deep political conviction (and anger), did not really have an ‘activist’ tone, but rather seemed like a regulars’ table for discussing the viciousness of the US political landscape. Another three years later, as I am writing these lines, this might raise the question of where to go from here. Is not *everything* this book discussed now history?

Yes and no. On the one hand, it is of course true that both the changing socio-political environment in the USA and the inner contradictions of the protest mobilizations make it highly unlikely that these protest mobilizations will simply reappear. In that sense, the TP and OWS are history. However, many of the social conditions of possibility of the protest-practices are still in force—most importantly, the political economic contradictions at the heart of the Great Recession and with them the precarious socioeconomic position and the corresponding discontent of the social classes that drove the protests. This means that even if the concrete practices can be considered history, the logics which were identified as driving and shaping these practices are not. In the conclusion of my PhD thesis, on which this book is based, I argued that the primary campaigns of Bernie Sanders and Donald Trump were clear signs that the conflicts and predispositions reconstructed as driving and shaping OWS and the TP would continue to resurface and to shape US politics with force. Before I defended my thesis, Donald Trump was elected president.

In a manner that I surely had not hoped for, this proved the lasting importance of understanding how the US American petty bourgeoisie experiences and processes its crisis and how this interacts with the different social fields that together shape politics in the USA. After this conclusion summarized the findings on the social determinants of the protest-practices on the different levels of abstraction, as they were addressed in the individual chapters, it therefore closes with an epilogue that sketches out how some of these social determinants can help us to understand what happened in the last years in the political field in the USA and draw some careful and preliminary conclusions on how the corresponding challenges might be taken up by a critically engaged social science.

8.1 Conclusion

The starting point of my argument was the observation that the USA (as with many countries around the globe) saw large right- and left-wing protest mobilizations in the wake of the Great Recession. These protest mobilizations grew explosively despite their often vague or contradictory messages and their respective growth followed clear socio-demographic patterns. Even though many authors writing on these protests implicated some sort of causal connection between the Great Recession and the occurrence of these protests, this assumed connection was not reconstructed in a systematic and comparative manner thus far. Furthermore, no empirical study hitherto had used qualitative, reconstructive methods to understand why specific socio-demographic groups were so responsive to the protest mobilization of OWS. The research question that was formulated to address these gaps was: *How can the lived experience of the Great Recession by the social classes that drove these mass protests be understood as shaping and informing their very protest-practice?*

Theoretically, this question was addressed through the conceptual lens of the Bourdieusian theory of practice. The protests, defined as collectively enacted social practices, were shaped by how their constituencies experienced the social developments around the Great Recession—both through their socially specific exposure to the dynamics of the crisis and through their respective habitus patterning this *being-exposed-to* as a *meaningful-experience-of*. In this sense, I also formulated the research question in an inverted manner. *How can the protests as a social practice be interpreted as a symptom of the socioeconomic crisis?* Thus, the protests are not only analyzed as something to be explained for its own sake—their explanation itself is something that helps us to better understand 'our times'.

Empirically, the base of my argument was the comparison of the early, explosive phase of OWS and the TP. OWS was carried out by the young cohorts or aspirants of the new petty bourgeoisie. The TP mobilized a different class generational unit experiencing the Great Recession in the USA, namely, the older cohorts of the classical petty bourgeoisie. It was shown that the rise and fall of the protest mobilizations was closely connected to the convulsions that the Great Recession sent through the social space of the USA. Furthermore, their practice was decisively shaped by the way in which the habitus of their core constituencies structured both their experience of the crisis and the protest-practices through which they articulated their discontent—across all the different levels of abstraction that were addressed throughout this book.

Every understanding of the crisis protests implies an understanding of the 'crisis', since it both structures our perception of what the protesters are reacting to and provides the background against which we measure the criticism they articulate. At the highest level of abstraction, the second chapter, "The Structural Crisis and the Emerging Patterns of Class Conflict", therefore outlined my understanding of the Great Recession—as an acute stage of the structural crisis of the finance-dominated accumulation regime. It sketched out the impacts of this crisis on the political economy of the USA and the emerging lines of class conflict that the crisis brought to the fore, especially in regard to different factions of capital. This accumulation regime had 'solved' the crisis of Fordism's declining rate of profit with a combination of wage suppression and offshoring—thereby creating a demand gap that was filled by investment in aggressive market expansion which was accompanied by the creation of ever higher amounts of fictitious capital. The growth of the latter increasingly diverged from growth in production, until the Great Recession threatened to violently iron out this discrepancy.

The political polarization of US society around the election of President Barack Obama highlighted diverging interests between different factions of capital. On the one side, the proponents of a "Green New Deal", in which green energy, high-technology sectors would assume the productive locomotive function in the national economy, stood behind Obama's presidential bid. On the other side stood the actors from those economic sectors fearing that such a restructuring of the national economy would be at their expense—especially the extractive industries and the inflation-sensitive owners of monetary capital. This very abstract sketch allowed for highlighting important features of the 'condition of possibility' of the protest mobilization. The TP had explosive momentum because its calls against redistributive politics and ecologically and socially sustainable development tapped into conflict within capital itself. OWS emerged in the crisis of legitimacy that arose when (partially because of the TP) this conflict's solution was forestalled through austerity by gridlock.

The third chapter, "The Demographics of the Mobilized: the Core Constituency of the Protests", concretized this abstract background in regard to how the specific social classes that formed the core constituencies of the protests were exposed to the developments described in the second chapter. It brought together the results of different surveys and studies on the demographic composition of the protest mobilizations for (i) identifying their respective core constituencies and (ii) sketching out the way in which these class-generational units were exposed to the dynamics of the Great Recession and how their position in social space had changed in the years before and after it.

The TP's core constituency, the classical petty bourgeoisie, had lived through the Great Recession with relatively little or no losses in income but experienced a severe devaluation of their safety assets—most prominently their houses—and a darkening of their economic horizon. While the boom in real estate and finance had cushioned the secular decline of this social class in the years after 2001, these sectors, in which many TP activists had their businesses, contracted most strongly during the Great Recession. As the core constituency of OWS, I identified the members of the aspiring young cohort of the new petty bourgeoisie who found their cultural capital—which defines their political economic position as a class—massively devaluated. Having just left institutions of higher education that had prepared them for a career in the educational or cultural sector or in administration, they were hit by the Great Recession right when they were about to enter the labor market. The combination of decreasing economic returns on investment in education (both through exploding costs and stagnating or falling wages) in tandem with a rapidly contracting labor market for younger people in the USA created a situation for this class-generational unit that led me to call them the *proletarianized aspirants of the new petty bourgeoisie* (Table 8.1).

This helps to explain the geographic distribution of the protest activities of Occupy and the TP. The fact that protest activities of the former were concentrated in college towns and larger cities, and overall in areas with relatively low unemployment and poverty rates, does not contradict the finding that those active in OWS reacted to the experience of economic

Table 8.1 Summary

Chapter	------------	*The Tea Party*	*Occupy Wall Str.*
3: Class-generational-unit and exposure to crisis dynamics	**Core constituency**	Classical petty bourgeoisie and administrative petty bourgeoisie, >45 years old	Proletarianized/ biographically blocked young new petty bourgeoisie, 25–35 years old
	Socio-biographical trajectory	Shock-like devaluation of economic capital, insecurity about future wealth	Creeping devaluation of cultural capital accelerated in 2007/08
5: Habitus reconstruction	**Negative horizon**	Collapse of order, loss of status	*Vague*: Loss of perspective, non-resonant environment
	Positive horizon	*Vague*: Restoring the "right framework"	Fulfilled life, mutual recognition, shaping society.
	Potential for enactment	*None*, delegating agency to others.	*None*, displaced into either redirection or acting out.
	Practical unfolding	Disappointment without disillusionment, repairing reality.	Impossible exodus, redirection activity.
6: The thick opportunity structures of the protests	**Social field of articulation**	*Quasi-field*, spanned by conflict in other fields	*Proto-field*, secession from social movement field in crisis

insecurity, but is most likely a consequence of its core constituency living exactly in these types of locations. The TP, on the other hand, is concentrated in suburban counties and more specifically in those that experienced high rates of foreclosure and low rates of unemployment. The latter fits with the findings on the way the classical petty bourgeoisie was impacted by the crisis—not primarily through a loss of employment or income but rather through the devaluation of long-term safety assets. This strongly supports one of my initial assumptions, namely, that the Great Recession indeed had a decisive influence on the TP's emergence and activism—in contrast to Skocpol and Williamson's argument that the Great Recession was a secondary trait (Skocpol and Williamson 2012, 205).

The fourth chapter, "Theoretical and Methodological Considerations: Habitus and Habitus Reconstruction", presented the methodology and the results of the reconstruction of the habitually structured experience of the crisis and the respective protests as they were lived through by the core constituencies of the protest mobilizations. This part explained the category of the habitus and the documentary method for habitus reconstruction. While the second chapter provided the abstract background of crisis and the second chapter specified what aspects of the crisis the core constituencies of the protests were subjected to, this chapter introduced the habitus as a category that allows us to understand how this socially specific being-exposed-to the crisis was transformed into the meaningful, lived experience of the protesting subjects and how they translated this lived experience into discontent and critique.

The fifth chapter, "Experiencing the Crisis: Results of the Habitus Reconstruction", formed the empirical and conceptual heart of this book. It presented the results of the reconstruction of the habitus of the core constituencies from open group discussions and interviews with participants in the protests. The analysis of the habitus of the TP's and OWS's core constituencies was then further nuanced by interpreting pictures used in two exemplary propaganda materials taken from these protest mobilizations.

The TP activists' habitus was reconstructed (in Sect. 5.1) as spanned between a negative horizon, defined by a deep fear of vanishing 'natural' differences and a loss of status and security, and a very vague positive horizon, defined by the longing for the reinstatement of the 'right framework'—the complex of 'natural' rules that would secure one's position and orientation within social space. The Great Recession and the election of President Obama was experienced as a kind of "waking up" to the realization that one's social and economic position was undermined—a realization which, however, was interpreted by the TP activists in a very peculiar way, which I labelled ***disappointment while refusing to be disillusioned***.

The suspicion that the 'American Dream' of material wealth and social recognition might prove unfeasible is neither understood as pointing to socio-structural reasons, such as a crisis of the capitalist political economy in its current form, nor to personal shortcomings or simple misfortune. This reflects a class ethos according to which everyone forges his own destiny, and which therefore legitimizes social inequality as ultimately 'just', as it is confronted with a reality that constantly defies this expectation in the sense that one does not get what one believes to deserve. The reasons for reality disappointing one's expectations are sought in the activities of hidden, subversive actors who purposely undermine the natural order of things, resulting in a 'conspiratorial mode of interpretation'. This interpretational pattern allows the angry insistence on a social order on which claims to wealth and social recognition are grounded, even when this very social order obviously fails to deliver on its promises.

Reoccurring patterns in the descriptions of these supposed subversive activities are, on the one hand, seeing an alliance between corrupted elites and the 'undeserving poor' to whom promises are made at the expense of the regular 'Middle American', thereby corrupting the order of the class society. On the other hand, the other orienting principle in the TP activists' symbolic universe posits an alliance of hidden players acting from outside the USA, which is undermining the nation state. Barack Obama as the first African-American president and 'social climber' functioned as a powerful symbol for both these ambivalences—which explains some of the anger and fear that was projected on him and his administration by TP activists.

The habitus of OWS' core constituency (reconstructed in Sect. 5.2) is spanned, on the one hand, by a positive horizon defined by a world that resonates with oneself—through mutual, dialogical relations to other people and through being involved in the discourse on the future of society. The negative horizon, on the other hand, remained rather vague but was discernible as the inversion of the positive horizon and is defined by a lack of resonance of society as a foreign and closed-off reality in which one does not have any say or agency. The negative horizon was documented especially in their accounts on their personal experience in the years before OWS, in which they mention the loneliness, detachment, and cynicism they felt during this period of time.

The positive horizon was documented especially in those passages of the interviews and discussions that dealt with OWS itself. In a sense, OWS functioned as a redirection activity for its core constituency—it in itself catered to those social needs whose lack of fulfillment had initially created the discontent that was then articulated through OWS. However, it was also shown that, even though OWS' protest-practice catered to those needs, it apparently did not satisfy them.

The result was a split relation to the protest-practice which was documented in the co-existence of two contradicting logics. Using the vocabulary of OWS' activists themselves, I called these two projects *prefiguration* and *protest*. The former relates to the activists' affective investment into OWS' practice as something rewarding in its own right, while the latter relates to the understanding of OWS as something that aimed at changing society overall.

In the group discussions and interviews with participants in OWS, such conflicting habitually patterned relations to the protest-practice were documented in the form of dilemmas that could only symbolically be 'solved' through jokes or wordplay. I also argued that the high prominence of the concept of "*Direct Action*" in OWS' discourse on its own practice must be understood in the light of the same contradiction. It, too, is to be read as the attempt to (symbolically) align the two conflicting logics of prefiguration and protest in one coherent protest-practice.

This understanding of OWS' core constituency's split relationship to the protest-practice and its rootedness in their lived experience of socio-biographical crisis dialectically solves the dispute if OWS is to be understood as a "New New Social Movement" (Langman 2013) or rather as the newest culmination point of the long trajectory of the NSM—be it as an example of "simulative democracy" (Blühdorn 2013, 2014) or as the "new spirit of the left" (Taylor 2013). It allows for reconstructing the rootedness of the ethos that unites OWS' practice with that of the NSM in the class-generational unit that decisively shaped this practice—the youth of the new petty bourgeoisie. The high affective investment of this class-generational unit in the *prefigurative* practices of OWS, however, also points to the fact that this class-generational unit finds itself confronted with an undermining of the very class position that this ethos was geared toward. I argue that this explains the prominence of questions of material redistribution in OWS' slogans and claims—questions that were traditionally not considered to be at the heart of the politics of the NSM.

These contradictions in both the TP's and OWS' core constituencies habitually patterned perception of the crisis and relation to the protests brought me to define them as 'crisis protests', in reference to Kerbo's concept of the "movements of crisis" (Kerbo 1982). Not only do participants react to a political economic crisis through protest, they also are themselves in the midst of (socio-biographical) crisis.

Section 5.3 further accentuated the way in which this shaped the relation of both OWS' and the TP's core constituency to their protest-practice through interpreting pictures used in propaganda materials by the two protest mobilizations. The results of this interpretation confirmed and accentuated the findings of the interpretation of the discussions and interviews.

The images were shown not only to document the contradictory relation that the constituencies had to their protest mobilizations but also to offer a kind of *affective premium* to those that identified with the subjectivity addressed through them. In the case of the TP, this was the *signing up for a higher authorities cause*, which would release one from the insecurity and guilt that resulted from feeling duped by the very social institutions one identifies with. In the case of OWS, it was the promise that even the resigned realization that the solution of the experienced social problems is beyond one's reach might still function as a *cultural competitive edge vis-à-vis others* that could grant some of the missing social recognition.

The sixth chapter, "Fields and Conjunctures: The Thick Opportunity Structure of the Mobilizations", which closes the 'analytical' part of the book, constructed the thick opportunity structure as the constellation of fields in which the protests unfolded. While the fourth and fifth chapters reconstructed the protesters' lived experience of the crisis and the way in which the habitus of the protests' core constituencies' not only structured this experience but also how it explains their resonance with peculiar protest-practices, this chapter now directed attention toward the socially structured environment in which their protest-practices took on their peculiar shapes and dynamics. It was shown that the cases were decisively shaped by the different socio-spatial environment in which their constituencies articulated their discontent. The chapter thereby provided the last step of concretion needed to answer the research question—how can the lived experience of the Great Recession by the social classes that drove these mass protests be understood as shaping their very protest-practice?

In the case of the TP (Sect. 6.1), Santelli's "rant heard 'round the world" was, other than the TP mythology suggests, not a spark that ignited a looming mass mobilization waiting to happen. Despite the discontent of its constituency, the lack of a 'social movement field' to which the actors were accustomed beforehand made them rather reluctant respondents at first (because protesting was "not in (their) DNA", as they themselves put it). The resonance of the TP mobilization with this constituency was made possible by a conjuncture of critical developments in a number of social fields which led to an alliance of actors that made sure that the 'rant' was in fact heard at all and which contributed to forming an audience ready to listen.

In the economic field, actors afraid that the Obama Administration's economic policies might initiate a restructuring of the field at their expense invested heavily in fueling protests to delegitimize the administration and thereby undermine its regulatory potential. In the political field, actors hitherto rather peripheral in the Republican Party seized the chance offered by this party's deep crisis following the electoral defeat in 2008 to better their own position within it by presenting themselves as "true Conservatives"—in contrast to party-establishment "RINOs" who had sold out to the "Socialist" Obama. Finally, in the journalistic field, a number of actors catering to the base of the Republican Party's electorate engaged in escalating condemnations of the administration which culminated in accusations that Obama is a "Racist" and the administration was "flirting with Fascism".

The protest-practice of the TP thus gained its explosive momentum from the dialectical interplay between this 'quasi-field' and the habitus of the mobilized constituency. The fear of losing both social recognition and wealth was stimulated and channeled by the conservative media's escalating condemnations of the administration as promoting socialism, which dovetailed with the economic actors' fear of a restructuring of the economic field at their expense. The reading of the world as a corrupted and skewed image of a 'true' reality in which 'real' Americans fight for how everything "was supposed to be" lent itself to the self-portrayal of the "TP candidates" among Republicans—an alliance also facilitated by the core constituency's inclination to rely on authority figures for reinforcing the 'rules' they felt were under threat.

However, this dialectic also set the expiration date for this explosive mobilization. When the main locus of conflict about economic policies shifted back into the realm of institutionalized congressional politics, the 'state of energy' in the quasi-field around the TP began to dissipate. The very ease with which the discontent of the core constituency found resonance in the political field early on (together with the habitual predisposition to delegate agency to 'higher authorities') provided little incentive for them to form independent organizational structures, meaning that the TP as an identifiable protest mobilization started to disintegrate soon after. On the one hand, this answers a question that was often asked in regard to the TP, namely, whether it is to be considered an 'authentic', "grassroots" social movement or if it was merely implemented top-down as "Astroturf" (e.g., Lo 2012; Frank 2012; Krugman 2009)—it was both—and why, nevertheless, the dissolution of the conjuncture 'on top' still meant the end of the mass mobilization, despite the persistence of the discontent feeding the mobilization.

In the case of OWS (Sect. 6.2), something like a social movement field, in which relevant parts of the core constituency developed their 'feeling for the game', did exist. However, the closing off of the political field toward this subfield and a number of developments especially in (though surely not limited to) NYC, such as decades of repressive protest policing, an increasing professionalization of activism in the tertiary sector, and a scarcity of time and material resources that young adults had at their disposal, brought this field itself into crisis.

Those planning OWS therefore developed a strategy which I called, in reference to Bourdieu, the *strategy of heresy*. Refusing to be part of what they perceived as the ritualistic and ossified status quo of the social movement field, they 'declared their independence' and presented OWS as a new, 'pure' social movement practice. This proved very attractive to those feeling resigned about the potential of political activism and, after initial mobilization successes, also to actors from the social movement field itself. However, after the eviction of the park, the low degree of institutionalization of this proto-field was not able to counter the centrifugal forces of the different factions that had come together in OWS.

The final, seventh chapter, "The Acid Test: Reconstructing the Meaning of the Park as a Socially Determined Practice of Protests", brought together all the findings from the preceding chapters to explain one peculiar practice of OWS, considered to be of high significance by many scholars that studied the protests in the wake of the Great Recession—the occupation of Zuccotti Park/Liberty Plaza that lent this protest mobilization its name.

While the decision to symbolically occupy a public space in NYC was inspired by the protests around the Mediterranean that had taken place since the winter of 2010–2011, it was not invested with high hopes as something that would actually last by those involved in its planning. The fact that it developed such an explosive momentum has to be understood through a specific conjuncture of social developments that partly contributed to the condition of possibility of this protest-practice resonating with this specific mass audience in the USA:

The core constituency of OWS, the youth of the new petty bourgeoisie, had experienced social isolation and a sense of socio-biographical loss of orientation in the years following 2008. The occupation of the park catered to their discontent in at least two ways. On the one hand, the dialogical and caring practices that formed the daily life of the occupation both allowed them to become active in a way that fit their blocked socio-biographical expectations by involving them in a discussion about the future of society. The inclusivity of the practice—which did not require any sort of 'membership' and was not based on a platform that one had to sign on to—and the permanent material presence in the park lowered the bar for highly individualistic and often anxious actors to overcome their skepticism and fears.

The park furthermore provided an interface facilitating contact to actors from other class-generational units, such as the unionized working class, social movement veterans (usually from the new petty bourgeoisie itself), and the urban precariat. As I illustrated with the example of the latter, however, these actors, with their different experiential backgrounds and the corresponding habitus, perceived the 'meaning' of the occupation in significantly different ways. These different perceptions (and the hopes and fears connected with them) contributed to escalating socio-political conflicts between the different groups as soon as the necessity of a change of strategy became a topic of discussion.

In combination with the mentioned crisis of the social movement field in NYC, differences ultimately hindered all attempts at reorganizing the structure of the protest mobilization, preventing the development of alternative practices besides occupying. After attempts at reoccupations failed, the protest mobilization disintegrated rather quickly and shrunk back to an enlarged group of core activists. The occupation therefore provided a means of overcoming obstacles to the mobilization of the discontent mainly of those young adults at the blocked threshold to the new petty bourgeoisie. However, it did so in a form that implicated high barriers against a further development of the protest mobilization, which—in the end—proved insurmountable.

In reconstructing how the different social determinants that contributed to both the explosive resonance of different social groups with this peculiar protest-practice and to the 'forbidden transition' of this protest-practice into new forms, this chapter functioned as a kind of acid test. It demonstrated not only that all the different findings of the chapters can be meaningfully combined into one coherent model, it also showed that the socio-analysis of this protest-practice can provide both a fresh perspective on the social logic of this practice and on the discontents and desires driving it.

8.2 Epilogue: First as Farce, Then as Tragedy

Interpreting the protests as a symptom of socioeconomic crisis rather than as an organizational ensemble aiming at social change (cf. Snow et al. 2006, 11)—although perhaps eluding questions of organizational continuities and discursive impacts—does illuminate social and political economic conflicts, which did not disappear when the protests ceased to exist as mass mobilizations. Rather, when these mobilizations were 'dried out' by the dissolution of the conjuncture that gave rise to them (TP) or reached a point of structural blockade (the 'forbidden transition' of OWS), these conflicts returned to latency. It did not take long for them to reemerge—maybe most spectacularly in the election campaigns of Bernie Sanders and Donald Trump. Albeit in a very different form, these campaigns document patterns of resonance very similar to those reconstructed throughout this book.

OWS' core constituency was strongly represented among the voters and supporters of Bernie Sanders, who was hugely successful in comparison to his contender Hillary Clinton among the young with degrees in higher education. However, as indicated by his strong performance in the so-called rust-belt states, his base also included important factions of the unionized working class. As the primaries developed, polls indicated that Sanders also gained more support among the 'non-white' parts of the working class—and not only in the industrial sector—according to the data of the center for responsive politics, by far the single largest sum of independent expenditures supporting his campaign came from the National Nurses Union (Opensecrets.org 2016).

This is a class alliance that in some sense was already prefigured around OWS. However, while the core constituency set the parameters for the everyday practices of occupied Liberty Plaza pretty much alone, the slogans and style of Sanders' primary campaign were more of a compromise, even if it explicitly used OWS as a point of reference and many participants in OWS presented their engagement with Sanders' campaign as a logical consequence of their engagement in OWS (McCreesh 2016; NBC News 2016; Robbins 2016; Krieg 2016). Sanders' supporters often declared that the organizing for his campaign was aimed at a grassroots mobilization that was supposed to outlive the campaign itself, and Sanders rhetorically affirmed this in his speeches when he, instead of explaining what he stands for, always emphasized what "we" are trying to achieve. However, the very form of a presidential campaign brings with it a degree of institutionalization that is in conflict with the anti-institutional predisposition of OWS' core constituency, as is documented in the angry and resolute public criticism by former OWS activists who refused to support Sanders' campaign (e.g., Holmes 2016).

Despite these criticisms, the surprising mobilization successes reveal that the rhetoric of "political revolution" and economic redistribution, which form the two main planks of Sanders' platform, resonate very well with both the working class and the youth of the new petty bourgeoisie. Sanders' successes also indicate that the crisis of the political field's relation to its audience, which had contributed to the rise of both the TP and OWS and which had polarized especially the Republican Party after 2008, now also makes itself felt as a polarization within the Democratic Party—and the future of this party will depend on how the party is able process this conflict. It is by no means clear if 'Bernie would have won', as some have claimed in the aftermath of the lost election. However, calls for 'unity' that aim at suppressing the conflict in the interest of the party's hitherto dominating factions will very likely forestall the necessary modernization that could allow for a sustaining victory against the accelerating regressive tendencies in US politics.

Understanding these tendencies also means to correctly identify the social classes which are their main popular driving force—and which are misidentified by many on the left and the right: Just as many commentators had subsumed the supporters of the TP under the category of the "lower middle class", they now declared Trump's base to be the "white working class" (e.g., Turney et al. 2017; Cox and Jones 2017). However, people who earn less than $50,000 per annum were as underrepresented among Trump supporters as they were among TP supporters. While this sum is only slightly below the median income, only a third of the supporters of Trump and the TP come from this half of the population (Lapinski et al. 2015; New York Times 2010).

The misidentification of Trump's base as the white working class rests mostly on a problematic but widespread statistical operationalization that equates not having completed a four-year college education with belonging to the working class (Walley 2017). Even as a rough measure, this is seriously misleading with regard to the class-generational units under scrutiny in this book. On the one hand, title inflation and the academization of large parts of the labor market make it increasingly probable that young people belong to the working class even *if* they have a college degree. On the other hand, and more importantly with regard to the supporters of

Donald Trump, for older cohorts, especially if working in the just mentioned economic sectors, college education might be an indicator for a relatively elevated class position, but not having a college education does not at all imply having a lower class position. And indeed, the American Election Study survey on the 2016 election revealed that almost two-thirds of those without a college degree that voted for Donald Trump did belong in the *upper* half of the income distribution (Carnes and Lupu 2017).[2] This also sheds a different light on the findings of research quoted in the NYT, which found a strong correlation between support for Trump and working in construction, trade, agriculture, and manufacturing (Irwin and Katz 2016): All this indicates that the class-generational unit from which the core constituency of Donald Trump's supporters is recruited is exactly the group that already was the main popular driving force behind the TP insurgency—the classical petty bourgeoisie.

Behind this is not mainly an organizational continuity. As a protest mobilization, the TP has almost completely dissolved after 2012, including most movement organizations. The affinity has to be understood rather as another case of habitus-practice resonance: Trump's message—with all its often-mocked inconsistencies and turnabouts—corresponds neatly with the basic orienting patterns identified for the TP's experience of the crisis. "Make America Great Again" is the document of the classical petty bourgeoisie's quintessential ideological fantasy of a return to the old order, in which everything was in its place. It allows to simultaneously articulate frustration about the dynamics of capitalist accumulation, in which the niches for the small businesses of the classical petty bourgeoisie get smaller with every economic bust, never recovering to their previous boom size before the next crisis, without having to call into question the basic social relations that connect the petty bourgeoisie's relative wealth with the very dynamic undermining it.

This fantasy of economic growth without accumulation and a market economy without asymmetrical competition is intimately linked with the undialectical contrasting of the "true" essence and the "false", corrupted realization of social relations which allows to make sinister, outside forces responsible for the perceived decay. Trumps posing against the "establishment", the insistence on him being his own financier, and the conspiratorial motive of the other candidates being directed from behind the scene resonated very well with these basic interpretational patterns as they are grounded in the classical petty bourgeoisie's interpretational predispositions. This also explains his constituency's proneness to believe in "alternative facts"—since, as I argued with regard to the 'birther conspiracy' and the TP, for many of them, ***reality itself has ceased to be real.***

Trump's self-portrayal as the 'tough guy' and 'strong leader' in the final battle against the forces of corruption, which he did not only cultivate during the campaign, but maybe even more so after he was inaugurated, likewise resonates closely with the habitus of the classical petty bourgeoisie as it was reconstructed in this book. It, on the one hand, allows to solve the problem that the conspiratorial mode of interpretation, albeit allowing for a rationalizing 'disappointment without disillusionment', at the same time undercuts one's agency—Trump is the figure on which this agency can now be delegated. On the other hand, this offers an 'affective premium': Along with the delegation of agency, one's fear and aggression resulting from the 'standing in line' are relegitimized as one is refashioned as a 'warrior' that "joins (Trump) in the trenches".[3] Interestingly, and maybe this is one if his biggest advantages vis-à-vis even a former TP candidate like Ted Cruz, who were not able to excite their audience to a comparable degree, he openly proposed measures that address the TP's core constituency's wish to turn back the wheel of capitalist accumulation cum internationalization through the canceling of Free Trade Agreements.

This points to the biggest difference to the TP party mobilization. While the latter had productively resonated with the crisis of the Republican Party in that the TP even helped to restabilize the Party's position in the political field to some degree, Trump's presidential campaign rather lead to a resonance failure of mutually reinforcing escalations. Although both the Republican Party and the conservative news networks reacted increasingly hastily to prevent a Trump candidacy, which they feared would threaten the party's relation to the dominating industrial faction in the economic field (which is only partially true) and risk losing even more younger voters to the Democrats (which also turned out to be only partially true) (Frum 2016), this time (in contrast to the case of the TP candidates in 2012), they proved unable to demobilize his campaign. Trump's economic resources made it difficult to dry him out, and the attempts of the party establishment and the media to delegitimize him instead invigorated his supporters' belief that he is 'one of us' against 'them'. It is not without a certain irony that during the final stretch of the presidential campaign, Charles Koch, who, like his brother, has been one of the most famous financiers of the think tanks and lobbying groups that fueled the TP, publicly considered that, given the choices in the Republican Party, Hillary Clinton (the Secretary of State in the administration that the TP had so deeply despised) might in fact be the best presidential candidate in 2016 (Trott 2016).

The story of the presidency of Donald Trump, with all its scandals and turnabouts, documents that the social contradictions that made his success possible now haunt his administration itself. Albeit being a striking climax of the story that began with the Great Recession, it is surely not its end. The interregnum of the crisis of the finance-dominated accumulation regime has been and will be marked by an escalation of the multiple, overlapping social contradictions: between factions of capital, different social classes, political actors that traditionally have represented certain, now shifting, alliances of social classes and capital factions, and many more. The main task of a critically engaged social science in this situation should be foremost to identify and analyze these contradictions and their rootedness in the dynamics of the current political-economic conjuncture. I hope this book is a useful contribution to this endeavor—and that I was able to show that especially a fresh and nuanced look at questions of social class can help to resolve a lot of riddles and paradoxes that make navigating this conjuncture so difficult.

Notes

1. A video recording of the people's gong in April 2012 can be found at: OccupySteve (2012).
2. This discrepancy becomes even starker if we consider that his voters disproportionately came from the Midwest and the South, where median incomes tend to be much lower than in states on the West- and Upper East Coast.
3. https://www.facebook.com/DonaldTrump/videos/10159158074630725/ (Accessed November 4, 2017).

Bibliography

Blühdorn, Ingolfur. 2013. *Simulative Demokratie: Neue Politik nach der postdemokratischen Wende*. Berlin: Suhrkamp.

———. 2014. A Massive Escalation of Truly Disruptive Action…? Bürger Protest und Nachhaltigkeit in der postdemokratischen Konstellation. *Forschungsjournal Neue Soziale Bewegungen* 2014 (1): 27–37.

Carnes, Nicholas, und Noam Lupu. "It's Time to Bust the Myth: Most Trump Voters Were Not Working Class." *Washington Post*, June 5 2017. https://www.washingtonpost.com/news/monkey-cage/wp/2017/06/05/itstimeto-bust-the-myth-most-trump-voters-were-not-working-class/?utm_term=.644391d3f6c7 (accessed February 24 2018).

Cox, Daniel, and Robert Jones. 2017. Beyond Economics: Fears of Cultural Displacement Pushed the White Working Class to Trump. (PRRI). https://www.prri.org/research/white-working-class-attitudes-economy-trade-immigration-election-donald-trump/. Accessed 4 Nov 2017.

Frank, Thomas. 2012. *Pity the Billionaire: The Hard-Times Swindle and the Unlikely Comeback of the Right*. New York: Metropolitan Books.

Frum, David. 2016. The Great Republican Revolt. *The Atlantic*, February. http://www.theatlantic.com/magazine/archive/2016/01/the-great-republican-revolt/419118/. Accessed 4 Nov 2017.

Holmes, Marisa. 2016. Mic Check! Bernie Sanders Swallows Occupy's Microphone. *International Times: The Newspaper of Resistance*, January 21. http://internationaltimes.it/mic-check-bernie-sanders-swallows-occupys-microphone/. Accessed 4 Nov 2017.

Irwin, Neil, and Josh Katz. 2016. The Geography of Trumpism. *The New York Times*, March 12. http://www.nytimes.com/2016/03/13/upshot/the-geography-of-trumpism.html. Accessed 4 Nov 2017.

Kerbo, Harold R. 1982. Movements of 'Crisis' and Movements of 'Affluence': A Critique of Deprivation and Resource Mobilization Theories. *Journal of Conflict Resolution* 26 (4): 645–663.

Krieg, Gregory. 2016. Occupy Wall Street Rises Up for Sanders. *CNN Politics*, April 13. http://edition.cnn.com/2016/04/13/politics/occupy-wall-street-bernie-sanders-new-york-primary/. Accessed 4 Nov 2017.

Krugman, Paul. 2009. Tea Parties Forever. *The New York Times*, April 13. http://www.nytimes.com/2009/04/13/opinion/13krugman.html. Accessed 4 Nov 2017.

Langman, Lauren. 2013. Occupy: A New New Social Movement. *Current Sociology* 61 (4): 510–524.

Lapinski, John, Josh Clinton, and Carrie Roush. 2015. The Deep Dive: Who Supports Donald Trump? (Data Points). http://www.msnbc.com/msnbc/the-deep-dive-who-supports-donald-trump. Accessed 4 Nov 2017.

Lo, Clarence Y.H. 2012. Astroturf versus Grass Roots: Scenes from Early Tea Party Mobilization. In *Steep. The Precipitous Rise of the Tea Party*, ed. Lawrence Rosenthal and Christine Trost, 98–129. Berkeley: University of California Press.

McCreesh, Shawn. 2016. 'March for Bernie' Is an Occupy Wall Street Homecoming. *Rolling Stone*, January 31. http://www.rollingstone.com/politics/news/march-for-bernie-is-an-occupy-wall-street-homecoming-20160131. Accessed 4 Nov 2017.

NBC News. 2016. Bernie Phone Bank Sets Up at Birthplace of Occupy Movement. *NBC News*. http://www.nbcnews.com/video/bernie-phone-bank-sets-up-at-birthplace-of-occupy-movement-653528643707. Accessed 4 Nov 2017.

New York Times. 2010. Polling the Tea Party. New York: *New York Times/CBS News Poll*. http://www.nytimes.com/interactive/2010/04/14/us/politics/20100414-tea-party-poll-graphic.html. Accessed 4 Nov 2017.

OccupySteve. 2012. *OWS Spring Training|The People's Gong*. https://www.youtube.com/watch?v=F_XxBs6IGNA. Accessed 4 Nov 2017.

Opensecrets.org. 2016. Independent Expenditures for Bernie Sanders, 2016 Cycle. https://www.opensecrets.org/pres16/indexp_indiv.php?cycle=2016&id=N00000528. Accessed 4 Nov 2017.

Robbins, Christopher. 2016. The Occupied Wall Street Journal Is Back in Print For Bernie Sanders. *The Gothamist*, April. http://gothamist.com/2016/04/13/bernie_sanders_occupy_wall_st.php. Accessed 4 Nov 2017.

Skocpol, Theda, and Vanessa Williamson. 2012. *The Tea Party and the Remaking of Republican Conservatism*. Oxford: Oxford University Press.

Snow, David A., Sarah A. Soule, and Hanspeter Kriesi. 2006. Mapping the Terrain. In *The Blackwell Companion to Social Movements*, 3–16. Malden: Blackwell.

Taylor, Blair. 2013. From Alterglobalization to Occupy Wall Street: Neoanarchism and the New Spirit of the Left. *City* 17 (6): 729–747.

Trott, Bill. 2016. Republican Financier Koch Says Clinton Might Make Better President. *Reuters*, April 24. http://www.reuters.com/article/us-usa-electon-koch-idUSKCN0XL01J. Accessed 4 Nov 2017.

Turney, Shad, Frank Levy, Jack Citrin, and Neil O'Brian. 2017. Waiting for Trump:The Move to the Right of White Working-Class Men, 1968–2016. *California Journal of Politics & Policy*, May. http://escholarship.org/uc/item/1cq9k81z. Accessed 4 Nov 2017.

Walley, Christine J. 2017. Trump's Election and the 'White Working Class': What We Missed. *American Ethnologist* 44 (2): 231–236.

Appendices

Appendix 1: Interviews and Group Discussions

(The list of interviews and discussions only includes those that were recorded and leaves aside informal conversations that were conducted during participant observations.)

Table A.1 Interviews and group discussions

Tea Party	TPG1 (3 participants)
	TPG2 (3 participants)
	TPG3 (8 participants)
	Ben and Mike
	Gary
	John
	Marco
	Matthew
	Patricia
	Sally
	Susan

(*continued*)

N. C. Kumkar, *The Tea Party, Occupy Wall Street, and the Great Recession*, Critical Political Theory and Radical Practice,
https://doi.org/10.1007/978-3-319-73688-4

Table A.1 (continued)

Occupy Wall Street	OWSG1 (3 participants) OWSG2 (4 participants) OWSG3 (8 participants) OWSG4 (3 participants) Amy Ann Anja Brenda Chris Daniel Danielle Elisabeth Erica Frederic Herman James John Leila Liz Louise Lucy and Lisa Mario Max Pepe Philip Susan

Appendix 2: Results of the Secondary Analysis of Hector Cordero-Guzman's Survey on Occupywallst.org

Table A.2 Results of the secondary analysis of Cordero-Guzman's survey on Occupywallst.org

			What is your age?				
< 18	18–24	25–34	35–44	45–54	55–64	> 65	Total:
40	466	688	333	322	278	94	2221
1.8	20.98%	30.98%	14.99%	14.50%	12.52%	4.32%	100%
			Which of the following best describes your race?				
White	Black	Asian	American Indian	Mixed	Others	Total:	
1820	40	45	10	116	156	2187	
83.22%	1.83%	2.06%	0.46%	5.3%	7.13%	100%	
			Which of the following best describes your education?				
No formal education	Grade school	High school	College educated, no degree	College degree	Graduate school, no degree	Graduate school degree	Total:
9	10	160	610	721	167	510	2187
0.41%	0.46%	7.32%	27.89%	32.97%	7.64%	23.32%	100%
			Are you employed?				
Full-time	Part-time	Unemployed	Retired	Disabled	Home-maker	Full-time student	Total:
973	518	295	107	43	55	193	2187
44.55%	23.72%	13.51%	4.9%	1.97%	2.52%	8.84%	100%
			Are you currently in school?				
Yes		No			Total:		
549		1638			2187		
25.1%		74.9%			100%		
			What is your individual employment income?				
<$24.999	$25.000–$49.999	$50.000–$74.999	$75.000–$99.999	$100.000–$149.999	$150.000–$249.999	>$250.00	Total:
1071	511	305	155	96	30	19	2187
48.97%	23.37%	13.95%	7.09%	4.39%	1.37%	0.87%	100%

Hector Cordero-Guzman's survey was conducted via an important webpage of OWS, 'occupywallst.org'. The following tables are based on the second wave of this survey, conducted between October 3 and 10, the dataset of which Cordero-Guzman was friendly enough to let me use. The survey included a question asking if one had participated in OWS, which could be answered with "I agree strongly", "I agree somewhat", "I neither agree/disagree", "I disagree somewhat", and "disagree strongly". For my secondary analysis, I reduced the responses to the subset of those that had reported that they "strongly agreed" or "somewhat agreed" with having participated, which includes 2221 of the 5124 valid responses in this wave, 2187 of which provided more than their ages.

Appendix 3

Exemplary Interpretation of a Focusing Metaphor: TPG2 "Standing in Line"

This appendix has two main purposes. For readers that found the methodological sketch on the documentary method for habitus reconstruction somewhat dry or abstract, it aims to provide a more concrete and nuanced impression of how this methodology is employed in the analysis of the actual material. Additionally, in order to increase the degree of intersubjective plausibility of the findings, this excursus offers a window into how I analyzed the material in a more concrete manner than in Chap. 5, which, for the sake of readability, focuses on summarizing and illustrating results of the interpretation process of immanent reconstruction of the habitual patterning of the group's discourse (Przyborski and Wohlrab-Sahr 2014, 401f.). The excursus begins with short summary on how I recruited participants for this group discussion before it turns to an extensive example of how I selected and analyzed passages from this discussion.

The passage interpreted below was taken from a TP group discussion held in April 2013 with members of one of the two TP groups I repeatedly visited during all three stays in the field. The recruitment of this discussion group was shaped by the way in which I approached and observed the TP group in the previous months. I found this TP group via the Internet site of one of the large, nationwide TP organizations, which provided a search function for TP groups in a given geographic area. The group itself had a webpage, which made it seem to be both a rather large and active group and geographically accessible to me. Both turned out to be true. I wrote an email to the press contact listed on the page, informing them that I was a German sociologist researching on the TP and asking them for the opportunity to get to know them a little. They answered with an invitation to their next meeting, which was also publicly advertised on the group's webpage. During my stays in the field, I returned to these meetings as often as possible.

After the first meeting, I had a short conversation with the person also listed as the group's press contact. The conversation mostly dealt with my research and my general impression of the meeting. At the end, we agreed to meet for an interview that would allow me to ask some questions about the history of the group. When two other members of the group's board, however, also showed up at the agreed time and place—a small roadside diner—I decided to have my first group discussion, TPG1, with these three, the founding trio of the group. The three participants in this discussion pretty much happened to fit the standard image of the TP activist—in their late 50s to mid-60s, and all of them were 'white'.

Even though this discussion was conducted in an open atmosphere, and I felt like I managed to establish a friendly relationship with these three, when I returned and visited some of their group meetings, I could never shake the feeling off that it would be impossible to overcome a basic mistrust on their part. When I sought to put together another discussion group during my second stay in the field, the group's board explained to me that they would prefer if the recruitment of the participants happened through them, citing their wish to make sure that the people I interviewed were really members of the group and not just someone who had just showed up to their meeting. This explanation did not really sound convincing to me, since I had already visited numerous meetings and chatted with several members of the group, thus giving me a relatively good impression who was a regular member and who was not. I therefore had the suspicion that their objection was motivated by a desire to maintain control over the image of the group presented in such a discussion. Indeed, already at their meetings, I had the feeling that they were somewhat suspicious if I sought out conversations with members of their group independently of them—an impression that was reinforced by the fact that the three people finally participating in the board's preselected discussion group demographically diverged notably from what I had seen in the actual group meetings. Two of the three preselected participants were 'non-white'. One of them, Patricia, was around 40 and the other, Marcos, was 30 years old.[1] Only the third member of the small group, Stephen, seemed at first sight to be a 'classic' TP member as defined by Skocpol and Williamson—he was 60 years old, 'white', and a convinced Republican since Ronald Reagan's presidential campaign in the early 1980s.

While I at first feared that the board's pre-selection might jeopardize the success of the discussion as a means to reconstruct the TP's habitus, in the end, it actually helped me sharpen my understanding of the decisive socio-structural dynamics of the genesis of the TPers habitus. It turned out in the discussion that the first two—both owners of small homes, one a plumber who had served in the military and was now striving to start his own business, and the other, an independent business accountant—repeatedly and collaboratively elaborated on propositions, which, in their basic structure, were very similar to those I found in the other two TP discussions I conducted.[2] Meanwhile, the latter, an autodidact with strong interest in libertarian theories who had worked for a large financial institution before being laid off in 2008, often seemed to initiate topics which were only reluctantly taken up by the others, indicating that his experiential background in important aspects diverged from that of the other two participants and, indeed, from those of the other TP discussion groups.[3] This indicated to me that, at least in this instance, the class background of the core constituency as a decisive element of the group's experiential background, and therefore its habitus, trumped even ethnicity and gender as group-constituting forces.

The discussion was conducted as an open group discussion (Bohnsack 2004, 2010, 207–10). Thus, I only provided the whole group with a discussion impulse question, otherwise letting the group discuss on its own without interfering either in the thematic development of the discourse or in the turn-taking among the participants. On the one hand, this served to allow them to process the topic according to their own relevance and, on the other, it let them 'home in' on shared centers of experience. Only after the group had 'exhaustively discussed' the respective topic did I initiate a new one, which, again, was then discussed by the group on its own.[4]

The passage I have chosen to demonstrate the basic steps of analysis is the first focusing metaphor that is both the climax and the conclusion of the first twenty minutes of the discussion. To identify this focusing metaphor, the fine transcript of the whole interview was subjected to a first, 'rough' formulating interpretation. For this, the content of the transcript of the whole discussion was paraphrased and the content's topical structure was identified. This included the identification of the paramount topic, the topics, subordinated topics, and sub-subordinated topics of this part of the discussion (Bohnsack 2010, 134, 220f.; Bohnsack and Schäffer 2007, 336f.). All group discussions and the majority of interviews I conducted in this project were subjected to this procedure. The result of this first formulating interpretation of the first twelve pages of the transcript, the "opening passage" of the discussion in which the group elaborates and concludes the first main theme, is presented below:[5]

A Formulating Interpretation: TPG2, "Opening Passage"

Opening question by the interviewer: "Alright, um, so, could you tell me what brought you to the Tea Party @.@ I mean, what, what happened, um, like I don't know, what were the reasons?"[6]

Turn-distribution: M grants P the 'privilege' to speak first

PT: One felt the urge to do something, because 'they' are taking away what one is striving for

T: One "woke up" politically.

ST: One was "desperate" because one did not find people to discuss the "political changes" with.

ST: The TP was a chance to "change things".

SST: One became "politically awake" and joined a TP group. As a patriot, one wanted to get involved and not just "slide down into a pit" with the rest of the country. One wanted to "get the message out".

SST: One is conservative and always had an interest in politics. When Obama got elected and Rick Santelli gave his speech, people started to get organized, and one joined because Obama was "heading in a wrong direction" and expected to be able to change this.

T: The politicians are jeopardizing what one thought to be safe.

ST: The bailout of GM was violating "the rule of law" since it dispossessed the stockholders.

ST: One had long silently accepted the erosion of the country, but now one felt the urgency to become part of "something bigger" to "change things".

ST: One is scared and angry because by "changing the framework of this country", "they" jeopardize everything that one thought is safe.

T: Empirically, one can see that Obama chose the wrong policies instead of "Reagan-like, free market" policies.

T: One is afraid that the country already has changed irreversibly.

ST: After the election one practically gave up, now one only stays with the TP because one "likes these people".

ST: The danger is that America has changed and one cannot convince the younger people anymore.

SST: One cannot even convince one's own nephews anymore.

SST: People are indoctrinated by "the progressive movement" in schools.

SST: That is why one should support school-choice politics.
SST: Homeschooling is also rising, but many children love school.

Conclusion: Being a TPer means one was standing in line and now one feels betrayed
Pause, participants ask for new question.

This step of the interpretation has three main purposes. First, it distances the interpreter from the text, dissolves the false sense of an unproblematic and immediate access to the meaning of the discussion's explicit content, and forces the interpreter to acknowledge that the suspension of the pragmatic shortcuts of everyday communication opens up hitherto unacknowledged 'wiggling space' for interpretation (cf. Schütz 1981, esp. 49, 99). At no point during the discussion, did I have the impression that I had any difficulty understanding what was said—however, as soon as I tried to paraphrase and structure it, I was forced to recognize that I quite often had difficulties 'pinning down' the actual meaning of that which was said. Second, in directing attention to the topical structure of that which is said, the focus shifts from the communicative-interactive process between the speakers toward the collaborative, joint process of elaborating propositions based on the shared understanding orienting them (Bohnsack 1989, 22). In the protocol of the formulating interpretation, I further emphasized this shift by erasing the different speakers, both by not indicating who said what (even some of the sub-subordinated topics were elaborated by more than one person) and by replacing 'I' and other clearly identifiable actors in the propositions with the impersonal 'one'.[7] Third, the structure of collaboratively elaborated themes also allows 'condensing' points of the passage to be identified—those subsections of the passage in which the greater theme of the passage is, in a certain sense, replicated *en miniature*. Bohnsack coined the term focusing metaphors (Bohnsack 1989, 23f., 284f.) for those synecdochal sequences of a discussion, which are often also marked by a high metaphorical and interactional density and in which the group in a certain sense "comes to terms with itself" (Loos and Schäffer 2001, 67). The interpretation of these focusing metaphors is the key to reconstructing the group's shared structure of experience—the habitus.

In order to identify the passages in which the group 'homes in' on such a center of shared experience, I will shortly summarize how the group's discourse unfolded during the first twenty minutes of the discussion: The discussion opens with an intentionally vague, hesitating impulse question. The interviewer's "um's", his laughter, and the "I don't know" signal a foreignness with regard to the field and thereby implicitly call the participants to elaborate even on those aspects of the initiated topics that they might otherwise consider obvious. Heightened by the stringing of three different sub-questions, the open—to some degree obscure—content of the impulse question furthermore leaves much space for interpretation, directing thereby as little as possible the way in which the participants process the initiated topics and leaving it up to them to unfold their own structures of relevance (Bohnsack 2010, 208f.). Probably because the genre of interaction they intuitively subsume this discussion under is that of the 'interview', the participants react at first by taking turns telling a short story of their way to the TP. The basic structure in response to the initial question involved each apparently recognizing that the USA was changing in a way they did not agree with and viewing the emerging TP movement as a promising venue to do something about this.

These stories seemed to be standardized narratives—including all the familiar ingredients: Obama, 'change', Santelli's rant, and the liberal/deluded majority one has to face—which were presented only with a very low degree of detail and contained little indication of emotional engagement in the story and thus were seemingly far removed from the actual lived experience of the participants. However, already the first proposition in regard to what the social changes that worried one actually were—namely, the mentioning of the bailout of GM and the indication that this bailout was unconstitutional—triggered a dynamic of a dramaturgically escalating collaborative elaboration which 'peaks' in the sub-topic of an all-encompassing material and social insecurity that results from "them" attempting to "change the framework of this country." Following this, S introduces a proposition that holds that the TPs political stance is a viable political alternative to Obama's policies. This, however, does not seem to resonate with the other two participants of the discussion, but instead only leads to a meandering excursus in the discussion, before Marcos finally returns to the original, shared theme and concludes it in an allegory which both other participants seem to accept as fitting and sufficient.

Because of the overall topical structure of the passage and the metaphorical density of the respective sequences, and finally because the analysis of other TP discussions and interviews lead to very similar condensing passages, the finale of the second topic and the conclusion of this paramount topic were identified as focusing metaphors (or, rather as a focusing metaphor with a 'cut-off' conclusion) and named "standing in line" after the concluding allegory. The interpretation of these sequences will be further illustrated in what remains of this excursus.

B Transcript TPG2: "Standing in Line"

M: You know, so on and so forth, we're seeing all these things, all these things that I guess, that are eroding our country. Slowly. And we've always said, oh you know, I maybe, let me, let me not, let me be quiet, I don't want to cause trouble. Um. You know, whatever, its um, it's not too big of a deal. But we've gotten us, we've gone to the point where we're saying no. We're, we're seeing our country slide down the tubes, and we have to stand up and do something. Because we will not stand idly by, while the rest of the country (.) goes off the cliff. So. We're, I guess that's ah, the biggest reason why we would join.

P: Yeah, and I, I think a little bit of it is a combination of, of, fear and an:nger. Because if you start shaking things like the rule of law and start creating new standards. If you wanna start saying that the constitution is a living, breathing document, and, and that there is no real foundation in it and you want to make new rules - than, what BINDS us? What, what, what is the measure of what can't be done if we don't want to follow the RULES. That means any politician or anybody can do anything they want and there is no consequence for it. And once THAT happens, (.) you know, it's chaos. And nobody is then safe anymore. You're not safe from, your, your, your personal property, your family, you don't opp-: you don't have any opportunity, to grow, I mean I think that was a big fear too, why you see, so many older people, who, who joined the Tea Party. Because (.) they're looking at all the things they built up. //M:mhm//all the securities that they thought were in place for their children and their grandchildren. And they're literally watching it disappear in front of their eyes.

M: yupp (.)

P: And then if, if, what are you living for, and what have all the things, you know, why, why did he serve his country, why do you have children, if, if, all those things you thought they could HAVE, they can't HAVE anymore! (.) Because people (.) want to set a whole new (.) standard of which is counter what we all believed and, and grew up in. You know, so-:

M: They want to change the paradigm of, or, of what our country, our countries original framework. Ah, was. or is.

(Deletion of approx. 5 Minutes)

M: Ah, the one thing I want to say, I guess to gather what a Tea Party member is in a nutshell? Um, picture yourself standing in, in line, um, to a movie, to, um, say anything. Sporting event. We're the person who has numerous times seen people cut in, cut in line, and just stood by and said, alright, it's not my problem, it's not my problem. You know, just. (..) Ah. we're, the Tea Party groups, are the ones that are finally saying, you know, enough is enough. You cut in line, this is not right, this is not, you are not playing by the rules. Whereas the left is the one that's saying, oh well, they, they are having a lawyer saying, they can cut the line because of X,Y,Z. We're the ones that are standing up

for what's right, as for how our framework, ah, is. In this country. I guess, I don't know if that's a
good analogy or not. But, that's who we are. We, we're, we finally had enough and we're standing up
for what's right. (..)
P, M: @.@
S: Another question?
M: @.@

The next step of the habitus reconstruction is the 'fine' or detailed formulating interpretation (Bohnsack and Schäffer 2007, 336ff.). The group's discourse is cut up in short sequences, which are paraphrased and identified as belonging to the three main genres of speech, which means they are identified as narratives, descriptions, or arguments. They are then analyzed with regard to their function in the topical structure of the discourse—that is, they are identified as propositions, or, for example, as affirmative or antithetical elaborations of propositions, or as concluding the elaboration of a proposition.[8] Since this step tends to produce great amounts of text which is rather dull to read, I will only present the fine formulating interpretation of the first eight lines as an illustrative example in the following:

C 'Fine' Formulating Interpretation, TPG2: "Standing in Line"

1: *Generalizing follow-up proposition in a descriptive mode:* What was said before could be extended to a larger image which one 'sees'.

1–2: *Elaboration of the sub-proposition 'larger image' in a descriptive mode:* The common denominator of all these things constituting the larger image is that they are all part of the creeping decline of 'our country'.

2–3: *Elaboration of the sub-proposition 'passive witnessing' in a descriptive mode with elements of argumentation:* Hitherto, one had only passively watched and not taken the initiative, since one did not want to 'cause trouble'.

3: *Elaboration of the sub-proposition in an argumentative mode*: One also did not say something because the changes were not perceived as threatening.

3–4: *Follow-up proposition 'becoming active' in a descriptive mode*: Now, however, one has reached a point in the general development where one gives up one's former reluctance and openly expresses one's disagreement.

4–5: *Elaboration of the proposition in an argumentative mode:* This change results from the dramatic development one is witnessing, which is the escalating decline of the whole country, which is perceived as a moral imperative: One has to risk being a 'troublemaker' and do something.

5–6: *Elaboration of the proposition in an argumentative mode:* One cannot simply accept the decline of the 'rest of the country', since this would qualify one as useless.

6–7: *Conclusion of the propositions "larger image" and "becoming active" into "reason for joining"*: This moral imperative resulting from one's perception of a general decline of the USA is the "main reason" that drove one to the TP.

7–8: *Specifying follow-up proposition "fear and anger" in a descriptive mode:* the perception of a general social decline triggered feelings of both fear and anger, which drove one to want to do something about the situation.

Already this explication of the discourse's structure gives a good impression of how the habitus' structuring of the participants' experiences underlying their engagement in the TP is documented in the text.

In the generalizing follow-up proposition, which opens the passage, M indicates that he perceives the event described before (the bailout of GM) as a *pars-pro-toto* encapsulating a general development (the decline of US society), which he feels forced to react to. In generalizing the particular event ('bailout') into a larger image (decline), he specifies the structural elements of the perception of the event that make this even thematically relevant for the group. This elaboration of the lived experience as a set of analogies (and in analogical form) is fairly typical for group discussions. This structure of the group's discourse as propositions analogous to other propositions, which together are specifications of analogously constructed encompassing propositions, is illustrated by Loos and Schäffer (2001, 67) with the image of a matryoshka doll. The structure of the discourse mirrors how the habitus structures the experience of the world around the subject as a "book, in which everything is read a metaphorical statement on everything else" (Bourdieu 1987, 142).

The detailed formulating interpretation of the focusing metaphors (selected based on the formulating interpretation) thus prepares the ground for the final step of the reconstruction, in which the identified propositions are then interpreted according to the orienting figures actually documented in them—or, in the terminology of the theory of practice, with regard to the homologies between the different 'objects' experienced by the actor that are taken up by the habitus in order to read them as metaphors for each other.

D Reflecting Interpretation, TPG2 "Standing in Line"

1–2: Follow-Up Proposition "GM's Bail-Out Was Only One Example of a Larger Trend of Social Decline Which One Is Observing"

> *You know, so on and so forth, we're seeing all these things, all these things that I guess, that are eroding our country. Slowly.*

During the discussion of the bailout of GM that formed the background of this proposition, none of the participants identified any direct relation between the bailout and their personal lives, but instead argued on the level of general political reasoning—it was simply wrong. This proposition now, however, indicates that the example of GM is relevant/problematic for the group's worldview because their perception of the bailout encapsulates a basic structural feature that appears generalizable to an overall social development, something that the story about the bailout is 'really about'. In generalizing from the particular event, the abstract discussions of which seem to tire him (as is indicated by the "so on and so forth"), M therefore specifies what about this event really triggers a negative reaction—or, in the methodological vocabulary of the documentary method, how it functions as a metaphor of the negative horizon of the group's orienting frame.

Although this negative horizon has not yet really been 'fleshed out', two peculiarities of how the proposition is articulated already provide some 'hints' to its structure. First, the "things", of which the bailout is but one example, are not pictured as 'bads' on their own (they do necessarily directly impact the living environment of the speaker) but as dangerous because they "erode" the country. The bailout is read as a sign to be interpreted and not as something immediately obvious to everyone. This is also one possible interpretation of the expression that "we're seeing all these things"—namely, that not everyone is seeing them—a hypothesis that would be consistent with the image of the "political awakening" that all three participants mentioned in their opening statement. Second, the image of "erosion" not only supports this interpretation in that it attributes a certain hidden and subversive character to the developments (also supported by the adverb "slowly", which attributes a certain 'creeping' quality to the process), it furthermore indicates a peculiar quality of the negative horizon implicated in this experience, namely, that it undermines the very ground one is standing on, making it both an uncanny and unsettling phenomenon.

2–3 Elaboration of the Sub-proposition: "One Remained Silent"

> *And we've always said, oh you know, I maybe, let me, let me not, let me be quiet, I don't want to cause trouble. Um. You know, whatever, its um, it's not too big of a deal.*

The elaboration documents what was only subtly indicated in the original proposition, namely, the passive relation toward the perceived decay, which one merely witnessed so far (one "sees" it). The legitimization presented for this behavior—which apparently is at odds with the graveness of the process described in the proposition—is twofold. On the one hand, it is stated that one shied away from the conflict actively intervening in the process of decline would have caused. Read as an ex-post rationalization, this could indicate the opposite of the intended self-presentation as a peaceful and calm character, in that it primarily is expressed to legitimize the anger and aggression that drives one's activism now. This reading would be supported by the specification that one "always" told this to oneself, which emphasizes how long and consistently one already suppressed the 'rightful urge' to finally do something.

On the other hand, read as a legitimization given from the viewpoint of the situation itself, it could also document an actual discomfort with conflict. Indeed, this would be consistent with the other element of the legitimization, namely, that the processes did not seem too severe in the beginning, which could very well be understood as something that one told oneself to suppress the urge to 'do' something that could cause conflict. Not only the analysis of the other discussions but also of the TP meetings and protest events I observed reveal that both hypotheses might very well be true. There is, on the one hand, a lot of aggression on the side of many TP activists that is negated in the self-presentation as the 'reluctant rebel'; on the other hand, there is an actual hesitancy toward exposing oneself to potential conflict, which is practically avoided by protest forms that grant a minimum of exposure to different opinions, such as 'roadside rallies', where the audience drives by in cars, or the participation in highly ritualized parades.

3–7 Follow-Up Proposition: "Becoming Active, Since One Had to"

> *But we've gotten us, we've gone to the point where we're saying no. We're, we're seeing our country slide down the tubes, and we have to stand up and do something. Because we will not stand idly by, while the rest of the country (.) goes off the cliff. So. we're, I guess that's ah, the biggest reason why we would join.*

The first interesting thing to note here is the tautological character of this follow-up proposition's explicit content: One was not active, and one is now active, because one reached a point where one felt the urge to become active. The information I would normally expect, namely, what *happened* at that point, is left out—after all, even in the case of a 'straw that broke the camel's back', one could reasonably expect information on the 'straw'. Although it is not possible to determine at this point, this silence might indicate some sort of difficulty to name the triggering event—either because it is not reflexively available to the speaker because it is for some reason at odds with his self-representation and therefore repressed from the speaker's discourse or, the other way around, because the 'event' itself never occurred, but is rather a necessary element of an ideological self-presentation whose position cannot be 'filled' by any actual experience of the speaker.

The problematic quality also could explain the contradictory relation of active and passive elements in this proposition. While M opens by beginning a sentence that seems to be stating that one has apparently gotten *oneself* into trouble ("*we've* gotten *us*"), he quickly corrects himself and finishes the sentence in a more neutral manner, merely stating that one did do something against 'it'. He then continues with a less engaged statement, namely that one watched the country decaying (which concerns one only because it is still 'one's' country) and finally concludes, in an even more distanced manner, that it is "the rest of the country" (apparently excluding oneself) that is going "off the cliff." While the very first mode implicates some sort of guilt through complicity and fear through involvement in the process, this seems to be pushed aside in a more and more heroic self-representation as someone who bravely stands up to save "the rest". The image reminiscent of a lemming "going off the cliff" supports this interpretation—and it also could be read as supporting the hypothesis developed apropos the first proposition, namely, that it documents a differentiation between oneself as one 'who knows' vis-à-vis the rest of society, which blindly leaps "off the cliff."

8 Specifying Follow-Up Proposition "Fear and Anger"

> *Yeah, and I, I think a little bit of it is a combination of, of, fear and an:nger.*

P explicates feelings she identifies as accompanying one's decision to join the TP, namely, 'fear' and 'anger'. At first, it seems a little odd that this specification is made in an affirmative manner, given that 'fear' as a driving force contradicts the heroic self-image of the brave activist standing up for the rest of the country as it was drawn out by M in the end of the last proposition.

It does, however, make sense if one connects it not to this last image—which, as was pointed out in the interpretation, to some degree seems forced upon M's own starting point in the elaboration of the proposition—but to the outlines of the negative horizon as an undermining of the ground one is standing on, as it was sketched out in the reflecting interpretation of the original proposition: "GM's bailout was only one example of the larger trend of social decline which one is observing" (1–2).

The mentioning of 'anger' seems to be more easily connected to the heroic self-representation. It does, however, also point to something absent in the preceding propositions—namely, who is to be held responsible for the development, a point that P, however, also does not really make explicit.

8–11 Follow-Up Proposition: "Shaking the Foundation"

> *Because if you start shaking things like the rule of law and start creating new standards. If you wanna start saying that the constitution is a living, breathing document,*[9] *and, and that there is no real foundation in it and you want to make new rules - than, what BINDS us?*

The follow-up proposition provides some more information on what is perceived as the "erosion of the country" triggering the aforementioned fear and anger. Apparently, what is experienced as threatening is the precariousness of the existing order, associated with "the law." The metaphor of the "real foundation" which is apparently in jeopardy takes up the motive of "erosion"—both refer to the feeling that the 'ground beneath one's feet' is not safe anymore.

Especially interesting is the juxtaposition of apparently small challenges (if you "wanna start", not necessarily meaning that you actually do it) with catastrophic fear ("then what BINDS us?"). This confirms that the described phenomena are still to be understood mainly on a metaphorical level. Such a fundamental fear as triggered here can hardly result only from the precariousness of the interpretation of the constitution, and even less so from a simple attempt to point out this precariousness. As in the case of the bailout of GM—the relevance of which for the group's experience can only be understood via it encapsulating a structural feature of the negative horizon orienting the group's lived experience of the situation they are in—such phenomena hint at a more basic experience of precariousness of the 'existing order', whose experiential core is yet to be identified.

However, the choice of these metaphors—of "rules", "law", and "the constitution"—provides at least a clue to situating where the discussants locate the responsibility for the threatening developments encapsulated in the proposition of the "erosion of the country". It is to be sought with powerful (because they can apparently challenge the existing order) and subversive (because they "want to" do so) actors, although it is not clear if they are attributed to a destructive or merely a misguided intention. In any case, this proposition validates the negative horizon hinted at in the first proposition of this passage, which is defined by a catastrophic fear of a collapse of order and orientation that apparently can already be triggered by minor changes.

11–14 Elaboration of the Follow-Up Proposition: "Shaking the Foundation"

> *What, what, what is the measure of what can't be done if we don't want to follow the RULES. That means any politician or anybody can do anything they want and there is no consequence for it. And once THAT happens, (.) you know, it's chaos. And nobody is then safe anymore.*

The elaboration of the proposition continues the rapid escalation from seemingly small challenges into catastrophic imaginaries, indicating that this passage indeed touches upon a focal point of the structuring of experience, even if the explicit content of the whole passage does not seem to directly capture any concrete experience of the actors but rather expresses the stereotypical form of these experiences itself. It also confirms that the experienced precariousness is perceived as related to a disregard for "rules" on the side of actors-perceived-as-powerful—the "politicians", who, by definition, make "rules".

This elaboration could indicate ambivalence toward the experience of social authority. On the one hand, the catastrophe is experienced as an overreach of authoritative figures that can "do anything they want". On the other hand, this very overreach is triggered by the suspension of the punishing capacity of an even higher authority endowed with the responsibility of keeping the "politicians" in check. Such ambivalence is not problematic on the level of the explicit content of the discourse, since the "rule of law" fulfills exactly this double function, as is the case in classical liberal theory. Since the discourse on "law" and "the constitution" has to be understood as a metaphor for an underlying experiential structure of the group, the ambivalence should at least be noted here.

The last, concluding sequence of this elaboration after the short break mainly documents the emotional density connected to the negative horizon of a total loss of orientation and security that structures how the situation is interpreted by the interviewees. It is, however, also an attempt to get the interviewer 'on board', discernible both in the opening "you know", indicating that the following is an illustration for somebody else, and in the emphasis on the fact that "nobody is then safe anymore", which means that everyone should be as worried as the speaker herself.

14–15: Elaboration of the Sub-proposition: "Nobody Is Then Safe Anymore"

> *You're not safe from, your, your, your personal property, your family, you don't opp-: you don't have any opportunity, to grow*

On the level of explicit content, this sentence at first seems opaque, since the speaker, who is apparently very upset, obviously struggles with its grammatical structure. What is literally said, namely, that one is not safe *from* one's property and family, clearly does not make much sense—at least in the context of the rest of the discussion, which nowhere indicates that TPers perceive property and family as an obstacle to personal growth. This grammatical confusion itself is, however, interesting because it again points to the great difficulties involved in concretizing the agentic side of the negative horizon. The speaker obviously opens by attempting to say what the threat actually is (so far we only know that "anybody can do anything"), however, naming the threat is too difficult, which initiates the shift toward what is under threat.

This small elaboration is especially interesting because, for the first time in this passage, it reveals something more concrete about *where* in the lived experience of the speaker the fundamental insecurity of the negative horizon is perceived as particularly threatening. Ruling out an 'anti-materialist' interpretation, what is meant is that personal (private) property, family, and an 'opportunity to grow' is experienced as threatened, with personal property being the first thing coming to mind. The negative horizon, which was so far only described as rather abstract 'chaos', the 'erosion' of the ground one is standing on, and a 'disregard of the rules', is apparently at least also connected to a (threat of a) loss of material wealth and security, as well as the opportunity to accumulate more of it, which is a likely meaning of 'personal growth'.

15–18: Elaboration and Conclusion of the Sub-proposition

> *I mean I think that was a big fear too, why you see, so many older people, who, who joined the Tea Party. Because (.) they're looking at all the things they built up. //M:mhm// all the securities that they thought were in place for their children and their grandchildren. And they're literally watching it disappear in front of their eyes. //M: yupp (.)//And then if, if, what are you living for, and what have all the things, you know, why, why did he serve his country, why do you have children, if, if, all those things you thought they could HAVE, they can't HAVE anymore!*

The first, elaborating part of this sequence redirects a central experience of the speaker (the centrality of which is clearly indicated by the still very high emotional density—a density that now apparently also carries M away with it) onto another social figure, in this case, the caring "older people". That M and P, neither of whom has children or grandchildren, and who are well below the average age of TP activists, both find this explanation so convincing and agitating can be understood through the structural similarity of the experience described with that reconstructed as the core of the fear as articulated in the last sequence. Again, it is a matter of material wealth and security ("all the things they built up") that is perceived as endangered, a danger that extends to the realm of the family, which in this sequence seems to be primarily a carrier of material security. Additionally, as in all the propositions connected to the negative horizon, the process described is surprisingly 'agent-less'.

While this seems to confirm what was reconstructed so far, the second, concluding part of the sequence adds another dimension of the experience that was thus far 'silent'. First, it is interesting to note that the perspective again shifts. The modus of the discourse remains that of an argument, yet the explicit addressee is not the interviewer or the generalized other (who both should sympathize with the worried elderly people) but the other two participants—M, who had served in the military, and S, who raised children. These two—and by implication P as well—are united in having been robbed of the purpose they 'live' for. Apparently, in the one instance, "all the things" they did are to be understood as the perceived sacrifices and abstinences that, in the other instance, supposedly granted "all those things" to them and their children. The strong emphasis on "having" "all those things" again seems to document that what is meant is primarily material wealth.

22–25: Conclusion of the Proposition: "Shaking the Foundation"

> *Because people (.) want to set a whole new (.) standard of which is counter what we all believed and, and grew up in. You know, so- //M: They want to change the paradigm of, or, of what our country, our country's original framework. Ah, was. or is.*

This collaborative conclusion closes the circle at least back to the original proposition in 8–11. In the first sequence, the hesitation and vagueness of P's contribution documents the difficulty of really naming the moving force behind the negative horizon. Whereas the discourse escalates very quickly when it comes to elaborating on one's feeling of threat and loss of orientation, it becomes slow and fragmented as soon as it comes to rationalizing what is actually happening. M's standardized rationalization is also to be read rather as covering up this difficulty than as addressing it, discernible in the no less general and vague formulation of the "paradigm" or the "framework" of the country, and especially of "them", as those who apparently have an interest in changing it.

However, even if the conclusion fades somewhat into vagueness—which might also be a reason why S then felt the urge to switch topics, leading to the thematic meandering I skipped over here for the sake of readability—the mentioning of the three metaphors of the "standard", the "paradigm", and the "original framework" at this point of the group's discourse nevertheless helps to better understand the metaphorical potential of the rule of law that was indicated but remained unspecified in the reflecting interpretation of 8–14. The fundamental insecurity articulated in the context of a disregard for the rule of law is to be understood as documenting the negative horizon of a loss of (present or future) material wealth and security. Material wealth is perceived as being that which gives one's lifelong abstinences and sacrifices a meaning, since it functions as the vanishing point of one's life's trajectory, maybe even projected to be fully realized only beyond one's death, through one's children and grandchildren. In this sense, the "rule of law" is a metaphor for the rules of the 'game' which one feels one should rightfully be 'winning' yet isn't. Since one always played 'by the rules' (had children, served in the military), someone *must* be manipulating the rules—even if it is not possible to actually say who exactly that is and why they are doing it.

29–41 Conclusion of the Thematic Passage: "What Brought You to the Tea Party" in the Allegory of "Standing in Line"

> *Ah, the one thing I want to say, I guess to gather what a Tea Party member is in a nutshell? Um, picture yourself standing in, in line, Um, to a movie, to, Um, say anything. Sporting event. We're the person who has numerous times seen people cut in, cut in line, and just stood by and said, alright, it's not my problem, it's not my problem. You know, just. (..) Ah. we're, the Tea Party groups, are the ones that are finally saying, you know, enough is enough. You cut in line, this is not right, this is not, you are not playing by the rules. Whereas the left is the one that's saying, oh well, they, they are having a lawyer saying, they can cut the line because of X, Y, Z. We're the ones that are standing up for what's right, as for how our framework, ah, is. In this country. I guess, I don't know if that's a good analogy or not. But, that's who we are. We, we're, we finally had enough and we're standing up for what's right. (..)*

I included M's allegory into this interpretation because it concludes the whole thematic passage leading up to it and was accepted as a conclusion for it by all participants. Consensus on this statement was indicated by a pause, which is ended with laughter, and by the demand for another question directed at the interviewer. Apparently, none of the other participants felt the need to contradict or correct M, and, in contrast to the preceding sequences, the topic appears 'complete' to them—there is nothing to add, the question what brought them to the TP is, for now, sufficiently answered in the elaboration what a TP member is. And, indeed, the reflecting interpretation of the passage reveals almost all the structural elements through which the orienting frame of the participants' could be documented in the preceding propositions.

The basic pattern is the frustration about 'all this' leading to nothing. The image of the "line" symbolizes a life full of abstinences that were supposed to be retroactively deemed meaningful by a promised fulfillment of reaching the head of the line. This line, "the framework" of this country, or, even more basic "the rules," is constantly corrupted by people cutting in line, to the point where one is "finally saying, (…) enough is enough." Interestingly, the reason why this is happening at the exact moment it is happening is again left unclear. The allegory instead suggests that corruption is as old as the actors' experience of the line itself—in a sense, he always felt duped. The fear that there might be no tickets left once he arrives at the cashier is left implicit.

As reconstructed above, the negative horizon—the collapse of order on which one has built one's claims for social recognition and material wealth—is also documented as orienting this proposition. The positive horizon on the other side—the restoring of the 'right' order, in which everyone gets 'what they deserve'—is, here, as in the preceding sequences, only present as a vague afterimage. And the final element of the orienting frame—the enactment potential—can also be estimated from what is presented here. The very passive way in which the experience of the decay is described and the somewhat helpless 'call to order' with which the subversion of order is answered both indicate the very low degree to which the situation is experienced as one about which one can do much—besides acting out the gesture of 'standing up for what's right'.

E Summary of Some Elements of the Orienting Frame as Documented in TPG2: "Standing in Line"

The passage interpreted in this appendix is the culminating point of the group's discourse on why they became active in the TP. Its character as a focusing metaphor of this thematic passage is indicated by two elements: firstly, its thematic relation to the overall thematic structure of the passage, which concludes with an allegory that takes up the basic structural features of the propositions of the focusing metaphor, and, secondly, its emotional density and the quick escalation into the description of an apocalyptic scenario of impending chaos. This implies that this passage documents central structural elements of the group's lived experience—and the interpretation demonstrated how especially the negative horizon of the group's orienting frame can be reconstructed.

The *negative horizon is defined by a loss of security and orientation*, an 'undermining of the ground one is standing on', and a threat to that which apparently gives one's life a purpose—namely, the wealth and security expected as the reward for one's sacrifices and abstinences. The allegory in which M sums this up is that of standing in a line that leads nowhere because everyone else unfairly 'cuts in'.

The social developments associated with decay are described in an apersonal and sometimes uncanny terminology, which is one feature of the discourse that documents that the overall orienting frame of the group is invested with a *low or non-existent potential for enactment*. The only references to an activity of one's own are the highly abstract motives of "standing up" and "saying no" or that one "joined the TP".

This is consistent with the observation that *the positive horizon of the orienting frame is barely discernible* in the passage. Expressed only as a vague afterimage of the negative horizon, it might be inferred that it is defined by the reestablishing of an order that grants one that which one feels entitled to—tickets to a sporting event, wealth, and a family.

Other noteworthy elements of the group's shared experience documented in this passage and that were only touched upon in this interpretation but that become more nuanced and defined in the analysis of other passages and discussions are an ambivalent relation to authority, for example, in the affirmation of 'the law' while simultaneously rejecting 'legalism' and in the fear of politicians' power and the wish to have somebody or something keeping them 'in check' and so on, a presentation of oneself as 'in the know' in contrast to the majority of 'blind' people, and an oscillating between fear, anger, guilt, and aggression.

Notes

1. This means that two of the three 'non-whites' I had seen in the 50-person meeting of the larger TP group were present in this small group, and to my estimates, the youngest person was present in this discussion as well.
2. The third discussion, conducted with members of a different TP group, was an eight-person group that much more closely resembled the demographic composition of TPG1 and the TP more generally.
3. Unfortunately, he was the only participant that did not agree to participate in a follow-up interview afterward, so that a contrasting reconstruction of his orienting frame was not possible.
4. Probably only because the actual 'group' within the discussion group was only a dyad, did I even have to suggest other topics. In the discussion TPG3—as in OWSG2 and OWSG4—the groups discussed for two hours without me intervening at all after the first discussion impulse. The thematic reconstruction of the groups' discourse, however, suggested that in their case, just as in that of TPG2, the length of the respective discourse on one topic was about 20 minutes each. However, the larger groups apparently had less difficulty coming up with new topics on their own.

5. To present the transcript of this whole passage would exceed the limitations of this excursus. However, short parts of the transcript will be presented when the next steps of analysis are presented below.
6. The opening question is not paraphrased but taken directly from the transcription of the discussion.
7. This corresponds with the documentary method's methodological orientation on the collective rather than the individual. Of course one has to be very careful to not silently 'inject' a notion of collectivity that then non-consciously guides the following steps of interpretation. In this case however (and in most passages of the group discussion), the 'I' was used in an exemplary rather than in an autobiographical sense, which is discernible for example in the fact that the passage concludes with a description what "a Tea Party member is, in a nutshell" (p. 230).
8. Bohnsack and Schäffer subsume the reconstruction of the dramaturgy of the discourse under the step of the reflecting interpretation rather than under that of the formulating interpretation. This is methodologically more correct since it clearly goes beyond a mere paraphrasing of the content. Pragmatically, however, since I had the support of an interpretation group for the reflecting interpretation of core passages of the group discussion and it turned out that these discussions were more fruitful when this step was already done as part of the preparation, I most often included it in the step of the formulating interpretation (cf. Bohnsack and Schäffer 2007).
9. From the formulating interpretation: The constitution as a living (breathing) document is a figure of speech referring to a non-originalist reading of the constitution and can thus be paraphrased as 'the constitution should be interpreted in the light of contemporary society'.

Bibliography

Bohnsack, Ralf. 1989. *Generation, Milieu und Geschlecht*. Opladen: Leske + Budrich.

———. 2004. Group Discussion and Focus Group. In *A Companion to Qualitative Research*, ed. Uwe Flick, Ernst von Kardoff, and Ines Steinke, 214–221. London: Sage.

———. 2010. *Rekonstruktive Sozialforschung*. Opladen: Barbara Budrich.

Bohnsack, Ralf, and Burkhard Schäffer. 2007. Exemplarische Textinterpretation: Diskursorganisation und dokumentarische Methode. In *Die dokumentarische Methode und ihre Forschungspraxis*, 331–346. Wiesbaden: VS Verlag für Sozialwissenschaften.

Bourdieu, Pierre. 1987. *Sozialer Sinn: Kritik der theoretischen Vernunft*. Frankfurt am Main: Suhrkamp.

Loos, Peter, and Burkhard Schäffer. 2001. *Das Gruppendiskussionsverfahren: theoretische Grundlagen und empirische Anwendung*. Opladen: Leske + Budrich.

Przyborski, Aglaja, and Monika Wohlrab-Sahr. 2014. *Qualitative Sozialforschung: Ein Arbeitsbuch*. München: Oldenbourg.

Schütz, Alfred. 1981. *Der sinnhafte Aufbau der Sozialen Welt: Eine Einleitung in die verstehende Soziologie*. Frankfurt am Main: Suhrkamp.

N. C. Kumkar, *The Tea Party, Occupy Wall Street, and the Great Recession*, Critical Political Theory and Radical Practice,
https://doi.org/10.1007/978-3-319-73688-4

Index[1]

[1] Note: Page numbers followed by 'n' refer to notes.

N. C. Kumkar, *The Tea Party, Occupy Wall Street, and the Great Recession*, Critical Political Theory and Radical Practice,
https://doi.org/10.1007/978-3-319-73688-4

The manufacturer's authorised representative in the EU is Springer Nature Customer Service Centre GmbH, Europaplatz 3, 69115 Heidelberg, Germany. If you have any concerns regarding our products, please contact ProductSafety@springernature.com

Printed and bound by CPI Group (UK) Ltd, Croydon, CR0 4YY

30/09/2026

02225654-0001